"Professors Bharadwaj and Rath present an in-depth look at the highly relevant topic of communication and persuasion. They compile a wonderful collection of concepts, research insights, case examples, and exercises for practice and reflection. This is a must-read for everyone who would like to improve their impression and impact on other people."

Johannes Habel, Associate Professor, European School of Management and Technology (ESMT) Berlin, Germany.

Communication Strategies for Corporate Leaders

Communication is the key to success in every aspect of life and ever so in a competitive business environment. This book examines managerial communication from seminal theoretical and demonstrative vantage points through an interdisciplinary amalgamation of sciences and the liberal arts. It presents new paradigms of managerial communication in the form of manoeuvres that can act as game changers in tug-of-war business situations, including difficult negotiations, conflicts and interpersonal dissonance that characterise the day-to-day corporate workplace tenor. This volume:

- Develops persuasion strategies based on argumentation tactics derived, for example, from legal cross-examination.
- Introduces "problematisation" and "deconstruction" as effective communication tools into mainstream managerial discourse.
- Employs Harvard Business School cases to demonstrate problem-solving skills, which will further serve as a guide to writing business reports, plans and proposals.
- Positions business writing methods as taxonomical tenets that can help tackle complex business scenarios.
- Draws business diagnostic procedures from diverse fields such as Sherlock Holmes from popular culture, and Jared M. Diamond from ecology.

This book will be a significant resource for business communication practitioners, especially corporate managers and leaders, sales and marketing professionals, and policymakers. It will be of interest to teachers and students alike, in business communication, organization behaviour, human resource management and marketing communications. It will act as a useful aid for classroom efficacy for teachers and academics.

Pragyan Rath is Assistant Professor in Business Ethics and Communication group at the Indian Institute of Management Calcutta (IIMC), Kolkata, India. She holds an MPhil and PhD in verbal-visual artistic relations. She has authored *The "I" and the "Eye": The Verbal and the Visual in Post-Renaissance Western Aesthetics* (2011) and has researched extensively on visual culture with related publications in national and international journals and paper presentations. She is currently developing a new model for corporate communications entitled "ekphrastic technology" based on the verbal representation of graphic designs.

Apoorva Bharadwaj is Associate Professor in the Business Ethics and Communication group at the Indian Institute of Management Calcutta (IIMC), Kolkata, India. A gold medallist in MA in English Literature, she holds a PhD in American Fiction. She has published research papers focusing on marketing communications, organizational communications, literature and management, Shakespeare and leadership, and inter-cultural communications in reputed national and international journals. She has authored a book entitled *The Narcissism Conundrum: Mapping the Mindscape of Ernest Hemingway through His Epistolary and Literary Corpus* (2013). Currently she is working on using fiction theories to decode advertising texts to develop new narrative models.

Contemporary Themes in Business and Management

Series Editor: Anindya Sen
Professor of Economics,
Indian Institute of Management Calcutta,
Kolkata, West Bengal, India

Business and management are shaped by both external and internal forces. The external forces are driven by the way society at large views the role of business and management in contributing to the social goals. The internal forces are driven by the changing nature of management thinking and research. These forces raise important recurring debates: should private corporates be left to their own devices or should there be monitoring and channelization of their activities? How intrusive should the state be in this respect? How to communicate more effectively within the organization and to the outside world? How to create new markets for basic survival as well as for completely new products?

This series will critically examine some of these themes and issues which have acquired urgency in the contemporary world. It will deal with currently relevant topics with the richness that they deserve and simultaneously eschew fashionable jargon to present lucid and rigorous studies with sound theoretical foundations. The individual volumes will be comprehensive and authoritative resources and will explore major debates from fresh perspectives on economics, management, international business, public policy, development studies and finance.

For a full list of titles in this series, please visit www.routledge.com/Contemporary-Themes-in-Business-and-Management/book-series/CTBM

Books in this series

Indian Business
Notions and Practices of Responsibility
by Nimruji Jammulamadaka

Communication Strategies for Corporate Leaders
Implications for the Global Market
by Pragyan Rath and Apoorva Bharadwaj

Communication Strategies for Corporate Leaders

Implications for the Global Market

Pragyan Rath
and Apoorva Bharadwaj

Routledge
Taylor & Francis Group

LONDON AND NEW YORK

First published 2018 by Routledge

2 Park Square, Milton Park, Abingdon, Oxfordshire OX14 4RN

52 Vanderbilt Avenue, New York, NY 10017

Routledge is an imprint of the Taylor & Francis Group, an informa business

First issued in paperback 2019

British Library Cataloguing-in-Publication Data
A catalogue record for this book is available from the British Library

Library of Congress Cataloging-in-Publication Data
A catalog record for this book has been requested

ISBN: 978-1-138-04791-4 (hbk)
ISBN: 978-0-367-88936-4 (pbk)

Typeset in Sabon
by Apex CoVantage, LLC

Contents

Figures

Tables

Scripts

Commentaries and explanations

Commentary on Script

Explanation

Case studies and caselets

Acknowledgements

We thank the Indian Institute of Management Calcutta for providing financial support to our project "A Study of Theoretical Frameworks from Critical Humanities to Develop New Communication Frameworks for Management Practitioners" which culminated into the constitution of this book.

Many thanks to Professor Anindya Sen, who could infuse in us the confidence of authoring this work with his persistent motivation.

We also acknowledge the help proffered by Harvard Business School for facilitating the intellectual import of two Harvard business cases, "The CEO's Private Investigation" by Joseph Finder and "Taking the Cake" by Ben Gerson.

Thanks for theming our think tank.

Chapter 1

Prelude to communication strategies for global corporate leaders

In today's volatile business world with its multitudes of vicissitudes, the leaders all the more need persuasion skills to bind their workforces and lead them by their high-minded missions. Communication is the most pivotal tool of persuasion which can mobilise the immovable, inspire the mundane and galvanise the inertia that cripple the proficiency of progressive ambitions. The art and skill of communication have inspired the process of metamorphosis through centuries and have helped leaders worldwide from different walks of life – politicians, sportsmen, artists, corporate heads, scientists and many others – to stimulate new thought processes, to initiate new ways of life and to impart new meanings to human philosophy. Communication is a human *need* and a human *deed* that can lead the people *indeed*! Here is your manual of communication that can help you operationalise your visions and missions through transmissions that can provide a new visionary lens to the myopic world.

The aim of this volume is to develop content that can fill the void in communication literature available in the managerial domain. Most communication literature currently used by academic/industry practitioners in management has its thrust on presentation skills and authoring business messages primarily in conventional formats. Most do not cover detailed studies of case analysis, an integral part of contemporary managerial training in decision-making processes. In our work, we have evolved new strategic frameworks of communication and applied them to diverse corporate situations through numerous cases and examples, both domestic and international. The work covers a wide gamut of solved hypothetical Indian episodes, as well as Harvard business cases which act as its major differentiating factor in global communication discourse.

Readership

We have developed the book that intends to reach out to diverse audiences by offering them multiple takeaways:

- Students can benefit from intensively worked out case studies from various managerial domains that relate to their career building endeavours.
- Communication instructors in management academia can benefit from the conceptual frameworks built and their detailed applications which can be used to make the process of teaching-learning more efficacious.
- Corporate professionals can use the communication manuals developed in the work for their daily transactions.
- Researchers can apply the theoretical contexts used in the work to develop new communication projects. As a majority of communication books (both Indian and international) have their content focus on formats and terminologies, this work intends to demonstrate how concepts have been evolved which rationally culminate into format designs, frameworks and terminologies that further add to the quintessential basis of managerial communications.
- Interdisciplinary scholars will find the work interesting since they would be able to comprehend how to use and apply their niche expertise in developing mainstream corporate communication literature.
- International students pursuing global careers can use this work to understand Indian markets and the application of interdisciplinary techniques of communication in the Indian as well as global contexts.

Methodology

We have sought to apply theories from variegated disciplines like humanities, social sciences and theoretical sciences to develop novel strategies and principles which can be used for communication practices. Contributions from landmark thinkers like Samuel Coleridge and Roland Barthes from Literary Studies, Pierre Bourdieu and Jean-Francois Lyotard from Sociology, J. Freedman and S. Fraser from Psychology, Einstein from Physics and even the Sophist rhetorician Protagoras, among others, have informed the conceptualisation of new communication frameworks that the authors have developed. The existing scholarship in the area of managerial communication, including the works of authors like Mary Munter, Peter Cardon, Robyn Walker, Michael Gamble, Jane Thomas and Courtland L. Bovee (to name a few), have also been used as reference material to build up this research work. Hence, the rationale behind our project has been to offer new perspectives and frameworks as considerable departures from conventional literature available for managerial communication.

Highlights

The unique profile of this book is characterised by the following features:

- It is positioned as the only book of its kind which delineates powerful communication strategies and their applications unlike many mainstream books on communication which either do not cover communication strategies at all, or just theorise on these strategies without presenting their applicability in corporate scenarios.

- This book presents new paradigms of persuasion in the form of manoeuvres that can act as game changers in tug-of-war business situations comprising difficult conversations like negotiations, conflicts and interpersonal dissonance that characterise day-to-day corporate workplace tenor. It equips communicators with argumentation skills that can retrieve a lost argument. For the first time, persuasion strategies have been "insourced" from argumentation tactics

  (a) used by lawyers to frame and position their wit to win a point (for instance, cross-examination);
  (b) used by Critical Discourse theorists to frame and position their new theoretical inputs (for instance, Judith Butler positioning Body Theory in feminist discourse and Derrida positioning Deconstruction in Poststructural discourse).

- The book breaks the stereotypical taxonomy of business messages which routinely use four categories – routine, good news, bad news and persuasive. The book brings a comprehensive string of business situations that call for strategic *responses* rather than staying with formatting protocols. We have elevated the process of writing messages from a formal routine etiquette or duty to a strategic tool for tackling critically intricate business scenarios. We have identified certain business situations not in regular circulation and used them to show how writing strategically becomes a powerful tool in the hands of the manager.

- It is the only book in the global market to take up case studies as one of its major learnings. Harvard business cases which are used worldwide in management institutes have been employed for the first time in a book on communications (both in India and outside) to demonstrate problem solving skills which also act as precursors to writing business reports, plans and proposals. As an addendum to this toolkit of **solved** Harvard cases, we also add some hypothetical but familiar domestic situations that call for critical thinking skills that contribute to intelligent configuration of business reports, plans and proposals. We deploy diagnostic procedures from medical sciences as well as taxonomical tenets from zoology and botany as guiding principles for scrutinising situations of corporate investigations. Sherlock Holmes and the evolutionary ecologist Jared M. Diamond have been invoked to give a new perspective to the investigative function of scrutinising not-so-obvious or camouflaged managerial problems to derive insightful problem statements and use them to present targeted solutions.

Preview: chapter snapshots

- Chapter 1: Prelude to communication strategies for global corporate leaders

The on-going chapter is a kind of orientation for readers as an initiating exercise into the content of the book. It provides a preview of the contents of the book, along with its highlights. It also informs the readers

(a) how diverse audiences – students, teachers, researchers and corporate professionals, both Indian and international – can benefit from the book;

(b) how the book is uniquely positioned as the only work of its kind imparting innovative concepts and frameworks with their pragmatic applications delivered.

- Chapter 2: Walk the talk: application of communication strategy

The chapter presents a toolkit of communication strategies based on theoretical inputs from diverse disciplines to enable managers to handle business situations. It is also rich in examples drawn from bureaucracy, media, business, entertainment, history and culture to bring alive these abstract concepts.

- Chapter 3: Checkmate: persuade to win

The chapter describes persuasion as an act of game changing manoeuvre deploying a "selling apparatus" for attaining desired targets in Catch-22 as well as dead-end situations. It equips readers with skills that can enable them to win lost battles. This chapter also introduces new terminologies not prevalent in managerial discourse, like problematisation and deconstruction, to redefine and reposition persuasion as warfare to be won through the subtle demolition of audience defence and resistance. In addition, it offers new insights to career builders for handling their recruitment communications for clinching a deal with their dream companies.

- Chapter 4: You've got mail: strategy in style

The chapter looks at the act of writing messages not just as exchange of information but as strategic responses to challenging business problems. It introduces a new taxonomy of messaging situations along with new strategic frameworks, concepts and terminologies. For each situation, email write-ups have been presented as tutorials in strategic writing skills. As the contemporary corporate scenario is beset with numerous raging controversies, which call for immediate tactful redressal, the chapter presents hypothetical controversial situations akin to real ones, for presenting a writing drill that entails application of new strategies not discussed hitherto in popular communication books.

- Chapter 5: Sherlock Holmes in action: managerial investigations (cases, reports, proposals, plans)

The chapter showcases Harvard business cases as well as hypothetical domestic cases as "texts" for launching investigations using new diagnostic tools to unearth latent intricate business problems and solve them. New innovative concepts have been deployed for case analysis, like

(a) domestication of problem through Anna Karenina Principle (evolutionary ecologist, Jared M. Diamond);
(b) verification and falsification through medical patterns of diagnosis (medical practitioner and novelist, Sir Arthur Conan Doyle);
(c) historicisation (New Historicism).

The chapter also covers writing analytical reports and business proposals along with authoring business plans as entrepreneurial tools for attracting venture capitalists.
    The salient attractions of the chapter include:

(a) two Harvard Business cases analysed and presented in the form of corporate reports;
(b) two indigenous business cases analysed and presented in the format of submission ready corporate reports; and
(c) one business plan and one business proposal completely drafted based on a hypothetical new business offering pitched in for funding.

In sum, the book offers a whole lot of new and exciting experiences and perspectives that are significant in a career builder's life in a contemporary business scenario.

Strategies for global corporate leaders
Stimulating the curious minds of diverse readers
Steeped in the dense theories of the erudite past
For contemporary managers in the world, furious and fast.

Chapter 2

Walk the talk

Application of communication strategy

Communication strategy is the cornerstone of all communication episodes in managerial scenarios. Imagine that you are a Vice President in a multinational giant. You have recently won a bid on a very coveted overseas assignment. Now you have to accomplish a competitive delivery in a short stint of time. But the flip side of the bid is there are no immediate incentives you can offer to your team. Now the challenge is to steer a team of *these* employees towards your big ticket goals without rewarding them with anything. You know that you are on a sticky wicket. Then what are your options? See Figure 2.1 for the sticky wicket options.

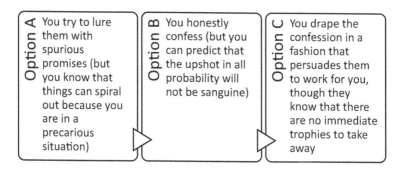

Figure 2.1 Sticky wicket options

Source: All figures, boxes and tables are by authors, unless otherwise mentioned.

When you elect and exercise Option C, you are acting as a Communication Strategist. How do we define a Communication Strategist? A Communication Strategist is a communicator who is *persuasive for being productive.* In other words, s/he knows how to talk in a way that makes others walk the talk. The architect of this walk-the-talk model is a noted researcher and teacher in the Tuck School of Business in Dartmouth College. Prof. Mary Munter[1] has made walk-the-talk easier for all management practitioners by building a universal grammar for productive managerial conversations.

In an Indian context, the application of Communication Strategy is all the more relevant as managers have to grapple with multiple issues of resource deficits, both financial and human. The inherent problem for the Indian workplace has been to mobilise people from heterogeneous sub cultures, which is a stupendous task. Indians work when they are forced, owing to fear of punitive action, or even if they work of their own volition, their sub cultural pluralities make the workplace narratives more rhizomatic and, hence, chaotic. As managing people in Indian organisations is a supremely challenging task for any manager, Munter's grammar can give them a structured paradigm to formulate *their own* professional dialogues for positive outcomes from convoluted situational dilemmas.

Engineering the walk-the-talk grammar

You need appropriate tools in your toolkit to manoeuvre your drive on the communication highway. One of the biggest misconceptions that we as communicators need to fight springs from our self-obsession bubble. We invest a lot of our time thinking about our attire, our presentation style, our content, our delivery and our preparation, and in the middle of all these activities we forget that the most important player in this game is the audience. Why? Because *the liberty to respond or to reject, to explore or to ignore, to select or to neglect* lies solely with the audience.

During the 1960s and the 1970s in the Occidental academia, there was a strong movement in philosophical thought gravitating towards the primacy of the reader on an equalitarian footing with the author in developing meanings in the process of reading the text. The zenith of this movement was reached when the French Literary theorist Roland Barthes came out with his seminal work "The Death of the Author"[2] in 1967. His work totally exterminated the grandiose that an author enjoyed till then and, for the first time, instituted the Reader as the new acknowledged legislator of the literary world. In the same vein, now the audience is the acknowledged legislator of successful communications. It is all the more true in the managerial context as the actor of the desired outcome intended by the speaker is the listener.

The first question that should intrigue you as a strategic communicator is not what will be your content, but why the audience would listen to you. So imagine yourself navigating through this trilogy of initial questions before you even gear up to walk the talk, as illustrated in Figure 2.2

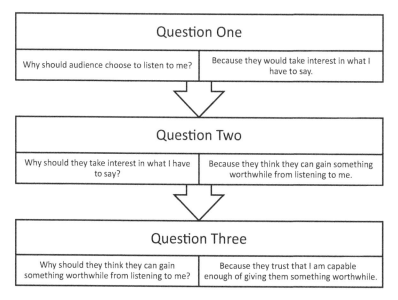

Figure 2.2 Hypothetical dialogue

This hypothetical dialogue helps develop your credibility, which is your first tool as a Communication Strategist. This tool is the Credibility Builder.

Let me imagine I am Mukesh Ambani. Do I need to build credibility? The immediate answer is "no". The world is at my feet, because I have proved my credentials already. I walk-the-talk with my baggage of credentials, wherever I go. I need not announce that *I am Reliance*, because the world vociferates that *Reliance is Me*. This is my Initial Credibility, my multi million bank account, a brilliant metaphor used by Munter to explain the concept of credibility. As I speak, I am using my currency. But every time I use my currency, my savings get depleted if I do not replenish it. In other words, is it enough to be Mukesh Ambani always? Is it possible that post my speech as Mukesh Ambani, I find my audience exclaiming, "I expected more!" The audience expectation would be even more for a celebrity because her Initial Credibility is very high. The more the credibility, the more risk of criticism. So what do I do as Mukesh Ambani, and even more, what do I do if I am *not* Mukesh Ambani? For both, the answer is the same. Don't stop at Initial Credibility. Build more and more. And build more while communicating. In other words, my communication should create credibility irrespective of the fact that I may or may not have Initial Credibility. In short, credibility is not given, it is manufactured, and the act of manufacturing credibility is called acquiring credibility. So, let us look at the manual of how to manufacture credibility, which will move your communication towards your motive.

The master kit of Credibility Building tools includes the following, as documented in Figure 2.3.

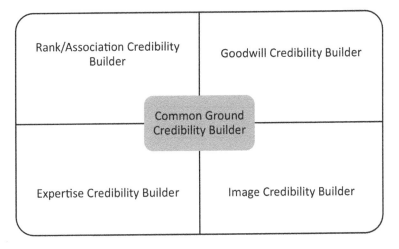

Figure 2.3 Credibility building toolkit

Rank/association credibility builder

If you are CEO of a transnational conglomerate, citing your rank itself will win your audience attention. But now the problem is that you do not have C or E or O in your rank profile. Then the question of how to build credibility might haunt you. The answer lies in this script culled from an award winning speech delivered by Priyanka Chopra when she clinched the *black lady* as the Best Actor (Female) for her role in *Fashion*, a 2008 woman-centric Hindi blockbuster. We quote a few lines from her acceptance speech in Script 2.1.

Script 2.1 Priyanka Chopra's *Filmfare* acceptance speech, 2009

Priyanka Chopra's *Filmfare* acceptance speech, 2009

• . . . To Ronnie, thank you for taking chances and making cinema that means a lot . . . to UTV, the team of UTV, who have put their hearts and souls into so many movies, specially *Fashion*. To Madhur . . ., thank you for believing I could be Meghna Mathur even when I didn't.

Source: Speech transcribed from "Priyanka Chopra Speech Filmfare". Rajesh Chopra. YouTube video uploaded on 27 Jun 2009. Accessed on 30 January 2016 <www.youtube.com/watch?v=Xk0C2-UqyuQ>.

At its epidermal level, the text seems to be all about Priyanka Chopra awarding credit to Ronnie Screwvala, UTV team and Madhur Bhandarkar. But while billing credit, she is building her own credibility as well. We can easily transcribe the credibility-building attempt into its strategic outcomes, as attempted in our commentary on Script 2.1.

Commentary on Script 2.1 Credibility building episode in Chopra's speech

To Madhur . . ., thank you for believing I could be Meghna Mathur

• Mandhur Bhandarkar, who has already proved his mettle as a national award-winning director, who is well-known for producing woman-centric movies, has had the faith in her talent to have cast her in an author-backed role of Meghna Mathur, who is the prime leader in the script of the movie. Unlike other movies, where the male gets the meaty role, here it is a woman who is the protagonist, and that woman is me.

> **thank you for believing I could be Meghna Mathur even when I didn't**

- Her downplaying her potential all the more highlights the same, when she credits the great director to have had belief in her talent, and not in her confidence in herself. (The emphasis is not on Bhandarkar here, but on his trustworthy choice – herself.)

> **thank you for taking chances and making cinema that means a lot**

- UTV makes meaningful cinema. It took its chance by creating a woman-centric movie which had precarious box office prospects. And such an enterprising production house has chosen her to essay the protagonist of its movie. (The stress is on the choice made for a challenging job.)

> **the team of UTV, who have put their hearts and souls into so many movies**

- UTV is a prolific production house, and she is working with them. (Again, the emphasis is on the choice made by a prolific production house.)

How many times when you author your curriculum vitae (CV) are you tempted to cite as your mentor for some summer internship project the title of an IIM/IIT professor to build your own credibility, since you did not have the privilege to secure admission in prestigious, coveted institutes? If you scan your own interview responses, you may be surprised to discover that scores of times you intuitively feel like citing you worked with some experienced or highly *ranked* professional from your domain to give the message to your interviewers that you have established yourself as a budding expert. You may recall a young doctor telling you how s/he worked with an experienced surgeon to win your faith in her credibility.

All these exercises display the use of Rank/Association Credibility. Rank is not simply a position. It is hierarchy. I am above someone in an organisation by dint of my merit. A rank derives its power not from its designation, but from this hierarchical number game.

Because society generally gives credence to this competitive number game, *rank* becomes the power calculator of any individual's stature. In this calibration system, the endeavour of the communicator *then* should be to position oneself in the top echelons of one's domain in the audience perception. What matters is how an audience profiles me on the basis of rank. But unfortunately, most of us may find that we do not have attractive ranks on our business cards. Then how does one manufacture credibility in this rank system? Credibility Builder is the answer.

I must scan my own background to discover and identify my credibility-building agents. For Priyanka Chopra, it was Madhur Bhandarkar. For the budding IT professional, it could be Ankit Fadia, the renowned ethical hacker from India. For the young cardiovascular surgeon, it could be Naresh Trehan, who operated on the erstwhile Indian premier Manmohan Singh. My credibility as a surgeon comes because of my association with Dr. Trehan, but a highly ranked doctor himself also *borrows* credibility from his renowned patient. So, a doctor also gains from her association with patients. Dr. Nandita Palshetkar is well esteemed because of her medical background. Yet a renowned model, Diana Hayden, has catapulted Dr. Palshetkar's status from a known doctor within her coterie to a national name in a newspaper, and this is all because of *association*. Diana Hayden used her own frozen eggs (frozen long back) to give birth to a baby at the ripe age of 42. And this was possible because of Dr. Palshetkar. Knowingly or unknowingly, we have all been borrowing credibility from our network of strong players to influence our audience.

It was the twentieth-century French Sociologist – Pierre Bourdieu – who in his "Forms of Capital" introduced the concept of "Social Capital".[3] Thus, your associations are also forms of capital such that your contact has the economic potential of gain for you. In the light of Bourdieu, "conscious borrowing" becomes a powerful strategy in profiling your own credentials in the mind space of your audience.

Goodwill credibility builder

Let us consider an episode of a routine social interaction. Today, Ms. Anita Chauhan came to your organisation to deliver her expert talk. Before the inception of her speech, she came and shook hands with all of you, enquiring about your name and your background. You were enormously impressed by her amiable disposition. When she actually mounted the pedestal to take charge of the podium to deliver her talk, you were already favourably inclined to listen to her. Her each and every word sounded to you sagacious. During the course of her speech, you were pleasantly surprised when she quoted one of your ideas which you had discussed with her in the morning over a cup of coffee. She named you publically as the originator of that idea. At the end of the day, you had tremendous *goodwill* for Ms. Anita Chauhan.

Another example: Today is February 3. What's special about this day? It's not February 14, Valentine's Day. It is precisely the reason why you are sad, because nobody remembers what is special about this day. Then, suddenly, there is a beep on your smartphone. Your face lights up as you think that your mobile click will take you to a conversation by someone near and dear on this special day. And what do you see? It's a Happy Birthday from *Wills Lifestyle* with a special discount which is valid for "x" number of days, a discount which you might never use. But what *Wills Lifestyle* has used is *Goodwill Credibility*.

Or, look at the following Script 2.2, which has some portions from an email you may still have in your inbox.

Script 2.2 ICICI: you've got mail

Just visit www.giftalivelihood.com, fill in basic details of the candidate you wish to refer and the Academy will do the rest. The cost of training and providing placement opportunities to the candidate will be entirely borne by ICICI Foundation.

I urge you to be a part of this program and help change the life of an underprivileged youth today.

With best wishes,

Chanda Kochhar,
MD & CEO, ICICI Bank

Source: Some portions are extracted from authors' personal correspondence.

Or when you listen to *CNN* News, you believe the tidings travelling to you from all corners not because Christiane Amanpour, Richard Austin Quest, Maggie Lake or Kristie Lu Stout are the news anchors, but because what keeps on ringing again and again in your mind is the iteration of the message against a black background: "CNN 30: Three decades that changed our world".[4]

Or, you like *Tag Heuer* not just because of its technology of chronology, but also because of its chronology of technology, particularly when it says, "Swiss avant-garde since 1860".[5]

Or, if you want to win a bet, the surest way of winning it is to bet on the answer your question would elicit when you ask any set of informed Indians which is the organisation that commands extraordinary goodwill in India. And the answer would be a four lettered word: TATA. This answer is obvious: TATA has earned its goodwill owing to a long history of relentless philanthropic work. When we view their advertisements, the focus is on themes of social upliftment, education, scientific development, religious harmony, patriotism and communal cooperation. It is only at the end that the climactic tag line comes: "We also make steel."

All these examples show the deployment of a goodwill credibility builder. When Anita Chauhan builds rapport with you and talks about you subsequently, she is building a relationship with you, a goodwill gesture. When *Wills Lifestyle* wishes you a happy birthday, this is also a goodwill act since there is an attempt at building a relationship at the personal level so that you do not feel lost in the faceless crowd of their anonymous customers. On a similar plane, when you get an email from Chanda Kochhar – the CEO and MD of ICICI, the name which you are used to seeing only in magazines and newspapers – it is yet another attempt at building a relationship between a farfetched corporate honcho and a commoner with its mediocre banking needs. As seen in the letter, apart from philanthropy, what strikes us is the presence of a celebrated signature which is tantamount to an autograph. Thus, goodwill involves a mutually beneficial symbiotic reciprocal relationship between the communicator and the listener. The listener feels benefitted because s/he has been identified, and the communicator gets the benefit of attracting the interest of the listener. Thus, the key concept of goodwill is a good relationship. But there is more to a relationship, as is the case with all relationships. A good relationship always stands the test of time. A 25th marriage anniversary is a proclamation to the world that see, we have been together for the last 25 years. It is no mean feat. In a similar way, when you as a communicator inform your audience that you have been working on a certain research project for last five years, exhibit your ability to sustain your interest in one particular area for a good amount of time. Here, we introduce the other vital element of goodwill: the relationship track record.

When *CNN* iterates on your television screen the image of "CNN 30", it is also a goodwill exercise by virtue of which credibility is built in the brand which has existed in the news market for the last 30 years. They make sure that you remember that *CNN* has been around for the last 30 years. In the twenty-first century, *Tag Heuer* is even more special because it deliberately clocks you back to an era of antiquity of the Victorian age of 1860. Interestingly, it is this historical distance of the product from our contemporaneity that gets translated as *Tag Heuer*'s market price, which, by the way, is exorbitantly luxurious.

Now we play the devil's advocate again. Track record means longevity of time. What if I have yet to kick start a track record of cumulative achievements? What if I cannot sponsor any social initiative or philanthropy? Merely personalising is not necessarily a ticket to goodwill. You may press the delete button when you see a mail from Chanda Kochhar next time because you know this is from an automated author. So, is this what goodwill is all about? There is more in this bag of tricks. To gain success is it only necessary to showcase your accomplishments, or can your worst debacle give you the best moment with your audience? You may be surprised to know how many have built successful relationships with their audience by using not their chronicles of success, but their narratives of failure.

What do you expect when you imagine Oprah Winfrey, the globally celebrated philanthropist and iconic talk show anchor, delivering a "thank you" speech on receiving the prestigious Bob Hope Humanitarian award, on September 22, 2002? Probably you would imagine her emoting, how her heart bled for the underprivileged people existing on the fringes of society. But here comes the surprise in Script 2.3.

Script 2.3 Excerpt from Oprah's thank you speech

Excerpt from Oprah's thank you speech

- I grew up in Nashville with a father who owned a barbershop, Winfrey's Barber Shop. He still does; I can't get him to retire. And every holiday, every holiday, all of the transients and the guys who I thought were just losers who hung out at the shop, and were always bumming haircuts from my father and borrowing money from my dad, all those guys always ended up at our dinner table. They were a cast of real characters – it was Fox and Shorty and Bootsy and Slim. And I would say, "Bootsy, could you pass the peas, please?" And I would often say to my father afterwards, "Dad, why can't we just have regular people at our Christmas dinner?" because I was looking for the Currier & Ives version. And my father said to me, "They are regular people. They're just like you. They want the same thing you want." And I would say, "What?" And he'd say, "To be fed." And at the time, I just thought he was talking about dinner. But I have since learned how profound he really was, because we all are just regular people seeking the same thing. The guy on the street, the woman in the classroom, the Israeli, the Afghani, the Zuni, the Apache, the Irish, the Protestant, the Catholic, the gay, the straight, you, me – we all just want to know that we matter. We want validation. We want the same things. We want safety and we want to live a long life. We want to find somebody to love. Stedman, thank you. We want to find somebody to laugh with and have the power and the place to cry with when necessary.

Source: Excerpt from "Oprah Winfrey's Speech." Accessed on 31 January 2016 <www.famous-speeches-and-speech-topics.info/famous-speeches-by-women/oprah-winfrey-speech.htm>.

When we migrate from the Occidental world to the Oriental, from the contemporary to the ancient past, we have the same experience. Emperor Ashoka, the invincible warrior who became a votary of Dhamma, could have disseminated this enlightened vision by merely issuing an injunction in an imperial fashion. But look how he chose to communicate through his now famous rock edict, no. 13, as excerpt from 13 is transcribed in Script 2.4.

Script 2.4 Ashoka's rock edict

Ashoka's rock edict

- Indeed, Beloved-of-the-Gods is deeply pained by the killing, dying and deportation that take place when an unconquered country is conquered. But Beloved-of-the-Gods is pained even more by this – that Brahmans, ascetics, and householders of different religions who live in those countries, and who are respectful to superiors, to mother and father, to elders, and who behave properly and have strong loyalty towards friends, acquaintances, companions, relatives, servants and employees – that they are injured, killed or separated from their loved ones. Even those who are not affected (by all this) suffer when they see friends, acquaintances, companions and relatives affected. These misfortunes befall all (as a result of war), and this pains Beloved-of-the-Gods.

- There is no country, except among the Greeks, where these two groups, Brahmans and ascetics, are not found, and there is no country where people are not devoted to one or another religion.[26] Therefore the killing, death or deportation of a hundredth, or even a thousandth part of those who died during the conquest of Kalinga now pains Beloved-of-the-Gods. Now Beloved-of-the-Gods thinks that even those who do wrong should be forgiven where forgiveness is possible . . .

- I have had this Dhamma edict written so that my sons and great-grandsons may not consider making new conquests, or that if military conquests are made, that they be done with forbearance and light punishment, or better still, that they consider making conquest by Dhamma only, for that bears fruit in this world and the next. May all their intense devotion be given to this which has a result in this world and the next.

Source: Excerpt from Rock Edict 13, from *The Edicts of King Ashoka: An English Rendering by Ven. S. Dhammika*. Kandy Sri Lanka: Wheel Publication, 1993. Accessed on 31 January 2016 <www.cs.colostate.edu/~malaiya/ashoka.html>.

We all know Gandhi's famous *Autobiography: The Story of My Experiments with Truth*.[6] The book which italicises truth by making it the title of the great man's work ironically recounts a tissue of lies by this legendary leader.

The common motif which threads these diverse examples from heterogeneous cultures and times together is that in all these cases the communicators (Winfrey, Ashoka, Gandhi) could strike a chord in the hearts of their audience not by limelighting their miraculous successes, but by highlighting their failures or foibles (Winfrey – prejudice, Ashoka – carnage, Gandhi – lies). The reason why failures have succeeded in these cases is because most of us may or may not have succeeded in our lives, but all of us have definitely failed once or many times. This common connect cements the relationship between the communicator and the communicatee. The psychological advantage of this powerless posturing is magical!

One feels more comfortable with people having the same vulnerability quotient. Knowing that even Gandhi had lied mitigates the feeling of guilt that one has because of lying; listening to Winfrey's confession that she was also prejudiced makes our prejudices look less sinful. The comfort also emanates from the fact that with people beleaguered with the same troubles, weaknesses and struggles, we feel less judged; we feel they are *also* like us.

Sometimes failure glorifies, elevates, exalts and even romanticises your profile by means of the trajectory you portray as you recount your struggle from abject past to the glorious present. Emperor Ashoka has been scripted on and off for scores of films and television serials *only* because he started his mortal journey as one of us who have massive material mania, and then he transmuted himself into a mediator monk. Any emperor by virtue of being an emperor commands legitimate right to combat and conquer. Until the Kalinga episode, Ashoka, like any other great ruler, was an invincible warrior. Instead of immortalising his conquests, his edict blatantly advertises his sinful overtures; it is like presenting the casualty list officially by owning the responsibility of the carnage authored by him. Yet the word "remorse" becomes all the more effective because it is contextualised against the backdrop of the heinous casualty list. And this makes the remorse look real. And it makes teaching of Dhamma not look like pious preaching. If a drug addict post rehabilitation exhorts the youngsters not to indulge in a similar vice, it sounds more authentic than a social worker discoursing on the same. Busting the popular myth that to impress your audience you should always try to look better than them, what works is when you look *like* them; that's how *Being Human* works more.

Imagine if Narendra Modi, the prime minister of India, would have been the son of a multi millionaire tea company owner. Do you think you would have been able to relate to him? Perhaps yes, because he is *aspirational*. But his humble origins of a *chai wala* background (tea maker-seller) make him more *inspirational*. This exemplifies how one can glamourise one's humble origins. In the light of such social valorisation of failures, you can now decode the magic of the often recorded famous openers, as in Script 2.5 and Script 2.6.

Script 2.5 Steve Jobs' opening lines

> **Steve Jobs' opening lines**
>
> • Truth be told, this is the closest I've ever gotten to a college graduation.

Source: Excerpt from "'You've got to find what you love,' Jobs says." *Stanford Report* 14 June 2005. Accessed on 31 January 2016 <http://news.stanford.edu/news/2005/june15/jobs-061505.html>.

Script 2.6 Bill Gates' opening lines

> **Bill Gates' opening lines**
>
> • I applaud the graduates today for taking a much more direct route to your degrees. For my part, I'm just happy that the Crimson has called me "Harvard's most successful dropout." I guess that makes me valedictorian of my own special class . . . I did the best of everyone who failed.

Source: Excerpt from "Microsoft's Bill Gates: Harvard commencement speech transcript." *NetworkWorld* 8 June 2007. Accessed on 31 January 2016 <www.networkworld.com/article/2291053/software/microsoft-s-bill-gates – harvard-commencement-speech-transcript.html>.

Thus Goodwill Credibility is all about relating with the audience through relationship, time and common experiences of failures.

Expertise credibility builder

Expertise credibility is important everywhere, both in flat as well as hierarchical organisations. But it is of prime importance particularly in flat organisations where hierarchal superiority alone cannot persuade people. How can one showcase one's expertise? The factors that can act as expertise credibility builders comprise rank, degree, training and experience. Let us see how expertise can be demonstrated without an avowed pronouncement of the vainglorious verbiage, "I am an expert." If one has rank, degree, training or experience, one can state them at the outset without appearing to be reading one's CV credentials in simple and laconic fashion to win audience credibility. The problem arises when we find that we do not have any of these in one's kit. Then how does one construct this credibility?

One way of shaping credibility is to go for sourcing. What is sourcing? If I tell my audience, "70% of Indian men residing in metropolitan cities are smokers," will you buy this statement? Perhaps not! Why should you rely on my data? How did I get this data? It came in my dreams? So, what do I *need* to prove my credentials, or even prove that I have credible information? Have I done some research on this subject? Am I an expert statistician, or a doctor, or a sociologist? If I am none of these, which is most likely the case, then what do I do? If I revise my statement and say, "According to a survey conducted in 2014 as mentioned in the *Journal of Indian Medical Association*, Volume X, Issue 6, 2015,[7] 70% of Indian men residing in metropolitan cities are smokers," will this give me more credibility? The answer is a big YES.

The importance of research and the need to show that I did mine is what we do not realise when juggling with our data. Sourcing of the data and that of accurate sourcing can fortify the strength of our deliveries. You can make the aforementioned statement even more impactful by stating, "According to a survey conducted in 2014 as mentioned in the *Journal of Indian Medical Association*, on page no. 24, Volume X, Issue 6, 2015, 70% of Indian men residing in metropolitan cities are smokers." The accuracy at this level makes it even more credible and may stage me as an expert on the subject. I can further accentuate my impact by citing not just one, but also four to five sources validating my assertion.

We constantly keep on witnessing without identifying a similar play of expert credibility in televised commercials. When products are promoted on the grounds that they are accredited, endorsed or recommended by the *Indian Medical Association*, the attempt is being made to play this credibility factor, and we all know that it works because the customer pays by buying these products. It is this factor of authority on skill and knowledge that a simple product like *Lizol*, a mopping agent, is made to look like a serious thought-provoking issue since it maintains hygiene recommended by doctors. You sure must not be thinking that *that* woman in the print poster is *actually* a doctor.

Other ways of enhancing expert quotients are issues related to delivery. The more you speak spontaneously, without taking support of speaking notes, and the more specialised jargon you use (of course, you should be able to explain them), the more would be your expertise as calibrated by your audience. As a finance expert, you simply cannot do away with the word "leverage". As a poet, can you get away from "metre" and "stress"? As a market researcher, you must know "core competencies" and as a human resource manager, you should have read your Maslow's Hierarchy. Any physicist will enjoy Christopher Nolan's 2014 *Interstellar* for the almost exact depiction of the Black Hole concept. The chemist knows her "bonding", and the biologist her "plasmas".

You can also quote experts if you are not an expert. If you are in a discourse on the Zika virus, and you are not a doctor, you can quote a doctor's comment to support your statements. But do not forget to establish your doctor's credibility. For example, establish your doctor's status by apprising your audience that he is "a nationally renowned medical practitioner working in AIMS Delhi as Chief Medical Officer". This pronouncement is known as building expertise of the expert, sourcing the source or referencing the reference. In other words, if your expert is well known, say you are invoking Einstein to back up your stance, then you need not educate your audience on who Einstein is. But you can still work better by stating something like, "as asserted by Einstein in his fifth manuscript titled XXX on page no. xxx".

Image credibility builder

Usually image is something which is related to charisma – either you are born with it or you do not have it. But this take on image as charisma being natural and not cultivated is a myth. Image can be created. It can be created through the attire you wear, the accessories you carry, the attitude you sport, the voice you command and the style you display. Image can also be developed by creating perceptions. If you mention to your audience that you are a follower of Mahatma Gandhi, you create a certain perception about your personality. Maybe people will imagine you as someone who is doggedly persistent, is poised, believes in the preservation of harmony and has strong set of values. But if you tell them that you are an impassioned votary of Hitler, there will be a complete overhaul in the image you create of yourself. They will now picture you as belligerent, overwhelmingly ambitious, a relentless leader and a hard-core, incorrigible dictator, or even maybe a man of action, a man with vision and a patriotic leader with great oratory skills. Thus, when you know that this is how you can create and recreate your image, use this technique strategically in your communication.

You can appear to be a connoisseur, say, of music. For instance, if in lieu of telling the audience that you are an ardent admirer of Michael Jackson, you set up your image as an admirer of popular culture. It is interesting consumer research that many IIT (Indian Institutes of technology) pass-outs make it a point to cite *Coldplay*, *Red Hot Chili Peppers* or *Pink Floyd* to establish a deeper and more nuanced connection with Western music. The difference in perception between a Jackson lover and a Floyd admirer is exquisite and deliberate!

An image can also deliver a classy lift to a product as exemplified by the following *Audi* print commercial. *Mona Lisa* dominates the view, relegating *Audi* to a puny space in the corner.[8] The message is louder than any body text – if you own an Audi, your tastes are classy. The values that the *Mona Lisa* (the classic painting by the eternal favourite sixteenth-century Renaissance painter, Leonardo da Vinci) portrays are transferred to *Audi*. The marketer knows her consumers well. She knows their tastes and their needs. Who owns an *Audi*? I must have money to buy an *Audi*. And *Mona Lisa* is a classic, but a classic that is worth a billion. The rich can afford a classy taste, and a classy taste needs money to be physically enjoyed and exhibited. Not many could afford a *Mona Lisa*. Similarly, not many could afford an *Audi*. So, the image is that of a unique, exclusive, invaluable, world class product, and the target consumer is, of course, a buyer with classy taste, but also a buyer who can afford a classy product.

Similarly, one can notice that the commercials of *Thums Up* invariably cast the Hindi cinema bigwigs like Salman Khan or Akshay Kumar to create the image of a *Thums Up* consumer – an adventurous, daredevil, macho icon. In the case of cosmetics of *Patanjali* – face wash, fairness cream and similar kinds – Kohl always conjures up the image of Baba Ramdev (the local Indian Yoga expert), and hence creates the feel of herbals, whereas *L'Oreal* always brings before your mental screen the image of Aishwarya

Rai, the Hindi cinema actress and her vocal acceptance of the glamorous brand that uses strong chemicals. Since image creation is such an important phenomenon, there are products which use the same brand ambassadors for years, like *Kent Water Purifier* with the veteran Hindi cinema actress Hema Malini (cinestars lend their image values to the product and help create perceptions). There is an advertisement showing Shahrukh Khan, popularly known as SRK in Hindi cinema, promoting a product like *Navratna* oil, which by its name might seem to you a run-of-the-mill product used in the rural belt of India, but with his powerhouse star value he "uplifts" the product image to make its possession desirable, even for urban users. So *Navratna* is now "cool"! And so is the refrain in their television commercials: "Cool! Cool!"[9]

Images can go a long way in instilling, inspiring and inculcating views. That is why many educational institutions have lecture halls named after Einstein, Chanakya and other path-breaking thinkers instead of being mechanically numbered as N-22. It is not just in names and star values. Your dress gives you an image. A sari (the Indian apparel) will give you a far different image than jeans if you are going for that crucial interview. Hence, the choice of attire also plays a vital role in creating image credibility. Mahatma Gandhi wore apparel that made him look like a representative of a country which is inhabited by a majority of farmers. Jawaharlal Nehru, though a contemporary of Gandhi, created an image totally different to that of Gandhi, which was in sync with his foreign education and rather Anglicised tastes. But the rose bud in his collared *kurta* (coat) did all the magic. Today his buttoned *kurta* is a fashion to reckon with – the Nehru Coat!

Images can also be built by storytelling. If you narrate the story of the famous Indian epic – *Ramayana* – you come across as the votary of value-oriented leadership; conversely, if you yarn the narration of another equally famous epic – *Mahabharata* – you may seem to be endorsing strategic leadership.

If there are images, there are image makeovers. Ratan Tata himself admitted that promoting Nano as a cheap car was a mistake: "Nano was made to reach out to people, (but) it never has. It is meant to be reachable throughout India with our dealerships. But we made our bunch of mistakes [. . .]."[10] Then the organisation went the whole hog to reconstruct the image of the car from its erstwhile perception of a low-income family car to an automobile fast tracking college-going youngsters. By sponsoring a 2012 movie called *Student of the Year,* Nano fortified its youthful image further by appealing to the youth brigade of the country – a story of a complete makeover of the image.[11]

Finally, we have the case of *Aqua Guard,* water purifier, which employs dual credibility – image credibility of the famous Hindi cinema czarina, Madhuri Dixit, with her doctor husband, the cardiac surgeon Dr. Sriram Nene, lending his expert credibility to the product as a medical practitioner and, hence, the vanguard of a healthy lifestyle. Many commercials, instead of employing movie stars and cricketers, just present on-screen models attired as doctors to build that image of expert credibility by underlining the medical benefits of using the products advertised. The audiences, though aware of this counterfeit act of seeing models as doctors, still tend to buy the products by practicing the nineteenth century renowned English poet and literary critic Samuel Taylor Coleridge's concept of the "willing suspension of disbelief" coined in 1817[12] in his literary discourse. Since then marketers are using this concept to sell their products. In sum, you get carried away by the potency of images created – this is the power of Image Credibility.

Common ground credibility builder

When you meet a stranger from the city to which you belong, you feel an instant connection, even though you may have never seen her before! Is it possible for you to decipher this sudden connection which may give credibility to your newfound relationship? We may call this connect the Common Ground Credibility – there is a common binding force which brings people together. The traditional practice of inviting an alumnus to inaugurate the orientation programme in educational institutes for welcoming new students is based on this concept of common ground. You are happy to hear from the alumnus rather than an illustrious personage from your field because the alumnus has a stronger connection with you. S/he proclaims, so to say, "I was like you. Been there, done it! You will be like me in years to come."

Here are certain ways to use this tool to get the audience on your side. First and foremost, you can easily use cultural values as your common ground. When you read about President Obama greeting Prime Minister Modi with the words *"kem cho"* making headlines in newspapers,[13] it demonstrates the power of expending cultural subtleties – that to, at the level of sub culture – like the

Indian Gujarati greeting, in this case. Nations, organisations, educational institutions, etc. all have some cultural values which they nurture, specific to them. One of the easiest ways of building common ground credibility is to explore the repertoire of these cultural values and use it as a connector to your audience. For instance, if you come to know that in an institute the way of applauding is not clapping but thumping on the desk, and you follow this customary way of applause, particularly when you are an outsider, you will easily be able to strike a chord in the hearts of your audience. It is like telling your audience, "I want to be like you because I respect what you like."

Common ground is all the more effective in negative situations, particularly failures. If you are addressing people beset by certain predicaments and you tell this crestfallen audience that once upon a time you had faced a similar type of problem, and then motivate them by narrating how you overcame those very problems, your audience will immediately respond to you with verve and vivacity. It is like telling your audience, "I was like you." That is why we see a towering figure like Amitabh Bachchan making an indelible impact by telling his story of how during the fatal accident he met on the sets of his film *Coolie* in 1983 he needed transfusions of blood to recover from his injuries. He goes on to add with a deep sense of agony as to how one of the samples of blood transfused in his body was affected with Hepatitis B, which affected his liver so much that now he is surviving on one-fourth of his liver. This story gives him that common ground factor which he uses to urge to his viewers that they should undertake Hepatitis B vaccination for their newborns. His lines are enough to endear him to all of us, and bring all of us on one stage where we stand united in mortality: "So, if I am standing here today, you are looking at a person who is surviving with 25% of liver. That is the bad part. The good part is you can survive even with 12%. But no one wants to get to that stage [. . .]."[14]

The entire campaign of *Incredible India* uses that common ground of collective shame when it issues its exhortation to Indians not to indulge in acts that disfigure the image of India in the eyes of foreigners. It would not be difficult for us to connect with embarrassing acts that we have all been a part of, perhaps visually been witness to, or deep down we know we have been guilty of doing the same at some point of time – spitting paan syrup on walls; throwing domestic (particularly kitchen) leftovers, otherwise popularly known as *kachra* (garbage), down balconies, or on to water bodies; using isolated grassy patches for bowel movements, and even urinating in every possible "*nukkad*" and "*gali*" (colonies and streets); even eve-teasing or perhaps ogling at foreign tourists. It feels great when the Indian protagonist dissuades Indians from indulging in these shameful habits. More than the responsibility projected by the brand ambassador of *Incredible India*, what impacts us is a sense of collective shame, which we feel as Indians.

Turning to politics, we get scores of election campaigns run on this common ground motif. The nomenclature of an Indian political organisation – *Aam Admi Party*, or the common man party – is also grounded in this common ground theory. Politicians have won elections from their pet constituencies using the common ground for years, mesmerising their voters by convincing them with assurances of belonging to the same place. Hence, they are induced to vote for an insider ousting the outsiders. The rhetoric of "insider" has won several elections.

Not just in elections, but also in marketing campaigns we get scores of successful episodes of the usage of this common ground theme. In fact, look at the *utterly butterly* campaign of *Amul* Butter advertisements; they are always reminding Indians about every great Indian incident that went into the making of our popular culture. In the words of the journalist Sylvester Dacunha, "The ads represent a history of modern India acted out by a little heroine, healthy and confident about the future."[15] When the *Lok Pal* bill became a rage in India, *Amul* cleverly used the topical issue to market its product by alloying with another popular expression – "lock *kiya jaye* (lock the answer)" – from the television blockbuster *Kaun Banega Crorepati* (Who will be the millionaire?), or *KBC*.[16] Or, it even used the celebrity gossip that defines the Indian teatime routine with the much-publicised slap allegedly administered by Shahrukh Khan to Shirish Kunder, husband of the celebrated director-choreographer, Farah Khan. The poster had the hilarious tag line "Please maar Khan" ("maar" in English is "slap"), playing on the name of the movie directed by Kunder – *Tees Maar Khan*.[17] Thus, historically *Amul* has been using popular discourse to connect to the Indian audience by giving it a sometimes humorous, sometimes hilarious and sometimes sarcastic twist as a common ground factor.

Cine stars become stars owing to this common ground factor and not that enviable X factor *alone*. Amitabh Bachchan could become a legendary superstar owing to his penchant for essaying characters of a common man – an ordinary coolie, a struggling labourer, a thief, and the list is endless. It has been a commonly accepted premise in Film Studies that Bachchan cinematically stood for the labour unionisation phenomena in the late 1970s naxal-ridden Indian diaspora, where the anti-capitalist labour movement was cinematically spiced up with indispensable Indian sentiment that can *only* come from quintessential Indian culture, as is evident from this popular dialogue of the 1970s blockbuster *Deewar* (The Wall). The context is the dialogue between two brothers, one who is an anti-establishment rebel (Bachchan) and the younger sibling (Shashi Kapoor), who is serving the system as police personnel. When the elder is flaunting his material status, the younger with only one dialogue demolishes the colossal ego of the elder by showcasing his priceless possession that *only* an Indian can value: "You might have bungalows, cars, money, but, *mere pass maa hai* (I have mother with me!)." The poignancy of a motherless son makes Bachchan's character subject to more sympathy for Indian masses despite his anti-establishment career. The southern sensation Rajnikant has been elevated to the pedestal of demigod owing to this common man image that binds him with his aficionados. His meteoric and mythical rise from a conductor to a cinema A-lister has a lot to do with his attractive yet easily imitable style of tossing the cigarette and juggling his shades. These mannerisms have been followed by the masses. By the way, these two superstars do not have the-so-called drop-dead Greek-God looks, and yet they are popular *only* because a common man thinks they are like him. The common man metaphor has been the silver lining for many celebrities that play to the gallery. Shahrukh Khan's *Chennai Express* set cash registers ringing with the famous dialogue: "Never underestimate the power of the common man."

So find more and more common ground factors to link you with your audience and create your X factor.

Thus, in this post trust era where it is difficult to gain faith, these credibility tools can assist you in establishing your credentials as an authentic communicator, even with the most sceptical audience. But appearing authentic is not enough. In today's corporatised world, where everyone is looking to satisfy her commercial interests, catering to their needs is as important as building your credibility. Let us transition from credibility building tools to the audience benefit distributor kit, another invaluable asset to good strategic communication.

Audience benefit distributor kit

Rewinding back to the reader response theory, we have to *now* think of the other important component of strategic communication, and that is the audience. Not that we have not been doing that with our Credibility Builder Kit. After all, it is all about connecting with our audience, and hence we need to work on creating, manifesting and boosting our credibility through our communication, and more so in the eyes of our audience. But we are *also* talking about productive persuasion, and hence, *merely* appearing compatible with the audience is not enough. Yes, compatibility is significant in striking a chord, but we are also interested in getting results, and that too, results from the audience. So, we need to do more than strike a chord; we need to *move* them so that *they* do what we want them to do. And that is possible when *they* feel they are getting something out of this entire exercise of listening and being a meaningful part of the communication activity.

What has been popularly noted as the WIIFT or "what is in it for us" is equivalent to Munter's framework of the Audience Benefit. Why would I (the audience) listen to anyone? For the simple reason that I feel I benefit in some way or the other; I feel that the outcome of what I hear makes for a positive change in my life. In other words, the managerial communicator is the strategic Santa Claus, who *distributes* goodies. At a deeper level, we already know the agenda of such distribution, do we not? So, here are some tips for great audience benefit distribution through strategic communication, as illustrated in Figure 2.4.

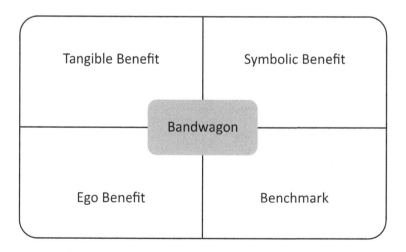

Figure 2.4 Audience benefit distributor kit

Tangible benefit distributor

It would be interesting to relook at your HR policies by your organisation, for its employees and for you! Has it ever occurred to you why you have been *requested by your organisation* to attend a particular workshop to learn a certain programme, language or theory? Or how many times after a conference or special meeting you get accessories *gifted* to you – accessories like bags, mugs or even stationery – or even *free* dinners, lunches, edibles? Or, for doing a project well, your organisation *gifts* you a bonus? Let us look at the web page of *Marks & Spencer*. The words are *right* there on your face: "Why Work for Us?"[18] We have picked up some interesting lines that adorn their Career Scope discourse with the tag line "Say yes to *M&S*". See Script 2.7.

Script 2.7 *M&S recruitment communication*

M&S Recruitment Communication

- There's a sense of camaraderie here; a feeling of belonging – probably because we go out of our way to listen to and involve all of our people. And because we want to be the best, we want you to be your best. The size and scope of our business means that the opportunities on offer are as diverse as the people that work here. If you're ready to play your part, you'll be richly rewarded too. From competitive salaries, bonus schemes and flexible working options to opportunities to volunteer in the community, there really is something for everyone.

Source: Excerpt from "M&S Careers." Accessed on 7 February 2016 <http://careers.marksandspencer.com/why-work-here>.

What do organisations really think about? Profit. And from where does the profit emerge? From good work. And from where does good work emerge? From employees. Hence, human resource is a significant strength for the good health of any organisation worth its salt, and subsequently the greatest profit-making tool. Every organisation needs to *take care* of their human resource. A *happy* employee is a *motivated* employee, and a *motivated* employee is pro-organisation. So, the most *visible* or *recognisable* manner in which an employee may be motivated is through obvious forms of benefits, that is, benefits beyond the regular employment procedures like salary. What would these common forms of benefits be? Rewards, incentives, benefits – whatever you might call them – exist in palpable, materially available and measurable forms. In other words, they are *tangible* incentives which we as employees can feel, hear, sense, weigh, digest and obviously use for our personal and professional growth.

"I am sent to a workshop" means that a training programme makes me more equipped to perform better for my organisation, and the newly learnt efficiency would, perhaps, eventually translate into a salary hike or promotion. And a promotion is a definitive incentive, since my rank (remember rank credibility) translates into a better pay-check, and hence better lifestyle. While I am incentivised for my training, I am, by virtue of my training, better equipped to work for my organisation. The cycle of incentives continues, where the employee through her training brings in better incentives for the company and, in due process, is incentivised by the company as well.

In certain training programmes, memoirs in the shape of usable *things* – like mugs, stationery and even clothing, like tees – remind us of the programme. More so because the programme title, along with the employee name and the year, are inscribed onto the physicality of the materials distributed. In management training programmes, tees with the brand name calligraphed onto them, become tangible incentives for the registered participants, since they occupy enviable positions in society for those who have attended such programmes. Therefore, a management training in any of the premier management institutes in India is a matter of incentive that may translate into task and career profits later on. And these are definitely profitable activities, since they are markers of social envy, desire and aspiration.

Benefits are more than just targeting basic needs. It is easy to understand the complex, yet inevitable nature of tangible benefits when we consider the job-hunting process. Tangible benefits are the lifeblood of any organisation. If we, as interviewees, have to prove our credibility and expertise to an organisation during the job seeking process, another prime concern from the point of view of the organisation is "what IT offers to the job seeker". Thus, the entire job seeking process is an act of communicating benefits – the candidate who is being interviewed tries to demonstrate what benefits s/he can give to the organisation by virtue of her merit as presented in the CV while the organisation tries to market itself by communicating the job profile in a manner that looks beneficial to the interviewee. Thus, it is not just about the incentives an organisation offers, but also about how these incentives are communicated. It would be interesting to read company websites, company offer letters and even television commercials that companies air to understand how audience benefits are highlighted through strategic communication.

In other words, the organisation also has to worry about advertising what they have to offer to a desirable employee as much as the desirous employee wants to impress the organisation (remember *M&S* webpage here). An Indian civil service profile is glamorous not just because it offers positions of power and nationalistic narratives. It also provides important and tangible employment benefits that render the job profiles attractive: travel concessions, housing allowances, security and home service among many others. A government job will have its own set of tangible incentives, as will a corporate service. One of the popular incentives which features on the government offer letter is the facility of Leave Travel Allowance (LTA) – a sponsored travel with family that makes the job profile singularly alluring. Similarly, the retirement pension schemes of government jobs are very necessary criteria for job attractions. Thus, the very incentives for employees are indirect incentives for the organisations as well. Hence, a strategic communication can never be devoid of tangible benefits. Remarkably, tangible benefit distribution *also* leads to furthering businesses. There are many shops, boutiques and websites that host a range of very common products/activities familiar to most of us working in corporations. The goodies like mugs, pen stands and other quotidian items get *customised* as per the company/organisation, employee name and other particulars, as required. The irony is that the employees might compete for these tangible benefits!

Symbolic benefit distributor

It is at this juncture that we introduce another variation of tangible benefit. The tangibility is reduced while the symbolic value of the incentive is enhanced. The complexity of such a benefit is beautifully captured by the term "symbolic". If the customised mugs, calendars and shirts are not enough, let us fall back on the tried and tested method of exemplifications – those from popular culture.

For an Indian consumer, popular culture would typically consist of two strong competing products/services: cricket and movies. Let us start with cricket. What happens to a bat when it carries on its material body the coveted signature of Tendulkar? What would the likely owner of the bat do now? Play with it, or garner her show-case in her drawing room with the same? The bat ceases to be a regular bat, a tool used to hit a ball in a sport called cricket. It is now something more than a bat. It is a representation of Tendulkar himself. Hence, an ordinary bat transforms itself into a valuable asset that might no longer be used in a game; it needs to be framed and preserved for eternity. In fact, the value might translate into an invaluable legacy that needs to be handed down to the next-in-line in a family. In other words, it becomes an invaluable possession that needs to be definitely spelt in a will before the owner dies, so that there are no inheritance issues. The signed bat is *now* equivalent to great economic value, but exists primarily as a symbolic embellish-ment that is *never* traded for its economic one!

Let us consider the very popular Hindi blockbuster of 2009, *3 Idiots*. The head of the technological institute in his introductory remark to his new students displays a pen (for all you know, he might have bought it from a shop next door). He weaves a narrative around the pen, stating that it is a special pen with special attributes, *gifted* to him by a special person to celebrate his intelligence. But the strategic comment that arrests the attention of all the students ema-nates at the end of the narrative. Virus (nicknamed by the students) states that for the next 20 years, he has been searching for the next Virus, to whom he can proudly hand over the pen. Such a narrative transforms a mere pen from a common tool that is used for writing to a symbol of excellence, or even a symbol of unachievable excel-lence (the length of time has boosted the value of the pen infinitely). The more unachievable, the greater the desire to achieve the pen.

When a tangible product loses its materiality to adorn an immate-rial or incorporeal value, like that of intelligence, diligence, excellence and other such non-quantifiable qualities, such that they cease to be the original objects, they then become symbolic objects rather than just tangible ones. Karl Marx, in his critique of the nineteenth cen-tury political economy (*Das Kapital*), defined the crucial distinction between the use-value and the exchange-value of an object.[19] A pen is used for writing; hence writing is the use-value of the pen. The moment the pen is a product in the market, it has a new value – the exchange value – which is an abstract assessment of the pen. On a similar note, a symbol is also an abstract quality. A symbol represents an abstract value, and not necessarily the material. In fact, the qualitative value ironically evolves into a more envious existence (Sachin Tendulkar's signed bat would now have a massive cost, or owning an M. F. Hussain-painting would be a more desirable proposition than holding a colossal bank account). A symbolic value gets me something more than money: enviable position, pride, self-esteem or all of it.

No wonder the adage "money cannot buy everything" works in an Indian context, though, ironically, these intangible qualities when exchanged as saleable tangible goods would be priced exquisitely. Hence, there are times when benefits are more appealing for their qualitative value than for their quantitative charm. Yet, we *also* want to remind our readers to never forget the underlying tangible profit-value that the transformed symbolic assessment always retains. After all, this is about strategic incentive, where any incentive to the audience is *also* a possible and hopeful addition to personal, trade or organisational profit.

Ego benefit distributor

We have tangible benefits and symbolic benefits to distribute to our audience. But as the need of the audience varies, so would the nature of benefits. Let us look at some of the interesting lines (mostly opening) in speeches made by great Indian personalities from various backgrounds, as we make way for the next benefit. When the President of the United States of America, President Obama, on his three-day visit to India, addressed a joint sitting of both the Houses of Parliament, his opening lines were typical yet remarkable in the context they were being made. See Script 2.8.

Script 2.8 Obama's opening lines

Obama's opening lines to Indian parliament

- Mr. Vice President, Madame Speaker, Mr. Prime Minister, Members of the Lok Sabha and Rajya Sabha, and most of all, the people of India.

- I thank you for the great honor of addressing the representatives of more than one billion Indians and the world's largest democracy. I bring the greetings and friendship of the world's oldest democracy, the USA, including nearly three million proud and patriotic Indian Americans.

Source: "Full text of Obama speech in Parliament." *India Today* 8 November 2010. Accessed 19 February 2016 <http://indiatoday.intoday.in/story/full-text-of-obama-speech-in-parliament/1/119263.html>.

In a similar context, also read our former Prime Minister, Atal Bihari Vajpayee, talking about the Indo-US relationship at the Joint Meeting of Congress, US House of Representatives. See Script 2.9.

Script 2.9 Mr. Vajpayee's opening lines

Mr. Vajpayee's opening lines to the US house of chamber

- Mr Speaker,
- American people have shown that democracy and individual liberty provide the conditions in which knowledge progresses, science discovers, innovation occurs, enterprise thrives and, ultimately, people advance.
- To more than a million and half from my country, America is now home. In turn, their industry, enterprise and skills are contributing to the advancement of American society.
- I see in the outstanding success of the Indian community in America, a metaphor of the vast potential that exists in Indo-US relations, and what we can achieve together.

Source: "The Vajpayee Visit." *Rediff.com*. Accessed 19 February 2016 <www.rediff.com/news/2000/sep/14pm.htm>.

Or scroll through the Indian corporate giant Mr. Narayan Murthy's 2015 Convocation Lecture delivered at the Indian Institute of Science (IISc) in Bangalore. See Script 2.10.

Script 2.10 Narayan Murthy's opening lines

> **Narayan Murthy's opening lines during IISc convocation**
>
> - Science is about unravelling nature and engineering is about using those discoveries and inventions to make life better for human beings. IISc is at the forefront of scientific and engineering research in the country. IISc has produced students who have gone on to earn laurels in the most competitive places in the world. Your research is well cited. Therefore, IISc deserves to lead in the transformation of India by using the power of science and engineering.

Source: "Convocation Lecture." *Scroll.in* 16 July 2015. Accessed 19 February 2016 <http://scroll.in/article/741723/full-text-narayana-murthy-questions-the-contribution-of-iits-and-iisc-in-the-last-60-years>.

Or reflect on Indra Nooyi, who hardly needs an introduction to Indian management students, when she says, "Thank you", on receiving the NDTV Global Living Legends awards, as reproduced here in Script 2.11.

Script 2.11 Indra Nooyi's opening lines

> **Indra Nooyi's thank you to NDTV**
>
> - Mr. President and NDTV,
> - Thank you very much for this incredible honour. You know, Malcolm Gladwell in his book the *Outliers* said, "Who you are cannot be separated from where you came from." I left India 35 years ago, went on to the United States, and had tremendous success in that meritocracy. But none of that could have happened if I hadn't had a wonderful upbringing very much here in India. So I have a lot to thank India for.

Source: Transcribed from NDTV Video "Never be happy with what you know: Indra Nooyi." 14 December 2013. Accessed 19 February 2016 <www.ndtv.com/video/player/news/never-be-happy-with-what-you-know-indra-nooyi/301374>.

Or enjoy Saurav Ganguly's hilarious opening of the first session of the Speaker Series, Intaglio, 2013 in the Indian Institute of Management Calcutta auditorium, as documented in Script 2.12.

Script 2.12 Saurav Ganguly's opening lines

Saurav Ganguly at IIMC intaglio

- Prof. Banerjee, Prof. Bista . . . [audience laugh] . . .
- This is what happens when you watch an India Pakistan game the whole evening . . ., when India loses, we're on an open top around Eden Gardens, and then you go to bed at 1 o'clock in the night because you're so tired and then you're up among the best students in the world, one of the few of the best students in the country, I would say, early morning the next day. So please pardon me for the mistake.

Source: Transcribed from YouTube, "Saurav Ganguly speaks on Leadership at IIM Calcutta." 11 November 2013. Accessed 19 February 2016 <www.youtube.com/watch?v=t-w582VzJWI>.

It is worth considering the praise bestowed on India by the US President on his visit to the country. This is a diplomatic political visit, and the political relationship between the two nations is of deep significance. The global power cannot overlook India. And this political, economic, social and cultural importance that India has on the global summit is so very eloquently evident in the opening lines of Obama's speech. It is a homage paid by the oldest democracy to the largest democracy, and the economic thrust is strengthened multi-fold when the three million is compared to the one billion population. A salutation to such a large and growing population is inevitable for a representative of a nation whose *Pepsi* and *Cola* and even *Spiderman*, *Ironman*, *Batman* and countless other brands are so enormously and popularly consumed by a significant segment of the one billion. The recognition and respect to that one billion from the head of the three million is inevitable. Remarkably, these three million are patriotic American Indians!

When we as communicators bestow a special courtesy to our audience because of our appreciation of their qualities, this declared appreciation is also a special form of benefit. When Obama comes to India, he appreciates Indians. When Vajpayee addresses the Americans, he too appreciates the Americans; he does so by commending the American democracy. Or, when Narayan Murthy is the Chief Guest for the most prized occasion of any institute – the Convocation – he too begins by praising the merits of the outgoing students from as great and reputed an institute as IISc. Or, when the *Pepsi Co.* head, who has been living in America for more than three decades, is celebrated in India with a prestigious Indian honour and presented by the highest dignitary of the nation – the President – it takes no time for Indra to acknowledge India, and the major impact that India had on her career. Or, for the hilarious mistake that Ganguly makes when he mispronounces the presenter's name, and then he quickly comes back with an equally amazing appreciation for the very audience he is requesting forgiveness from. He says he was watching an India-Pakistan match, which is already a spirited experience to have, and then next morning to be standing amidst the world's best students can be quite a task for pronunciation mistakes! It is not about his exertion; it is about the huge *ego benefit* he delivers to his audience by creating an aura around them by pedestalling them to the stature of excellence not only nationally, but also globally. Thus, he translates his nervousness into an evidence of insuperable merit of the audience. This was a smart cover-up of his mistake by the tactful use of ego benefit.

The famous nineteenth and early twentieth-century Austrian psychologist, Sigmund Freud, established the important term "ego" that has seeped into popular discourse with various modifications. The word "egotistic" has a negative connotation, since it refers to anyone who thinks too highly of herself. But the word "ego" is a neutral identity. In Hinduism, ego would refer to "*aham*"; in Western psychological discourse, it refers to "self"; and in managerial communication, it refers to "self-esteem". So, ego benefit is all about appreciating the other; we make our audiences feel that *they* matter. Our audiences need to feel that their contribution is significant. As a project manager, how many times has your smile or even a thumbs-up to any of your teammates and even subordinates resulted in good partnership? As a teacher, how many times have you managed to win over a shy student when you praised her efforts to answer in class?

Ego benefit can be used in the most strategic way for encasing the most strategic points. Let us consider Murthy's convocation speech again. He praises the calibre of students from IISc. But, the speech in totality is actually an inquisitorial on the contribution of these bright students who pass out from bright institutions like the IITs! Or, look at Vajpayee's lines again. He praises America for their democratic ideals. Then, he intelligently switches over to Indians living in America and their contribution to America's growth. Let us call this the Circular Ego Benefit Strategy. We might have heard of circular reasoning, begging the question or in Latin, *circulus in probando*. The idea here is that if the reasoner states that P is true because Q is true, then Q is true because P is. Hence, the reasoning is circular, where the reasoner develops the credibility of P, such that P now becomes the expert to render credibility to us. In a similar manner, we may use the ego benefit to make our audience credible experts, who, in turn, vouch for our expertise. We do not blow our trumpets, but use the circular process of getting third party appreciation for our own organisation by first drawing their interest and respect by appreciating them as credible stakeholders. For example, when we have executive participants coming for management development programmes to our institute, we welcome them with an ego benefit: "It is our honour to teach experienced people like you!" But we can go one step ahead when we say, "Experienced people choose good institutions!" That is a much smarter way of developing credibility of one's own organisation than stating in clumsy statements, "We are the best organisation in management development programs." Alumnus culture of institutes is one of the finest examples of this strategic practice of symbiotic benefit – students use the platform of their home institute's reputation to launch their careers and the institute is helped by these students who now have become their successful alumni as brand ambassadors to sustain and advance its reputation. Hence, alumnus culture is so integral and significant for all big institutions. After all, we can only beg our own for our own benefit!

Benchmark benefit distributor

Now we come to our final two benefits, and they are related. A management institution takes all the trouble yearly to announce the successful number of students placed. And that is declared as a record; as a benchmark. Every athlete sets a record in her sport. Every blockbuster movie sets the benchmark for the business it does. Every company announces the benchmark that it has created, sustained or set. Every coaching centre sets the benchmark; many of their students ranked in the top 50, 100, 200 or even 1000 in coveted Indian entrance examinations like the Joint Engineering Examination (JEE) or the Common Admission Test (CAT). Benchmark is the benefit that is useful when you want to set standards. It is not only about announcing your credibility, but is also about setting the target for the next activity. If it's 90% this year, the signal to the audience is that we need to go beyond that – set a 90.1% perhaps for the next fiscal year.

As the popular axiom goes, records are meant to be broken. A benchmark is set to *motivate* competitive audiences to either sustain the level achieved or go beyond it and set a new one. A commendable target is not necessarily just a target but actually a motivating factor. Hence, a motivating factor translates into a required action of wanting to beat the best or proving one's worth, and this translation from wanting to achieve a target to actually achieving it is the benefit that a benchmark might fulfil. So, next time a standard is set, you know what it means. Subconsciously or otherwise, you are itching to push it and, thus, set a higher one. Such an event would naturally result in more tangible incentives for you, as well as for the organisation. There was a time when 2 G was a miracle in mobile technology. The moment there was the 2 G buzz, trust us when we say that technicians were already working on the next what's-better-than-2 G project? The moment a film sets a gigantic business prospect of 100 million, the next big producer or the same production company is working with greater zeal to *raise the bar*. The art of *raising the bar* is the benchmark benefit, or rather the benefit the act of benchmarking is expected to motivate to achieve! It is no mean feat that we have come from 2 G to 4 G in a short time, and the count is still on!

Bandwagon benefit distributor

And if benchmarking sets the tone, then bandwagoning is the inevitable trap! What is a bandwagon, literally? Imagine a Western countryside. A carriage on four wheels crosses the pavement. A band of musicians are seated in the carriage doing the thing they do best. The music, the colour and the rhythm gets the kids excited, and as the carriage dashes through the town, all the kids run after it, hoping to jump on to the carriage. Bandwagoning, in fact, comes from a negative phrase – heard of the "herd mentality" syndrome? The shepherd's job is to see that a sheep does not wonder astray and stays with its herd. Herd mentality is when I do something *only* because *everyone* is doing the same. In a way, I am following the crowd. Now, the negative connotation originates in the possibility of the herd not always being right, and following a crowd is not necessarily following your instincts. So why do we do this? Why do we not follow our instincts, but do what the crowd seems to do, like what the crowd seems to like or hate what the crowd seems to hate? For the simple reason that I am scared I will be left behind, or even worse, I am losing out on something that everyone else is enjoying the *benefit* of! Herd mentality is all about hiding one's insecurity, or overcoming the feeling of being left insecure and alone. So the negative positioning of herd mentality is given a positive twist in corporate practice and then we have our very own bandwagoning.

For example: A movie releases on a Friday, and by the weekend all the posters set the benchmark – 65 million rupees earned for the first time in the history of the weekend movie business. Sixty-five million rupees is not just the business figure. Where does that figure come from? Obviously from the number of people who have bought tickets and seen the film. The movie is *popular*. So, what does that do to me, who is sitting at home, looking at television commercials, posters, newspapers or any other form of media that announces the benchmark of 65 million rupees? I start feeling that I am missing out on something big, which everyone else is getting to see, hear and experience. Eventually, I book my tickets for a Wednesday, and finally do get to have my experience of the movie. I come out with a headache, but, by then, the movie business has soared to a fastest ever record of 100 million rupees.

From smartphones to *Kellog's* cornflakes to holding Twitter or Facebook accounts to "whatsapping"; we have countless corporate examples of lifestyle changes ushered in by bandwagoning. One of the greatest followerships created through bandwagoning in the Indian context of education is the fervent *fetishisation* of engineering, medical and management studies. From school onwards, parents plan tutorials for entrance examinations for their sons and daughters, such that children are lining up for lessons from their early teens to crack the Joint Entrance Examination (JEE) post their twelfth standard, the Common Admission Test (CAT) post their graduations, and the civil service examination post their Masters. They are hardly studying, and if they do, they study subjects like Mathematics and Science, or Economics in the Social Sciences. In fact, they study more in the *Agarwals, Brilliants, Times* and then *Chanakyas* in all their student lives than in proper universities or educational institutions. And this is not because these kids love these tutorials or career options, but because any other subject or career option is not presented to them as lucrative ventures. Their parents feel that if their sons are not engineers, job prospects would vapourise into thin air. And if you graduate with Arts as a major, the perception is that you have not been a good student or you failed in the coveted entrance examinations. The issue lies in the so-called intrinsic merit declared in such educations and their corresponding examinations. The issue is that this political coalition which has ripened between the operators of these coveted examinations and the institutions which use these examinations as their screening tools has resulted in a booming business of millions *only* owing to this practice of bandwagoning. As a result, all other career options look redundant.

If benchmarking is the incentive you would get if you *raised the bar*, bandwagoning is the incentive you would lose if you do not follow the rest who are in the business of *raising the bar*. At the end, the *bar does get raised* and your contribution in *raising the bar* is incentivised.

So here your tool kit is ready; a smart translation of a philosophical principle of reader response theory. See Table 2.1 for a quick reminiscence.

Table 2.1 Strategic communication tool kit

Credibility builder tool kit	Audience benefit distributor kit
Rank	Tangible
• Association	• Material valorisation
Goodwill	Symbolic
• Relationship	• Abstract qualifier
• Time	
• Failure	
Expertise	Ego
• Sourcing	• Self-esteem
• Sourcing the source	• Circular reasoning
Image	Benchmark
• Tastes	• Showcase standard achievements
• Preferences	• Motivate to raise the bar
Common ground	Bandwagon
• Sub cultural connotations	• Herd mentality

This tool kit is the product of the application of variegated interdisciplinary studies which have stood the test of time (remember goodwill credibility – time factor) as seminal path-breaking thought moulders with huge followings in different academic and industrial domains. Here is the record of these must-read works which have fused the various communication practices into a successful model in Table 2.2.

Table 2.2 Theoretical backgrounds of the communication techniques discussed

Thinker	Nationality/ designation	Year	Text	Term/philosophical movement	Communication technique derived
Roland Barthes	French literary theorist	1967	"The Death of the Author"	Participation of the reader in building meanings in a text	Importance of audience in authoring the outcomes in communication episodes
Pierre Bourdieu	French sociologist	1986	"The Forms of Capital"	Social Capital	Rank/Association Credibility
Samuel Taylor Coleridge	English poet and literary critic	1817	Biographia Literaria or the Biographical Sketches of MY LITERARY LIFE and OPINIONS	Willing Suspension of Disbelief	Image Credibility
Karl Marx	German sociologist	1867–1883	Das Kapital, Kritik der politischen Ökonomie (Capital: Critique of Political Economy)	Use-Value and Exchange-Value	Symbolic Value
Sigmund Freud	Austrian psychoanalyst	1920 essay	"Beyond the Pleasure Principle"	Ego	Ego Benefit as Self-Esteem

Notes

1 Mary Munter, *Guide to Managerial Communication: Effective Business Writing and Speaking*. Upper Saddle River, NJ: Prentice, 2012.
2 Roland Barthes, "The Death of the Author." *Image/Music/Text*. Trans. Stephen Heath. New York: Hill and Wang, 1977, 142–147.
3 Pierre Bourdieu, "The Forms of Capital." *Handbook of Theory and Research for the Sociology of Education*. Ed. J. Richardson. New York: Greenwood, 1986, 241–258.
4 Tag line from poster, accessed on 30 January 2016 <http://3.bp.blogspot. com/-LQZEjD2VoLI/VjBg3HVb1uI/AAAAAAAARiI/rFg9bvu9O9s/ s1600/CNN%2B30%2B%25E2%2580%2593%2BThree%2BDecad es%2Bthat%2BChanged%2BOur%2BWorld%25E2%2580%2599. png>.
5 Tag line from poster, accessed on 30 January 2016 <http://upscaleliv- ingmag.com/wp-content/uploads/2015/01/534041915FB00009_TAG_ Heuer_.jpg>.
6 Mahatma Gandhi, *Autobiography: The Story of My Experiments With Truth*. Trans. Mahadev Desai. Ahmedabad: Navajivan Mudranalaya, 1927.
7 The sourcing is a hypothetical example.
8 Image accessed on 20 February 2016 <http://files1.coloribus.com/files/ adsarchive/part_1191/11913755/file/audi-q7-mona-lisa-small-70886. jpg>.
9 Image accessed on 20 February 2016 <http://images.financialexpress. com/2015/06/emami780.jpg>.
10 K. V. Lakshmana, "Branding Nano as cheapest car was a big mistake: Ratan Tata." *Hindustan Times* 16 July 2015. 20 February 2016 <www. hindustantimes.com/business/branding-nano-as-cheapest-car-was-a- big-mistake-ratan-tata/story-wXlXfObW15qN890SyV1ACL.html>.
11 Image accessed on 20 February 2016 <http://bharathautos.com/wp- content/uploads/2012/09/tata_nano_student_of_the_year_contest. jpg>.
12 Coined in *Biographia Literaria* or the *Biographical Sketches of MY LITERARY LIFE and OPINIONS*.
13 "Kem Cho Mr. PM?" *The Times of India* 30 September 2014. 20 February 2016 <http://timesofindia.indiatimes.com/india/Kem-Cho- Mr-PM-Obama-asks-Modi-Michelle-Obama-not-present-at-dinner/ articleshow/43858623.cms>.
14 Sonup Sahadevan, "I am surviving only on 25 per cent of my liver today: Amitabh Bachchan." *The Indian Express* 10 December 2015. Accessed 20 February 2016 <http://indianexpress.com/article/entertainment/ bollywood/i-am-surviving-only-on-25-per-cent-of-my-liver-today- amitabh-bachchan/>.
15 Sylvester Dacunha, "The story behind Amul's 'utterly butterly' ads." 12 September 2012. 20 February 2016 <www.rediff.com/money/slide- show/slide-show-1-special-the-story-behind-amuls-utterly-butterly- ads/20120912.htm>.
16 Ibid.

17 Tag line from image accessed on 20 February 2016 <www.instablogs. com/wp-content/uploads/2012/07/amul_combined_ad_for_people_in_ corporate_image_title_lixaq.jpg>.

18 Excerpt from "M&S Careers." Accessed on 7 February 2016 <http:// careers.marksandspencer.com/why-work-here>.

19 Jim Powell, *Derrida for Beginners*. Orient Blackswan, 2000, 145.

Chapter 3

Checkmate

Persuade to win

The communication strategy toolkit serves to help the communicator engage in productive communication. But this is at a basic level. The toolkit is the armoury but not the master plan for outwitting an opponent. And it is this agenda of outwitting that needs something more than what a communication strategy toolkit can offer. You are equipped with the toolkit to outwit, but beyond the equipment you need a "style" of warfare. And for every style, a certain combination of armoury works.

In the corporate battlefield, there are two predominant styles of communication, as pointed out by Munter. There is "telling" and there is "selling". Who "tells"? The boss! Or the informant! To whom? The subordinate. But who "sells"? The persuader, the convincer, the influencer, the motivator, the stimulator. And to whom? The unmotivated, disinterested or uninformed audience. Hence, selling is not easy because you are dependent on the audience. And this "dependence" is the point of departure to access the act of selling as a productive form of communication. It is the communicator's Achilles' heel. Subsequently, Thetis, to save her son (ironically, who hardly can be saved), had asked the Greek blacksmith, Hephaistos, to build a shield that would protect the Greek hero from danger. We are the modern Hephaistos who want to protect the speaker from the Achilles' heel; namely, the dependence of the seller on the audience. We accept the irony that perhaps even Thetis knew about the impossibility of her undertaking. We are preparing armour that has the task to save the impossible. Yet, Thetis does order armour. And we, as researchers of communication, also present for such armour.[1]

In light of our task, we introduce two terminologies that would eventually have maximum currency in the corporate communication battlefield:

(a) Communicator's Achilles' heel – Audience dependency that has to be manoeuvred strategically for a productive output;
(b) Style Shield: Strategic game plan to outwit a difficult or non-negotiable audience.

Again, style shields are of two kinds:

• Telling Style Shield;
• Selling Style Shield.

A telling style shield is used to inform. The speaker merely needs to inform because s/he is not expected to worry about the audience reaction to her information. It is the decorative piece of warfare and used in those situations where the audience needs to be informed. The audience here is a need-based audience, an audience who is ready for information or even ready to act upon it, perhaps trained to act upon it – the high interest audience. For instance, in a military emergency, the army is called upon to act to save the nation. Generals and Admirals inform, instruct or simply "tell" the militia the game plan of action; the army is ready to act upon it, as they have been trained to do so, without question.

But look at some other instances where "instruction" does not work.

Instance 1: I am sitting in a mess waiting for food, surrounded by a bunch of young people. I want to discuss the problems of old age, but the crowd is too self-obsessed and living in the moment of youthful glory to bother to listen to me. My Achilles' heel is exposed and adds to my vulnerability because while I need the crowd to substantiate my ideas, they do not need my ideas or even me. What do I do? I remember my mother's instructions when I first started cooking. How does one make *Daal Tadka*? Let me not get into details as to how I boil lintels/pulses, assuming people know. Let me get to the *tadka*. We take a pan, and heat oil in it. As the oil gets hot, we add the *tadka* – mustard, cinnamon, chopped onions, chillies and other garnishes. It is here that any mother would automatically advise, "Step back from the pan when you add these garnishes into hot oil; they would splinter and fall on your face and burn it!" In our role of Hephaistos of communication strategy, we designate this act of splintering as STIMULATION.

The audience is like the pan with the oil. As speakers, we need to ignite their spirits, and to do that, we need to provide garnishes, the Indian form of *Tadka*. Suppose I tell my disinterested youthful audience who are completely ignoring me, "Youth is overrated! They should be laid off to help increase the retirement age for employment!" There is going to be massive outcry from the very bunch who earlier did not even bother to look at me. If the response to your *Tadka* is "Crap!", you should beam within because you have successfully manoeuvred them through your Achilles' heel and got the very crowd you are dependent upon to actually listen to you, even to process a negative judgement. Any judgement is better than zero interest, and stimulating is a method of instilling interest by provoking an audience. So, we see a "change" in an audience – from zero interest to provoked interest. We call this *Tadka* Style or Stimulating Style.

Instance 2: To understand this instance, we go back to our goodwill builder toolkit. Maya is down and out because she failed. I tell her that I failed too. Maya trusts me more because I have been through failure like her and have overcome it; so can she. Her trust materialises into a positive thought process; she wants to try again. From a low phase, she "transforms" into a positive space of mind. So, we see a "change" in an audience – from zero interest to motivated interest. We call this Motivation Style.

Instance 3: Salman Khan was out of form and almost out of the superstar league that consisted of the top three Hindi film industry Khans. It was 2010, and *Dabangg* was released. The rest is history. The actor with his goggles tucked behind his collar and trademark swagger became one of the most effective style actors of contemporary times, such that his style *alone* generated a guarantee into the X + 100 million prestigious club. Post *Dabangg*, wearing goggles tucked behind the collar became a common sight on streets. So, we see a "change" in an audience – from having been written off to garnering maximum followership. We call this Followership Style.

Instance 4: I am not sure if I want to join the navy. You tell me all the good reasons as to why I should. I am finally convinced. So, we see a "change" in an audience – from doubt to confidence. We call this the Style of Convincing.

Instance 5: In Shakespeare's *Julius Caesar*, when Caesar was killed and Brutus delivered a speech to the Roman citizens demonstrating why there was a national need to remove Caesar for the safety of Rome from a dictator's hands, the people bowed to Brutus. For welfare of the nation, Brutus even sacrificed his best friend. But when Mark Antony spoke, he turned the crowd from Brutus to Caesar, by repositioning all those qualities deemed negative by Brutus in Caesar into positive and pro-Rome qualities. So, we see a "change" in an audience – from Brutus to Caesar; from Pink to Blue; from Pepsi to Cola; from X to Y. We call this the Style of Persuading.

In each of these instances, the common thread that runs through every attempt at manoeuvring the Achilles' heel is the attempt to bring about a "change" in the minds of the audience so that the "change" would be reflected in the habits of the audience. And once the "customised change" is successfully ensured, then "selling" becomes "telling", because the audience has been transformed into a high-interest audience from a low-interest one. The youthful but sensitised audience is more open to old age care; Maya is motivated to do well against all odds; more goggles sell in the market thanks to Salman Khan's fan club; the confident navy aspirant will turn down a corporate career; and the crowd has favoured Caesar, and Antony as the avenger of Caesar, over the idealistic Brutus. As modern Hephaistos, we reintroduce our Style Shields as the quintessential armoury of our Selling Apparatus as a diagrammatic illustration in Figure 3.1.

Figure 3.1 clearly shows that the task is not easy. The intensity of strategy grows as we move from one style shield to another. The herculean task lies in the stumbling block already deeply cemented in the audience consciousness. We are talking about (a) X; (b) doubt; (c) no interest; and (d) despair. So, the first lesson that we need to learn even before using the Selling Apparatus is to identify the stumbling block. We need to know what we are fighting against. Then we can launch the first line of attack – always aimed at the stumbling block. Till X is not removed, they cannot like what I want them to like, which is Y. Until doubt is not dispelled, there is no chance for confidence in my product. Until "they" are not interested, I cannot expect followership. Until despair is not annihilated, where is the chance for hope? Thus, the seller has to first work hard to make a little space for herself in the consciousness of the audience, even before thinking of selling Y, or hope or even aiming at followership. And to make space, one has to "create" space in a place that has no space for the communicator. In this labyrinth of spaces, the style shield works its magic to first create space. That is what this shield is meant for. Once the space is created, the communication toolkit will come handy. But until then, the style shield apparatus "makes way" into the labyrinth. We have to learn to make way even before we walk the talk. And this chapter is all about how we "make way to walk the talk".

In managerial jargon, we have come across terms and phrases like negotiations, conflict management, mergers. In simple language

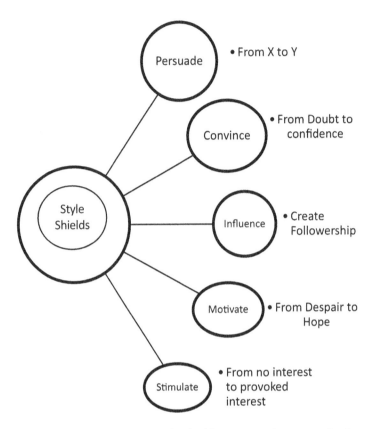

Figure 3.1 Selling apparatus: style shields in strategic communication
Source: All figures, boxes and tables are by authors, unless otherwise mentioned.

exercises, these big terms and phrases are offshoots of exercises on persuasion and argumentation. And in the present context, we are talking about "making way". At the end of the day, all these exercises are about "making way" for the speaker, the seller or the idea-generator. So, here we introduce various ways of making inroads into the audience consciousness – the various assets of the selling apparatus.

Assets of the selling apparatus

- Asset 1: Balance Theory

Which vocation thrives on persuasive tools of communication? Law. We start the description of the first asset of the selling apparatus using a

Hollywood movie that deals with the classic tool of legal persuasion –
cross-examination. The attorney is allowed to question the opposing
witness, and bit-by-bit breaks the credibility of the witness's testimony. *My Cousin Vinny* is a 1992 movie directed by Jonathan Lynn.
The plot is simple. Two young boys from New York, while travelling
through rural Alabama, enter a convenience store. When they come
out and start driving, one of the boys, Stan, remembers that he has
a tuna fish can which he forgot to bill. The memory is more vivid
because a patrol car follows them, and both the boys wonder how
much trouble they would get into for unknowingly lifting a tuna fish
can in the vicinity of a strict legal territory like that of Alabama. To
their utter surprise they get caught, and later are shocked to know
that they are the prime suspects in a murder case – the store clerk
was shot. The other boy, Bill Gambini, learns from his mother about
an attorney in his family – his cousin Vinny. The irony is that Vinny,
who definitely agrees to help his nephew, is himself *only* a personal
injury lawyer, has had no trial experience before, and failed the Law
examination six times. Vinny, along with his girlfriend, Mona Lisa
Vito, comes to Alabama to help save both these boys. How he does
help is the story of the movie. But we are more interested in a few
episodes in the movie that would enable us to elaborate upon a style
of persuasion that Munter calls Balance Theory.

Episode 1: Vinny and Vito have to get up early in the morning
in a hotel in Alabama because of the noise made by an early train.
They enter the breakfast arena, and question the cook about the
noise. What follows is a discussion about a breakfast dish, which
happens to be an Alabama favourite called grits (see Script 3.1).

Script 3.1 Screenplay on grits from *My Cousin Vinny*

All about grits

- Vinny: What's this over here?
- Cook: You never heard of grits?
- Vinny: Sure. Sure, I heard of grits. I just actually never seen
  a grit before.
- Honey, you gonna try it?
- Vito: You first.
- Vinny: What is a grit, anyways?
- Cook: It's made out of corn. [. . .]

- Vinny: How d'you cook it?
- Cook: Simmer it in water for 15 or 20 minutes, . . . put it on the plate and add butter.

Source: Excerpt from "My Cousin Vinny (1992) Movie Script." Accessed on 8 May 2016 <www.springfieldspringfield.co.uk/movie_script.php?movie=my-cousin-vinny>.

Episode 2: Of the three circumstantial witnesses who are certain that Bill and Stan are the culprits, we look at two testimonies in particular. One of them is the fat guy Sam Tipton. Here is his testimony culled directly from the screenplay in Script 3.2. Script 3.3 follows Script 3.1 and contains the testimonial of the final witness, Mr. Crane.

Script 3.2 Screenplay on Tipton's testimony from *My Cousin Vinny*

Sam Tipton's testimony

- I was makin' my breakfast.
- I saw them two boys go into the store.
- Then later I heard a gunshot.
- Looked out the window.
- They were running out.| Got into the car and drove off.
- Attorney: Is this the car?
- Witness: Yes. It is.
- Attorney: Thank you, sir.

Source: Excerpt from "My Cousin Vinny (1992) Movie Script." Accessed on 8 May 2016 <www.springfieldspringfield.co.uk/movie_script.php?movie=my-cousin-vinny>.

Script 3.3 Screenplay on Crane's testimony from *My Cousin Vinny*

Mr. Crane's testimony

- Attorney: Then you saw those two boys run out o' the Sac-o-Suds, jump in this car and take off?

- Third Witness: Yeah. They peeled away. Car was all over the road.
- Attorney: Thank you, sir.

Source: Excerpt from "My Cousin Vinny (1992) Movie Script." Accessed on 8 May 2016 <www.springfieldspringfield.co.uk/movie_script.php?movie=my-cousin-vinny>.

Episode 3: Stan doubts Vinny's calibre and decides to go for a more experienced attorney. To his utter dismay, Stan discovers that the public defender (PD) stammers. Despite that, PD starts off on a winning note, when he notices that Tipton has to wear glasses. The interrogation continues in the following Script 3.4:

Script 3.4 Screenplay on PD versus Tipton from *My Cousin Vinny*

Public defender versus Tipton

- Public Defender (PD): Now, when you viewed my clients, . . . how-how far away were you?
- Tipton: About 50 feet.
- PD: Now, do you think that that's close enough to make an accurate . . . i-i-i-identification?
- Tipton: Yes.
- PD: Mr Tipton, I see you wear eyeglasses.
- Tipton: Sometimes.
- PD: Would you care to show those eyeglasses to the jury, please? Thank you.
- PD: Thank you. Mr Tipton. Were you wearing them that day?
- Tipton: No.
- PD: You see! You were 50 feet away, you made a positive eyewitness identification, . . . and-and-and yet . . . you were not wearing your necessary prescription eyeglasses.
- Tipton: They're reading glasses.
- PD: Uh . . . Well, uh . . . Mr, uh . . . uh . . . Could you tell the court what colour eyes the defendants have?

- Tipton: Brown. Hazel green.
- PD: No more questions.

Source:Excerpt from"My CousinVinny (1992) Movie Script."Accessed on 8 May 2016
<www.springfieldspringfield.co.uk/movie_script.php?movie=my-cousin-vinny>.

What we see happening here is an argumentation fallacy, which we reinvent as the "fallacy of common sense". The most commonsensical point of approach for any attorney fighting the case for Bill and Stan would be to attack the witness head-on through the obvious choice of query, "how far were you when you saw the accused". The rationality behind the question is the power of "distance" and a good enough distance dilutes the confidence of assertion. Add to this commonsensical line of attack – a pair of glasses. The stereotyping of glasses as lack of eyesight is exemplary. What goes wrong here is exactly what we call a fallacy. And most attacks are nothing but fallacies. PD did not "make way", but jumped on obvious conclusions without undertaking his homework. As you read through Script 3.4, you realise that every pair of glasses is not an indicator of poor eyesight, and there are confident people who can identify the colour of eyes from a distance of 50 feet. Tipton was very sure about his identification, and he actually validated his confidence. These common assumptions were the PD's Achilles' heel.

What do we mean when we say "make your way" first, even before you think of the idea that you want to sell? Identify the audience's point of view, and then study that view closely to isolate the possibility of an audience's Achilles' heel. Watch Vinny do exactly that with Tipton in Script 3.5.

Script 3.5 Identification of Tipton's Achilles' heel from *My Cousin Vinny*

Tipton's Achilles' Heel

- Vinny: Is it possible the two defendants . . . entered the store, picked 22 specific items off of the shelves, . . . had the clerk take money, make change, then leave. Then, two different men drive up in a similar . . .

- [Tipton shakes his head, but Vinny shouts back confidently]
  Vinny: Don't shake your head. Wait till you hear the whole thing so you can understand. Two different men drive up in a similar-looking car, . . . go in, shoot the clerk, rob him and then leave?
  Tipton: No. They didn't have enough time.
  Vinny: How much time was they in the store?
- Tipton: Five minutes.
  Vinny: Five minutes? Did you look at your watch?
- Tipton: No.
  Vinny: Oh, I'm sorry. You testified earlier that the boys went into the store . . . and you had just begun to make breakfast. You were just ready to eat and you heard a gunshot. So obviously it takes you five minutes to make breakfast, so you knew that. Do you remember what you had?

  The unfamiliar zone for the confidant man begins

- Tipton: Eggs and grits.
  Vinny: Eggs and grits. I like grits, too. How do you cook your grits? You like 'em regular, creamy or al dente?
  Tipton: Just regular, I guess. [**Tipton starts looking confused for the first time**]
- Vinny: Regular. Instant grits?
  Tipton: No self-respectin' Southerner uses instant grits. I take pride in my grits.
  Vinny: So, Mr Tipton. How could it take you five minutes to cook your grits . . . when it takes the entire grit-eating world 20 minutes?
  Tipton: I dunno. I'm a fast cook, I guess.
  Vinny: I'm sorry, I was over here. I couldn't hear. Did you say you're a fast cook? That's it?! Are we to believe that boiling water soaks into a grit faster in your kitchen . . . than on any place on the face of the earth?
  Tipton: I don't know.
  Vinny: Perhaps the laws of physics cease to exist on your stove! Were these magic grits? Did you buy them from the same guy who sold Jack his beanstalk beans?
- Attorney: Objection, Your Honour.
- Judge: Sustained.
- Vinny: Are you sure about that five minutes?
- Tipton: I don't know.

- Judge: I think you made your point.
- Vinny: Are you sure about that five minutes?
- Tipton: I may have been mistaken.
- Vinny: I got no more use for this guy.
- (lone applause)

Source: Excerpt from "My Cousin Vinny (1992) Movie Script." Accessed on 8 May 2016 <www.springfieldspringfield.co.uk/movie_script.php?movie=my-cousin-vinny>.

The moment Vinny identifies Tipton's fallacy, the typical response of the shattered confidence of a man who was too sure before, is there for all to see:

"I dunno. I'm a fast cook, I guess."

Obviously, Mr. Tipton did not think about laws of physics. It is psychological reality that we cannot argue with a confident audience. Mr. Tipton is the typical protagonist we are looking for to represent the low interest audience. But it is also psychological truth that a confident man breaks like none other when self-doubt is injected into his assertive mind. The moment I lose trust in my own assertion, I lose my "balance", my confidence, my comfort zone. Hence the difference between

"Those are my reading glasses"

and

"I must be a fast cook".

Balance theory is a step-by-step method of unbalancing the confidence in an assertion by careful detection of the Achilles' heel in the assertion being made. And such an attack can only be made when you know that you stand for the truth, which Vinny knew – Bill and Stan were innocent. So there had to be a loophole in the witnesses' assertions, however confident they might appear.

Enjoy the disbalance of the third witness as well in Script 3.6.

Script 3.6 Mr. Crane's Achilles' heel from *My Cousin Vinny*

> **Achilles' heel in Mr. Crane**
>
> - Vinny: Hey, Mr Crane. What are these pictures of?
> - Crane: My house and stuff.

- Vinny: House and stuff. And what is this brown stuff on the windows?
- Crane: Dirt.
- Vinny: Dirt. What is this rusty, dusty, dirty-lookin' thing over your window?
- Crane: It's a screen.
- Vinny: A screen! It's a screen. What are these really big things right in the middle of your view . . . from the window of your kitchen to the Sac-o-Suds? What do we call these big things?
- Crane: Trees?
- Vinny: Trees, that's right. Don't be afraid. Just shout 'em out when you know. Now, what are these thousands of little things that are on trees?
- Crane: Leaves.
- Vinny: Leaves!
- (sniggering)
- Vinny: And these bushy things between the trees?
- Crane: Bushes.
- Vinny: Bushes! So, Mr Crane. You could positively identify the defendants for a moment of two seconds . . . looking through this dirty window, . . . this crud-covered screen, . . . these trees with all these leaves on them, . . . and I don't know how many bushes.
- Crane: Looks like five.
- Vinny: Uh-uh. Don't forget this one and this one.
- Crane: Seven bushes.
- Vinny: Seven bushes. So, what do you think? Is it possible you just saw two guys in a green convertible, . . . and not necessarily these two particular guys?
- Crane: I suppose.
- Vinny: I'm finished with this guy.

Source: Excerpt from "My Cousin Vinny (1992) Movie Script." Accessed on 8 May 2016 <www.springfieldspringfield.co.uk/movie_script.php?movie=my-cousin-vinny>.

Vinny wanted to prove only one thing:

"Is it possible you just saw two guys in a green convertible, . . . and not necessarily these two particular guys?"

But this deportment would have had no takers in the initial round of discussions because his audience was not ready for it; the audience was confident in its own assertions. So, what does Vinny do? He first takes on the audience's point of view. He "makes way"; he makes space. And how does he do that? By a step-by-step spelling out of the audience's Achilles' heel. When PD attacked Tipton with the distance problem, he lost. But when Vinny broke down an otherwise "uncomplicated description of distance" into distinct zones of unexpected detail, the technique of dis-balance began (see Figure 3.2).

The 50 feet now looks lengthy for a man who was so sure he had identified rightly. Balance theory is the process-wise breaking down of audience's dependence on their credibility anchors. When a confident audience breaks, they are left in a quandary. Human psychology says that in a confused state, particularly after rigorous

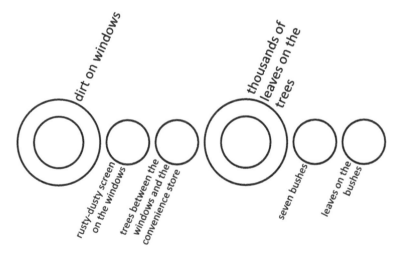

Figure 3.2 Fifty feet into distinct zones of unexpected details

self-doubt, an audience is more open to hearing your idea, which otherwise would have fallen on deaf ears. Nobody likes confusion, more so the confident audience. So, Crane's "I suppose" is the ultimate *checkmate* that you can hope for. What Balance Theory can do or does to business negotiations is any reader's guess, as is illustrated in Figure 3.3.

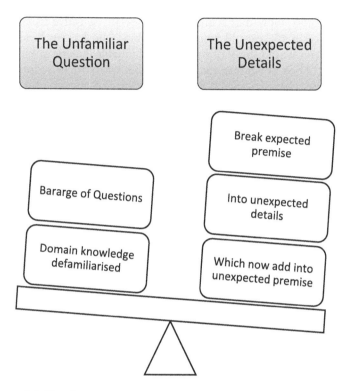

Figure 3.3 The diagrammatic approach to balance theory

- Asset 2: Problematisation

What happens when an argument is fool-proof, or makes sense as per any one perspective? Every argument or opinion cannot be a fallacy. When the Achilles' heel ceases to exist in the audience, the negotiator then is in a difficult position, a condition we call the Catch-22 situation. You cannot find fault with an opinion, but you cannot deny it as well. This is the case with Nick Naylor, the protagonist of *Thank You for Smoking*, a 2005 movie that has a reverential followership amongst most management students. Yet, what most of these students might have missed in the movie is the brilliant manoeuvre of a Catch-22 situation, or what we as modern Hephaistos propose is the problematisation of the Catch-22 condition. The opening scene of the movie explains the process exquisitely. There is a hostess, Oprah, and a reality show that is anchored on socially sensitive issues. She introduces a 15-year-old young boy Robin, who has his head tonsured. You would think of him as a fashionable American kid. But hold on! Look at her introduction of Robin with care in Script 3.7.

Script 3.7 Introduction of Robin by Oprah from *Thank You for Smoking*

Robin is introduced by Oprah

- Robin Williger is a 15-year-old freshman from Racine, Wisconsin. He likes studying history and he's on the debate team. Robin's future looked bright; however, recently he was diagnosed with Cancer. A very tough kind of Cancer. Robin tells me he has quit smoking though and no longer thinks cigarettes are cool.

Source: Excerpt from "Thank You for Smoking," screenplay by Jason Reitman, 7 September 2014. Accessed 9 May 2016 <www.screenplaydb.com/film/scripts/thankyouforsmoking.pdf>.

Now we know the story behind the tonsured head. As students of communication, and that of strategic communication, we would consider this introduction to be a very smart one indeed. A case is built for a serious attack on smoking. Had Robin been introduced with a one-liner – "he suffers from cancer because he smoked" – the effect would have been lost upon an impressionable audience. Rather, let us build the case for Robin in steps as illustrated in Figure 3.4.

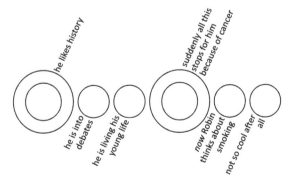

Figure 3.4 Robin's introduction in steps from *Thank You for Smoking*

What Oprah has actually done is "build the case" successfully for an unforgiving war against smoking. It is at this very profitable juncture that the hostess introduces one of her panel members invited for discussion – Nick Naylor, the Vice President of the Academy of Tobacco Studies – with an interesting sideline,

> "They are the tobacco industry's main lobby in Washington, DC and Mr. Naylor is their chief spokesman."[2]

Naylor is stamped for life! The description of the crowd is apt:

> "This is a very angry bunch of people. As we pass the FROZEN CROWD, we see PEOPLE: mid-scream, mid-spit, mid-gesture."[3]

This is a Catch-22 situation. What can Naylor do? He cannot deny the connection of tobacco with cancer. He cannot accept the connection because by virtue of being the lobbyist of the organisation, his work ethics would not permit him to. When you cannot say "yes" and you cannot say "no" you *then* have one choice left – you problematise the situation.

Problematisation is a critical tool derived from the Critical Humanities tradition. The premise of this tool is deep. We have a mono-rhetoric about everything: a dominant, singular and final opinion. The French sociologist Jean-François Lyotard called this mono-rhetoric the grand-narrative in his 1979 publication, *The Postmodern Condition: A Report on Knowledge.*[4] Not that the dominant opinion is wrong, but a critical thinker looks for layers of meanings. And "layers of meanings" cannot be equated to an Achilles' heel concept. The latter is as much a mono-rhetoric; it is a defined weakness ready to be attacked. The study of Hypertexts in Cyberspace, a subset of Social Media studies, has come up with the concept of the rhizomatic narrations, or the poly-rhetorical narrations. If rhetoric is speech, then mono is uni dimensional speech, and poly or rhizomatic is multi dimensional speech. Thus, any opinion that comes across as full and final might have multi-perspectives to it. And problematisation is the art of carving out these multi-perspectives; these rhizomatic narrations; these poly-rhetoric nuances. If you are faithful to a critical tradition, you problematise to "expose" multi-perspectives; if sceptical of critical traditions, you problematise to "escape" Catch-22 situations by "confusing" the audience even more by "creating" more problems and thereupon make a simple premise look complicated. But the utilitarian value of problematisation as a necessary art of persuasion cannot be denied. Look at Naylor's several attempts at problematisation in Script 3.8.

Script 3.8 Naylor nails the prop in *Thank You for Smoking*

> **Naylor problematises the prop**
>
> - Oprah, how on earth would "Big Tobacco" profit off of the loss of this young man? I hate to think in such callous terms, but if anything we'd be losing a customer. It's not only our hope but it's in our best interests to keep Robin alive and smoking.

Source: Excerpt from "Thank You for Smoking," screenplay by Jason Reitman, 7 September 2014. Accessed 9 May 2016 <www.screenplaydb.com/film/scripts/ thankyouforsmoking.pdf>.

As an astute communicator, Naylor does not forget the "prop" used by Oprah to influence public opinion – Robin. And then he takes a detour by lashing out at the government's role in these debates. Ron Good is the new senator, and Naylor has this to say about him (see Script 3.9).

Script 3.9 Naylor nails the accuser in *Thank You for Smoking*

> **Naylor problematises the accuser**
>
> - Let me tell you something, Oprah, and let me share something with the fine, concerned people in the audience today. The Ron Goodes of this world want the Robin Willigers to die. Awful, but true. I'm sorry, but it's a fact. And do you know why? I'll tell you why. So that their budgets will go up. This is nothing less than trafficking in human misery, and you, sir, ought to be ashamed of yourself.

Source: Excerpt from "Thank You for Smoking," screenplay by Jason Reitman, 7 September 2014. Accessed 9 May 2016 <www.screenplaydb.com/film/scripts/ thankyouforsmoking.pdf>.

The formula is simple. You cannot argue against a premise as familiar and acceptable as is the mathematical equation, $2 + 2 = 4$, unless you are a genius with numbers. But for lesser mortals, we can always say, "If $2 + 2 = 4$, then so and so would have been the consequence." In other words, you mean to say that "it is not the case," but by not uttering the contradictory statement directly, you do not commit to the truth claim, but aesthetically state the conditional claim. This is a famous grammatical condition, rule or law that we learn in school when studying basics in English language. It is known as a Subjunctive Mood – an imaginary, conditional or hypothetical or even a contradictory state of affairs; "Had smoking really killed smokers, nobody would have been alive to buy these products."

Naylor shows how advertising a victim is also "trafficking in human misery". The lobbyist has shifted the issue of contention from the "consequences of smoking" to the "prop" used. What first looked like a simple mono-rhetoric representation of a child-victim of smoking now has poly-rhetoric overtures – a case of trafficking in human misery. In one go, Naylor has brought in a sharp criticism on related areas of concern, beyond their stereotyped mono-rhetorical representations – he hints at profit agendas in social marketing, NGOs, bottom-of-the-pyramid discourses and corporate social responsibilities. He has steered the debate from the pros and cons of smoking and tobacco to the larger systemic issues of social and economic roles of victimisation in the political agendas of social services.

It is from Naylor that we derive two definitions of problematisation: one for the sceptic and one for the faithful learner. We name this the Two-Faced Problematising Technique after, of course, Harvey Dent in the insanely famous 2008 Christopher Nolan's *The Dark Knight* (see Figure 3.5).

Let us try a critically engaging illustration of problematisation, for the ever-faithful learner who would look down with contempt at artful artifice. Any form of violence against women has always been justifiably criticised by governing bodies and common people alike. There are blogs, slogans and write-ups about the inhumanity towards women, particularly in a patriarchal society. But, patriarchy is not the *only* guilty party in such heinous crimes. Do we *only* discuss the cause and the perpetuator of those causes that lead up to the crime? What should be done to those perpetuators, or are there *fringe* criminals as well? Let us review the generic case facts again.

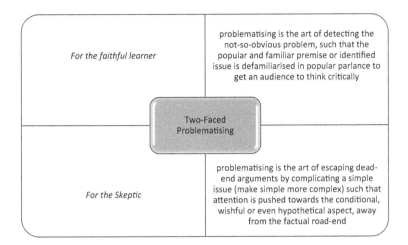

Figure 3.5 Harvey Dent problematising technique

- We come out of malls after watching late night movies. How many times, in various parts of various urban centres of our country, have we faced the difficulty of hiring a cab to take us back home? The typical excuse by cab drivers is the destination is too far and they will not get people to take back. Is this a patriarchal problem or a larger ethical problem?
- The victims, when found in despicable conditions on roadsides or public places, are shunned. Commoners like us do not help them get medical aid in time. But the public outcry is only against the patriarchy.
- Commoners are not brave enough to help these victims because they are scared of the bureaucratic system. Who wants to soil their hands in these police cases? We have been well fed with stories about bureaucratic abuse and ragging over time. But the public outcry is only against the patriarchy.

What first looks like a simple case of victims of a male-dominated world, now looks like a complicated systemic poly-rhetoric that needs concern at various points in various directions. Imagine how these analyses might affect our policy makers when they make policies for many aspects of public life.

Let us also try a clever artifice that a sceptic would always hold the art of problematising guilty of. We need to go back to Naylor. He attends his son's school. He asks his son's class whether they want to be lobbyists. The kids want to know what *that* means. He says: "I talk for a living."[5] Kid 2 asks, "What do you talk about?"[6] Naylor admits its cigarettes. Now the factual statement comes from a well-informed kid:

"My mom used to smoke. She says that cigarettes kill."[7]

This is again a 2 + 2 = 4 condition. So, what can Naylor do? Remember your credibility building toolkit and look at Naylor playing the devil's advocate in Script 3.10.

Script 3.10 Naylor nails expertise in *Thank You for Smoking*

> **Naylor problematises expertise credibility**
>
> * NICK (to Kid 3): Really? Is your mom a doctor?
> * KID 3: No.
> * NICK (to Kid 3): A scientific researcher of some kind?
> * KID 3: No.
> * NICK: Well, she doesn't exactly sound like a credible expert now, does she?
> * Kid 3 sinks in his seat.

Source: Excerpt from "Thank You for Smoking," screenplay by Jason Reitman, 7 September 2014. Accessed 9 May 2016 <www.screenplaydb.com/film/scripts/thankyouforsmoking.pdf>.

Naylor has problematised Kid 3's expertise credibility builder – the mother. Even look at the episode when Naylor's son has homework and comes to his father for suggestion, as in Script 3.11.

Script 3.11 Naylor nails criterion in *Thank You for Smoking*

> **Naylor problematises the criterion**
>
> * Joey: Dad, why is American government, the best government? [. . .]
> * Naylor: I mean, A. Does America have the best government? and B. What constitutes a best government? Crime?

> Poverty? Literacy? In America? Definitely not best. Perhaps not even better than most. (however) We do have a very entertaining government.

Source: Excerpt from "Thank You for Smoking," screenplay by Jason Reitman, 7 September 2014. Accessed 9 May 2016 <www.screenplaydb.com/film/scripts/thankyouforsmoking.pdf>.

How many times have we done the above to escape a direct answer that we do not want to give? It is a great tool in question/answer sessions. Michael Jackson sang, "Black or White", but a problematiser would prefer to root for the grey.

- Asset 3: Problem-Solution Structure

To be a winning persuader one needs to know how to pitch one's idea, framing it in a successful way. Usually people believe in the notion of selling hard their idea by elaborating its merits as much as possible. What they fail to understand is devoting a gargantuan space or time on belabouring the takeaways of their idea, which do not give them a winning edge. They need to comprehend how to position their idea so that it might be projected as the only panacea in the given matrix of complex circumstances.

Here comes in the next asset – shake your audience up. Do not talk about benefits, merits, plus the points of your proposal. First let them "see" a problem which is difficult to fix. The more intense the projection of the problem, the better your chances are of success. Spend considerable time on elucidating how grave is the problem. Once you are able to create furrows of anxiety on their relaxed brow, give them a reason to smile – there is a solution to it – the solution is your proposal, your idea, your recommendation which will salvage the situation. A classic case in point is the advertisements of *Dettol* sanitisers.

A few years ago, the cleansing agent for "dirty" hands was a tiny, inexpensive, innocent bar of soap lying near our washbasins. *Dettol* launched a rigorous onslaught on this tiny little thing by highlighting pictorially in its advertisements how this so-called cleansing agent itself is not clean. There is an optical diagnosis of this small cake of soap. You are shown through microscopic projection how this soap has been touched by numerous soiled hands and it is now itself mired in a pool of those deadly germs that cause an array of ailments. The spectacle of a contaminated soap "creates" a problem, the problem which never existed for us but now is created, magnified and given horrendous dimensions. When viewers get worried, it is time to sell a new idea – the liquid hand wash which will take care of this multi-hand contamination problem. There is no great talk about the benefits of the product; in fact, there is no need to talk about the merits it embodies because the portrayal of the problem itself ups its acceptance quotient. The more sombre the problem, the better are the chances that your idea gets sold out as the solution to this problem.

Dettol extended this strategy to the launch of their other allied products. Again, a problem was created – the bottle of handwash is also not virgin; it is touched by scores of sullied hands. But there is nothing to worry about, since now "the no-touch bottle" liberates you from the hassles of a contaminated nozzle. For washing hands you do not need to touch the bottle at all now. Product innovation gives a wondrous solution from this cauldron of sanitisation problems. Without touching the bottle you can still find the "pure" drop of *Dettol* falling into your hands and cleaning them up. But the success story does not end here. One more product from their kitty became a household need, thanks to this application of problem-solution structure they have been applying brilliantly to their commercial promotions. The cute little bottle of hand sanitiser found its way inside your handbags and your kids' school bags to give you salvation from another problem manufactured and solved by *Dettol*. You are travelling, enjoying your moments of outing. When hunger pangs strike you, you think of washing hands before you think of nibbling a morsel of your food. But again there is a problem (problem very well pictured for you by these fabulous advertisements of *Dettol*). There is no water; there are not wash rooms nearby. Now how do you sanitise your hands? The solution is simple: use a hand sanitiser which is bottled in a baby shape and is your convenient companion wherever you go. *Lifebuoy* was quick to adopt and modify this strategy by presenting it as *"tiffin ka best friend"* so that your kids do not forget to carry hand sanitisers along with their lunch boxes when they go to school.

Numerous other products got a lifeline on shelves of retail stores only because of the dexterous use of problem-solution structure. Again, rewinding to bygone days, we discover that one kind of soap was used for bathing entirely. No one thought about whether the skin of a leg was different, or the facial skin is delicate, so on and so forth. But now marketers educate us by presenting a long list of "serious" problems which cannot be overlooked – facial skin needs a different cleanser, hence use face wash. If you are a man you cannot use the face wash of your wife, buy men's face wash. Fairness is not just the need of women; men can also face rejection owing to dark skin, thereby demolishing the traditional attribute of an attractive Indian male – tall, dark and handsome. The solution to this problem is *Fair & Handsome* cream.

If marketers can use this strategy, why can't managers use it? You have a recommendation to make. Portray a problem in front of your management. Suddenly they will start seeing problems in the current system. They will get perturbed more and more as you detail out their problem with its dire consequences. When they are assailed by the trepidation of operating a "flawed" system, you present your recommendation as a solution to this problem. You ask for additional staff to help complete your projects under crash deadlines and management resists this idea since they do not want to spend money on recruiting additional human resources – paint a picture of the losses incurred by the company owing to paucity of staff. The story of the losses should be yarned first so that they are convinced that the crunch of staff is indeed a massive problem. Do not talk about your proposal of induction of new staff at all until you are sure they understand the gravity of the problem. When you are convinced that they are convinced that a problem exists, then give your recommendation of recruitment as a treatment for this "knotty" problem. This is how the problem-solution asset solves your problem.

The problem-solution structure is again a classic example of the Theory of Performativity from the Critical Humanities tradition. You make alive what you describe. The famous American Gender Studies theorist Judith Butler discusses the power that simple speech acts have. Any act of communication is an act in defining and, hence, shaping identities. In this capacity, a problem-solution structure is a performative act of communication – it shapes identities and lifestyles according to problems and solutions.[8]

- Asset 4: Inoculation Technique

The phenomenon of vaccination changed the course of medical history. The formula is interesting. You want to develop immunity against a disease, and disease means "enemy virus". So, what you do is ironical. To defeat the "enemy virus", you inject a small dose of the same into your body – a dangerous feat indeed! How many of us remember those tetanus injection pricks, and the subsequent rash or fever? The rash or fever is the reaction to that small lethal dose injected into our body. The white blood cells in our body, in the meantime, handle the situation and develop anti bodies that can fight the "enemy virus"; such is the perfection the human body is capable of. Once the immune formula is ready, the disease is no more a terror because we have developed immunity to combat it; we have been inoculated. Munter applied the same formulae in strategic communication. We add to Munter: start your argument from the "enemy virus".

It was in 2011 that the Indian superstar and perfectionist of the Hindi film industry took a detour. And we are talking about Aamir Khan before the "intolerance debate" era post 2015. He was at the peak of critical success because of his hugely appreciated directorial debut – *Taare Zameen Par*. The stars were at his feet, and he could do anything, since he had it all – the tags of being versatile, meaningful, intellectual and successful. But then, he changed tracks and decided to produce an adult certified movie; a coming-of-age movie for the youth of India – *Delhi Belly*. He is perhaps the first Indian movie producer who went from a television channel to warning on television a particular segment of Indian moviegoers that this movie was *not* meant for them. He openly "confessed" that the movie contained unparliamentary language (much before the movie was released) and *also* that it was *his* recommendation to the censor board to certify the movie as a feature film with adult content. He also named the segment of the audience he felt the movie was not appropriate for – family audience, women, children and other sensitive and impressionable segments. The warning did not stop there. The first promotional feature of the movie that had a wide release on social media as well as television was equally obedient to the warning mandate. Yet, let us relook at this first video, which we think is a classic selling shield of its kind.

The commercial begins with the producer Aamir Khan staring at you from the screen, worried and explaining: "Friends, I have produced a film, *Delhi Belly*, because of which I am very worried."[9]

- *Point to be noted*: The regional word he uses for "worried" is "*chintit*", which is a very upper class and sophisticated word that is not commonly used in daily conversations. Moreover, if he was "worried", he would not have ventured into making the movie.

He then continues to explain: "I am worried because the language in the movie is a bit vulgar; in fact, not just vulgar but disdainful."

- *Point to be noted*: Use of two words, "*ashleel*" and "*behuda*", almost synonymous, and deliberate highlighting of the negative aspect of the movie.

The warning continues: "For these reasons, this movie is not for those people who are a bit . . ."
Aamir Khan is obviously referring to family audiences, to women, to children, to all those expected segments of society (stereotypes) who "are expected to" dislike slang and adult content. But his voice trails off, as he is interrupted in his apology by the three young protagonists of his movie.
One of them says: "Those kinds who are tedious, miserly, boring . . . not for them."

- *Point to be noted*: use of words like "*pakao*", "*khadoos*" and "boring" are again stereotypes of the audience who do not use slang or even watch adult movies, again stereotypes entertained by the youth generation.

Another says: "These are not indecent, they are normal words, like [beep], [beep], [beep]."

- *Point to be noted*: "beep" is a tool used by a government body – the censor board, the agency that deems fit which movies should be watched by which segments of the audience. The so-called "normal" words uttered in the video have been deliberately beeped. When is a "beep" used? When you want to "tell" the audience that a word has been used, which should not be in circulation. But what really happens? Though the word is silenced behind a "beep", the "instruction" has a reverse impact. A child knows that a word has been used which the adult world thinks is not good enough for her to hear. The knowledge of the existence of such a word, even if not the direct use, thanks to a "beep" has an impact the censor board has never bothered to consider in its instructional policies. The child is curious to know the word; the "beep" accentuates the level of peculiarity! There are three "beeps" in this promo dialogue, which become three more when the third character translates these "daily use" words in English! Six "beeps" in all.

A worried Aamir Khan interrupts: "These people are going to destroy my reputation." To which one of the three protagonists jeeringly adds: "Yes! In the last 30 years, the respect my uncle has earned, he will lose it all." And the rest, repeat as a refrain, "He will lose it all."

- *Point to be noted*: If we remember the track record in our good-will toolkit, we can discern the underlying agenda of the jibe. After all, this movie is being produced by a man who has made a name for himself in the last 30 years, which is no small feat. Would he make nonsensical movies, an artist of the calibre of Aamir Khan? It's anyone's guess.

Aamir Khan gets angry at the jibes and retorts back, (un)fortunately with a "beep". The *last* "beep" is followed by a deafening silence as the other protagonists fade out, leaving Khan looking at us sheepishly. With the background music, comes the tag line of the promo – "Shit happens!" Now there are seven "beeps", one ironically contributed by the warner himself.

Will the readers now be able to define Inoculation? We will have another go at it.

In 2007, *Jab We Met* hit the Indian screens. Aditya Kashyap (Shahid Kapoor), the surviving legacy of the Kashyap Group of Industries, is up against a brick wall handling a failing corporation, which his parents, and principally his father, had steered to astounding heights. Let us look at the major blocks in Kashyap's life, as illustrated in Figure 3.6.

In Kashyap's journey to self-realisation, he meets Geet (Kareena Kapoor), and what happens there is anyone's guess. But the important episode here is in the boardroom of his office, when after having been missing for several weeks, he returns to face all and sundry. When the young Kashyap stands on the dais, what is expected of him to share with the very employees he left marooned, by opting out of the responsible role of headship? He is expected to say "sorry". But watch the amazing screenplay penned by Imtiaz Ali for the speech delivered by Aditya, as in Script 3.12.

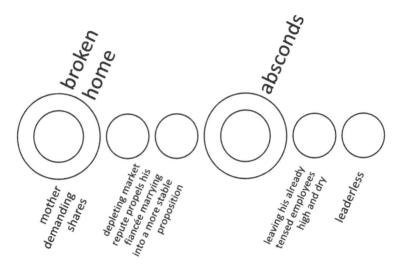

Figure 3.6 Blocks in Kashyap's life

Script 3.12 Aditya's apology from *Jab We Met*

> **Aditya's apology speech**
>
> - Good morning.
> - I hope all of you will not beat me up? Mehra Sir, please don't beat me up. But I agree, I have done something that deserves beating. I left without notifying. From the beginning the company is not doing well, and on top of that, me and my depressions. I am also aware the gossip about me being floated in the market. Aditya Kashyap cannot take his father's place. Company is on the verge of splitting. His girlfriend married someone else. He ran away from the town. So on and so on, and so on! All rumours…which **by the way are so true.**
> - (*Audience stunned and murmurs*)
> - So, our share prices are at all-time low; all new brands have miserably flopped; in other words, our condition is pathetic; boss, we are dead! **It cannot get worse than this, now only good can happen, and will happen!**

Begin with the Negative

Twist to the Positive

- (*Silence and motivated*)
- If we really wish for something, and this time, I really wish . . . actually . . . that I face every problem head-on; I complete every incomplete plan; and take this company there where even my dad could not dream of taking. I know you all love my dad a lot. He is here; he is watching us; so let us gear up and show him that boss, don't be so arrogant about yourself because this company can work without you, and work better than your expectations. Let's show him; what do you say?
- (*Applause*)

Source: Translated by the authors from the original screenplay of the movie from personal VCD.

This is a fine sample of a motivation speech. The audience, which had given up on the young CEO, was more into lamenting over the absence of the elder Mr. Kashyap, and gossiping about the deficiencies of the younger scion of the Kashyap family. But Aditya adroitly turned the table, and how? Inoculation! If the readers have yet not grasped the style, let us try a traditional illustration of the same. Let us go back to the famous speech of Mark Antony once more in *Julius Caesar,* which is one of the oft-quoted passages from the body corpus of Shakespearean work.

Mark Antony begins his fierce onslaught on the assassins of Julius Caesar with these words, "Friends, Romans, countrymen, lend me your ears;" (Act III, Scene 2, Line 73),[10] inviting his hostile audience to listen, and then he adroitly assures them: "I come to bury Caesar, not to praise him." Thus he begins with identifying the "common ground of agreement" before getting into the argument that is counter to his audience's biases, which makes his oration an exemplary model of persuasion. And then he strategically shifts his message, as is evident in Script 3.13.

Script 3.13 Mark Antony's speech

Mark Antony's speech

- The evil that men do lives after them;
- The good is oft interred with their bones;
- So let it be with Caesar. The noble Brutus

- Hath told you Caesar was ambitious:
- If it were so, it was a grievous fault,
- And grievously hath Caesar answer'd it.
- Julius Caesar (Act III, Scene 2, Lines 75–80)

Source: William Shakespeare. *Julius Caesar.* Ed. Samuel Thurber. Boston: Allyn and Bacon, 1919. Shakespeare Online 26 Feb. 2013 <www.shakespeare-online.com/plays/julius_3_2.html>.

Here Antony iterates Brutus' stance by stating that Caesar had to be assassinated because he was guilty of monstrous ambition. He cleverly uses "if" to initiate doubt about Caesar's mammoth motive of might. At the same time, he accepts the psychological reading of Caesar's mind by Brutus regarding his puissant ambition for power by declaring with emphatic usage of irony, "For Brutus is an honourable man . . ." and then he keeps on repeating "Brutus is an honourable man" as a refrain but not to impart mellifluous lilt to the passage but to build the force of argument.[11] See Script 3.14 for Antony's communication strategy.

Script 3.14 Mark Antony's speech (Continued)

Mark Antony's speech (Continued)

- He hath brought many captives home to Rome
- Whose ransoms did the general coffers fill:
- Did this in Caesar seem ambitious?

  - Julius Caesar (Act III, Scene 2, Lines 88–90)

- When that the poor have cried, Caesar hath wept:
- Ambition should be made of sterner stuff:

  - Julius Caesar (Act III, Scene 2, Lines 91–92)

- Yet Brutus says he was ambitious;
- And sure he is an honourable man.
- Julius Caesar (Act III, Scene 2, Lines 93–94)

Source: William Shakespeare. *Julius Caesar.* Ed. Samuel Thurber. Boston: Allyn and Bacon, 1919. Shakespeare Online 26 Feb. 2013 <www.shakespeare-online.com/plays/julius_3_2.html>.

"He is an honourable man" is an argument of opposition which Antony uses to build his own argument, thereby inoculating his audience and establishing his line of thinking. It is like moving into the opponent camp by first agreeing with their stance and then launching a counterargument that topples the opposition tooth and nail. This is exactly what the producer of *Delhi Belly* did. He began with all those opposing points that a typical audience would entertain about the type of movie he produces, that the language is "*ashleel*" and "*behuda*" for the family audiences. And he even perpended the governing audience – the censor board and its sur-veillance tool – the seven "beeps". So did Aditya Kashyap (Shahid Kapoor). He began in jest about getting beaten, even referring to a senior member in the crowd, Mr. Mehra, beating him up. Then he actually listed every negative point that was endorsed by the rumour market; and "rumour in the market" was no different from "gossip amidst his employees". He cleverly addressed the latter while naming the former. The list against him is formidable, as is evident in Figure 3.6. In sum, the company condition is pathetic. And yet look out for clever transitions in this self-depreciating act –

- I deserve to be beaten, as I have done that kind of work.
- These are all rumours, but all of them are so true!

Now if we refer back to the "failure" quotient used in the good-will credibility builder toolkit by King Ashoka, it is moulded in the same style. Ashoka "exposes" the casualty list, and admits that he is responsible for the unaccountable and uncalled for death in Kalinga and later has remorse; he then positions his request/order – "practice dhamma".

It is human nature to be defensive. It would have always been easy for Aditya to say, "You have not gone through what I have; my depressions, my loneliness". It would have been easy for Aamir Khan to say, "Slang words are everyday words; they are branded as unparliamentary; one needs to discern similar language used in the parliament." Antony could have said, "Brutus is wrong; Caesar was never ambitious; he was bleeding for Rome." It would all have been in vain, because the audience was hostile. Rather, they all began with the "enemy virus". For Antony, it was always that "Brutus was honourable, and if Brutus said that Caesar was ambitious, so he was." He worked harder repositioning "ambition" as a posi-tive quality rather than defending the accusation. For Aamir Khan, "*ashleel*" language deserved censorship. However, he repositioned adult movies rather than defend the accusation. For the young Kashyap, "rumours in the market" were right, and he could never be like his father. However, he actually comes to the point in his speech only in the middle, when he says that things have turned so bad that it cannot get worse, it can only get better. And then he repositions himself against his father, motivating his employees by saying that now is the time to show the senior Mr. Kashyap how much more they can all do, which even the senior scion could never have imagined.

Inoculation technique can become a powerful move in your game of persuasion to disarm your opponent by using her own point. The popular misconception about persuasion is one should only discourse vociferously about the merits of one's stand to reinforce one's position. But the reason why people do not succeed by describing just the takeaways of their idea is because they often completely overlook their adversarial viewpoint, which makes the advocacy status of their ideas more vulnerable. This debacle of advocacy is the upshot of numerous reasons. Firstly, you appear biased, as you are ignoring the flip side of your idea (in real life situations every idea you propose, or every recommendation you make, may be saddled with certain factors working counter to it). Secondly, you are likely to get bombarded with questions because you do not deal with the negative side of a certain issue at all. Your audience will then try to derail you by opposing your arguments, and then even if you have a strong argument in your favour, the going will get difficult now that their verbal duel with you has already graduated into a battle of ego. When people raise certain objections, withdrawing their points because someone else has a rational argument against it becomes all the more psychologically difficult, because it entails a self-demeaning feeling of defeat. To combat this problem, you just need one more manoeuvre, and that is using the inoculation technique.

To transcribe the same game plan in the world of business, imagine some insurance agent coming to persuade a batch of young people to buy the insurance policy. S/he can begin and end with the same theme – how the insurance plan can benefit them. But the long list of benefits may not be able to convert the young listeners into buyers because s/he does not touch upon the opposition. This opposition might soon be raised by one of the sceptic listeners who may ask the agent as to why s/he should buy the policy when at this age s/he can invest the same money in other lucrative plans. In that case, the agent may have to give a long monologue as to why insurance is a desirable item in the investment portfolios even for people who are young and yet to embark upon their family lives only to be refuted every time from this opponent who will not backtrack easily since s/he owns the position of the sceptic. But if this agent had used the inoculation technique, s/he would not have given anyone a chance to raise objections because they owned them first, thereby making the defence more difficult. Before anyone could have brought this point to the forefront, s/he would have begun like Mark Antony, starting with the common ground – agreeing with the audience position that insurance plans are not lucrative options to park monies at such a young age. Then, s/he could have slowly moved, again like Mark Antony, by making this opposition the strategic motif: "Yes, insurance does not give you handsome returns, but what it can give you is protective cover . . ." This can disarm your adversary as s/he is left with no points to counter. You employed the point of criticism to begin with and yet proved your point. Since nobody owns this antagonistic point against you – no feathers are ruffled, no egos are hurt – the audience finds it easy to surrender their own perspective and embrace your notion.

It is like using a two-sided format to present your idea – in lieu of starting with the pros of your position (which all of us are tempted to do), deliberately start with the cons of your stand, but do not spend much time on these cons and quickly deflect the audience attention towards the pros that now seem to outweigh the cons. But remember, do not dwell at length on the cons lest you reinforce the negative impression, which your audience may be harbouring; just touch upon the cons and then save more time for the discussion of your pros. This has a dual advantage – the audience gets satisfaction that you are a fair analyst who has considered kaleidoscopic perspectives on a certain issue and they are contented that their doubts were answered. Apply this technique at the outset of your talk so that you do not give anyone a chance to speak against you at all. This is how Munter's **two-sided cons/pros format** can work for you.

A variant of this technique is the strategy of **eliminating options**, a technique proposed by Peter Cardon in *Business Communication: Developing Leaders for a Networked World*.[12] If there is a problem and you want to propose an unconventional solution, to soften audience resistance first start by enumerating the solutions your audience is likely to suggest. Take up their suggested solutions one by one and demonstrate how they will not work. Do not talk about your recommended solution until they are convinced that the ideas they had in their minds will not work. Once you eliminate these options, space is created for you to step in and lay out your idea. This is then the ripe moment to launch your recommendation, which may now appear to your audience as the only plausible solution that might work, thereby bolstering the possibility of its acceptance.

Unlearn what you learnt at school. A debate *for the motion*, now entails *against the motion* points. We propose the four camouflaging manoeuvres that an effective inoculation must have **but** *only* to change the game in your favour (see Figure 3.7)!

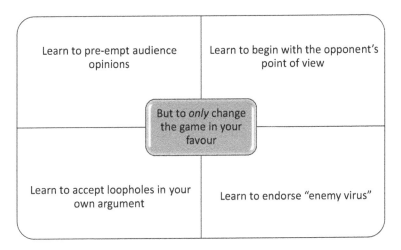

Figure 3.7 The inoculation mechanism

So, follow the opponent to be the opponent!

- Asset 5: Deconstruction

Let us revert back to the days of school physics when we were flummoxed by strange equations, dimensions and perspectives. And to top it all, we struggled through speed, vector and time exercises. But one example still stands out in our collective memory. We might forget the theory, but not the illustration. Passenger A is seated in a fast moving train. Passenger B is standing on a still platform. When the train car crosses passenger B, and there is a bolt of lightning, she notices the flashes at both ends of the train car concurrently. But for passenger A sitting inside the train, the front side lightning flash appears first, and then the rear one follows. So, who is correct – both flashes at the rear and the front happen simultaneously or the front one happens first and then the rear one? According to Einstein, both are correct! And the reason is that passenger A interprets from her point of reference, which is "within a moving train car", and passenger B from a different point of reference, "on a still platform". This is, for the nerds, Einstein's Special Relativity theory. For the lesser mortals, we resurrect the theory as the Theory of Perspectives.

According to Einstein, interpretations have truth value as per the perspective in which these interpretations are made, and perspectives, lenses or frames of reference (as we choose to call them) can be different; in fact, they are different for different individuals. We all cannot be sitting in a fast moving train car simultaneously, can we? Our theory of perspectives distorts the biggest myth of generic public knowledge – that there is an absolute meaning, an absolute concept of truth. We also understand why such myths need to be perpetuated in systems. Imagine a child thinks that s/he need not follow the attendance rule in school, because compellingly sitting in a class does not exactly amount to studying. The child is correct, but only as per her frame of reference. The school will have the unquestioned rule of compulsory attendance so that children are disciplined into attending classes, and "hopefully" discover interests which they might not have anticipated in that particular subject or class. School authorities are correct, but only as per their frame of reference. Now, in Einstein's words, there can never be a covenant on the simultaneity of events from different locus points. Accordingly, we grow up in environments of disciplines in education institutions, where law of attendance is gospel. If we question that, we are labelled outlaws, rebels, anti-institution, anti-nation and you can go on adding unlimited words to the prefix at your discretion.

We are not here to demonstrate how to bring about agreement on the simultaneity of events from different reference points. After all, our expert (Einstein) has previously declared such a feat as impossible. But, we use the expert to harpoon the singular point about value judgements; they are not absolute. They are valid as long as their frame of reference is valid. This is a very big philosophical statement to make, because it alters the dimension of value systems – everything becomes "relative". Welcome to the psychological world of relativity. And one of the greatest benefactors of this theory of relativity is the world of corporate communications. Will you imagine the power of sovereignty that is given to you as a communicator? Aamir Khan, through communication, repositioned the value judgment for adult movies. Mark Antony singlehandedly repositioned a defamed Caesar in the eyes of a Brutus-devoted audience, thus ousting Brutus in favour of the recently lost would-be emperor. Aditya Kashyap repositioned his previously doubtful "ability to lead" by clever comparison with his father, the crowd favourite – "that we can and must do more than what senior Kashyap could have ever dreamt of". And washing detergents today are repositioning "dirt" as good, courtesy *OMO/Surf Excel* (*"Daag achche hain"*). The philosophy of relativity thus allows tremendous agency to a communicator. For centuries artists, philosophers and theorists from other disciplines have been using similar theories of perspectives, but it was Einstein who popularised the concept of relativity by giving it a scientific definition.

Way back in the Greco-Roman era of history, when rulers had to speak, there was the need for instructors to tutor the likes of Cicero – the great Roman orator – to express effectively before large audiences. The genesis of oratory was in a discipline christened as rhetoric, and the teachers of rhetoric called themselves the Sophists; in Greek, the wise men. One of the famous Sophists, Protagoras, had laid down the premise for a good argument – that truth is nothing but that which is positioned well by a good argument. The underlying point was that if you argue well, you win the case, irrespective of the "real state of events". Or, more pronouncedly, you "construct" the truth or the "real state of things" through the craft of an argument. Protagoras was famous for holding that "man was the measure of all things".[13] It is another matter that the dangers of casting arguments within the sophist frame of reference had history condemning such teachings into exile within stockades of academic hermitage. Today, the likes of Munter find beautiful relevance of these same tricks and techniques of sophistry and rhetoric in circumstances where communication is the prerequisite of industrial, administrative and corporate negotiations; a world which is always about positions and repositions, parleys and inducements.

What started as a trend with Relativity Theory had its unique existence in the history of ideas because of the philosophical contribution of one maverick, who changed the course of philosophy altogether. We are talking about the Algerian thinker – Jacques Derrida. He, along with a few others, independently cemented certain patterns of interpretation, which later many historians of the history of ideas collated into one description of philosophy: the post structural school of thinking – a revolution that buzzed in and around European and American academia in the 1960s. In light of Derrida's contribution, let us provide another illustration in anthropology as a parallel to that of the physics dominated train graphic. Claude Lévi-Strauss, the French anthropologist, wrote in his "Writing Lesson" ethnographic records of the lives and times of the Nambikwara tribe. This was 1955. His pronouncement on the tribe is well reflected in these oft-read lines:

> That the Nambikwara could not write goes without saying. But they were also unable to draw, except for a few dots and zig-zags on their calabashes. I distributed pencils and paper among them, none the less, as I had done with the Caduveo. At first they made no use of them. Then, one day, I saw that they were all busy drawing wavy horizontal lines on the paper. What were they trying to do? I could only conclude that they were writing or, more exactly, that they were trying to do as I did with my pencils.[14]

The anthropologist's "Writing Lessons" is a historical marvel because it bared in a systematic manner (he went and lived there with the tribe) the behavioural patterns of tribes on exposure to the civilised Western world. Derrida deconstructed the "lesson" in his iconic 1967 release *Of Grammatology*[15] when he asked us all to wonder whether those "dots and zigzags" were *not* writing, just because the white European did not understand them. That "writing" is an educated word for the English speaking community does not necessarily mean that "ʃ"[16] is not expressive, just because the frame of allusion is not English. If this is philosophically too heavy, let us talk about activities with which we are more familiar.

There are Women's Achievers' awards – celebrating womanhood in an endeavour to proclaim that gender disparity is inconsequential. But apply the principle of deconstruction – if there are awards for women who achieve, the underlying implication could be that generally women do not achieve; hence women who achieve these awards need special felicitation. Thus, this act of deifying women by presenting those awards that are restricted to the she-gender is tantamount to demeaning their status. The subtext is that they cannot vie with the masculine gender; hereafter let them compete within themselves only.

On similar lines, let us deconstruct the Axis Bank commercial, where a man who has come to share his happiness of becoming a father with a pack of sweets is asked to give not one but two sweets since he is blessed with a daughter – again the subterranean meaning is those who father daughters need to be reassured of the positivity of "good" news by means of two pieces of sweets in lieu of just one. What does this say about the situation of that culture where you need extra ego benefit (from our strategy toolkit) to encourage a girl child as a credible practice? Or, when *LG* launches its unisex washing machine highlighting that the product is both for men and women – the unsaid text is washing is primarily a woman's job but now even men do it.

Discourses on women in their utmost earnestness to present a progressive take on the gender have fallen prey to the patriarchal habit, unfortunately unknowingly. It is not that the Women's Achievers' awards, the Axis Bank commercial or the *LG* unisex washing machine do not intend well for women, but their intention when applied in their professed progressive illustrations fail to progress for the very reason that they end up unwittingly reinforcing the patriarchal attributes all over again. You provide a deconstructionist a juicy bone to bite into. Look at one of our many cultural terminologies. Ma Durga is the goddess of good over evil. She was expressly created to annihilate the obnoxiously dreadful devil – Mahisasur. And she did. This mythological story is celebrated in a grand manner every year as *Durga Puja*. The celebration of good over evil also has a feminist streak with a woman finishing off an evil man. The intrepidity of womanhood is at its peak. But the moment you call Ma Durga in various affectionate and admirable names, one being "Mahisasurmardini" – the assassinator of Mahisasur – a deconstructionist would gleefully wait for a bite. The right to fame now lies in the act of assassination of the devil, and hence the devil is very significant in "constructing" the identity of the goddess. Imagine Ma Durga without Mahisasur. In fact, she had to be customised and created by various gods to kill the devil who was otherwise invincible.

It is not just the case with gender identities; the custom in our Indian culture that has many mythologies being celebrated for victory of the hero/heroine over the villain entails the nomenclature of the event or even the good protagonist after the villain. Ram is famous because he killed Ravan. Krishna helped the Pandavas in vanquishing the Kauravas. Even in a movie, the villain is very important. Management students ate out of the hands of Christopher Nolan in *The Dark Knight*. Ask them what they remember, and immediately the answer is Joker and not the protagonist, Batman. We do not know which would be the more unshakeable example of collective judgement: the Tatas as the king of CSR in India, or the Joker in *Dark Knight* as the most popular character in the global entertainment industry. One of the strongest criticisms for the science fiction attempt by SRK – *Ra One* – has been the lack of a strong villain to support the "construction" of a strong hero. *Sholay*, a legendary movie in B-town, is remembered and recast still, but not for its protagonists Jai/Veeru but for its villain Gabbar – whose twenty-first century versions like *Gabbar is Back* and many more prove that though the yesteryear blockbuster is popular for its portrayal of the debacle of the evil in the form of Gabbar, it is precisely *that* very Gabbar who is alive, even after his screen demise in the climax of the script; he carries the flag of the movie high and does not allow his memory to be erased from public commemoration.

If you still have the courage to remake *Sholay*, even after Ram Gopal Verma's *Aag*, any big hero today would want to play Gabbar. Have a look at some of the remakes of recent times of earlier movies, mythologies, classics – a very recent post-2000 phenomenon in the business of movie making. The attention is on what we want to designate for easy reference as the depiction of the "less preferred" from the original.

Mani Ratnam's *Raavan* released in the year 2010. It was the rehash of the mythological Ram, the god born in human form; Sita, the goddess born in human form and wife of Ram; and Raavan, the villain who abducts Sita. So Ram will fight Raavan to get Sita back. The good will fight the bad. Interestingly, the movie has Raavan play a Veerappan-style dacoit, who captures Sita, and Ram is the upright police officer. At the end, Sita chooses Raavan over Ram, because he had affection for her, notwithstanding his being an outlaw; while Ram was more about principles than love. Is this an alternate reading, or are there subtle hints and potentials for these interpretations in the original mythology, particularly with the strong episode of Sita having to prove her sanctity of being Ram's wife to her people, and Ram supporting the people's wish because his norm was that his subjects come first, then he?

Vishal Bharadwaj released *Haider* in 2014, inspired from Shakespeare's *Hamlet*. Nobody thought of Hamlet's mother, except as depicted – the selfish woman who married the murderer of Hamlet's father. But Bharadwaj thought of possible extensions of her character. Haider (Hamlet) loved his mother and father. But his father was more into the principles of freedom of Kashmir. The son is obsessed with his father and is unable to come to terms with his mother's marriage with the suspect, along with hints of his obsession for his mother. The suspect is calculative, but loves Haider's mother. This woman is so fated – trapped amidst an immoral lover, an idealistic husband and the confused son – yet she is the only positive character who wills to live amidst the follies! Is it possible to read these subtle potentials into Shakespeare's script? Nobody doubts that Tabu (she played the mother) was the real hero in *Haider*.

Reading "these subtle potentials" into an otherwise "innocent" text is the mark of a good deconstructionist. The likes of scholars – Jonathan Schroeder, Janet L. Borgerson, Douglas Holt and many others – have borrowed this philosophical interpretive model from academic disciplines like Culture Studies, Media Studies, Journalism, Literature, Art History and even Philosophy, and have developed a strong currency for its application in the managerial domains, particularly in Consumer Theory and in the study of Advertisements. Jonathan Schroeder does a classic piece of deconstruction in his 2006 "Critical Visual Analysis"[17] in his examination of the hugely iconic posters of *CK One* that released in 1994 to inaugurate the launch of a unisex perfume with the same name.

There is nothing path-breaking about a unisex perfume now, but in 1994, it was so. But for that, we need to understand the 1990s.

The 1990s are famous for the inaugural of multinational cultures over all the continents. With the MNC culture, there also emerged MNC vocabularies – "globalisation", "liberalisation". So, why liberalisation? How would an organisation get a North Korean, a South Korean, a West German, an East German, a Hispanic, an African, a white Caucasian, a Brahmin, a Dalit, a Muslim, a Jew and a Christian to work as a productive team, unless you do not broadcast an ideology that would best help cultivate good organisational atmosphere and hence profitable output? An undifferentiating labour force in terms of race, gender and class also means a lucrative workforce. If MNCs become the substantial character of the economic activities of a system, then the corresponding cultural characteristics will have values that will help such an economic system survive.

- First rule of deconstruction – always look for profit motives in ideological stances. Values have an economic agenda as well.

The next step is to understand the "construction" of an ideological stance. We will blaze the trail a bit more when we say that an ideology is not about what I believe in, as much as it is about what I "prefer", and over what. For instance, I might prefer filter coffee over instant coffee. Nobody objects to this line of thought. But we are not trained to think what the underlying interpretation of the following statement would be: "I believe in punctuality". It obviously means I am punctual, and I expect other people to be punctual. But it also means that I "prefer" this style of conduct over its opposite – "I dislike unpunctuality". Now it will be easy to understand each of the following premises of the ideological stances. I am capitalist – I am not for communism? I am socialist – I am anti-capitalist? I am religious – I am not an atheist? I am a feminist – I am anti-patriarchy? Thus, every ideological stance is a preference over its opposite, and this act of "preferring over" helps "construct" our identity. That I am a feminist is a "construction" of an identity that might have a patriarch look at you with reservations. What do we intend to say here? That the "preferred less" in your ideological stance gives value to the category that is preferred. Strictly speaking, without dishonesty, honesty as a value has no existence in a particular frame of reference.

In the critical studies phraseology, the preferred category is the "dominant" aspect of an ideological stance. The "category preferred over" is the "repressed" side of the same ideological stand. A deconstructionist always starts the analysis from the "repressed", "sidelined" or "silenced" side of a story.

- Second rule of deconstruction – always look for "less preferred" in an ideological projection.

But things do not end here. You need to have the knack of identifying the dominant point of view, and that entails the skill of spotting the unspottable, which we label as the process of identifying the ideology itself, even before you venture into finding the binary opposite of what is projected. A classic case is the *Mountain Dew* commercials. The tag line of the early phase of the Indian *Mountain Dew* commercials has been the famously quoted "*Dar ke aage jeet hain*" or "Beyond fear, is victory". So, the visible ideological belvedere of the brand is the repositioning of fear as good, because if you fear, then alone you will achieve victory, and hence fear is a stepping stone to courage. But we say "no"; this is not their stance. Just browse through the visual narratives of all their commercials. Do we have one where a kid recites the victory mantra and then goes for her school examination? Do we have a young teacher recite the victory mantra and then go for her class? Do we have a young mother recite the victory mantra and then go to the operation room for her delivery? What we have instead is the victory mantra recited by a fearing protagonist of the likes of Salman Khan and Hrithik Roshan, big action heroes of B-town, before indulging in bungee-jumping, paragliding, parachuting, trekking, diving and other adrenalin-pumping activities that denote machismo. The equivalent of victory in these commercials is machoism – the hidden ideology. It has to be since this is a soft drink product that has to attract a certain segment of society – the adolescents – who desire the macho appeal.

- Third rule of deconstruction – fish out the hidden ideology

And then what do you do? Simply deconstruct the "constructed" nature of identity as projected in the narrative. In short, the formula is simple, even if the philosophy isn't. If A is the projection (first identify A correctly), find its binary opposite B (in a frame of reference A will always have a B) and then detect how B survives as A. Videlicet, the agenda of profit, is for B through the camouflage provided by A (see Figure 3.8).

We hark back to the famous case of *CK One* through Schroeder again. The poster was released in 1994 to a shocked crowd. Today, the very same poster is housed in top museums, studied in many academic circles, and even followed by many other brands like *United Benetton*. The poster provided shock value in 1994 because it was the first of its kind, then. Today, it is a much accepted, imitated and even emulated version of advertisement. We look at two particular angles that the poster became (in)famous for – (a) multiculturalism and (b) gender role reversal. The famous model Kate Moss is made to stand in the poster, but not in the centre. She is surrounded by

Positioning of Ideology as
Preference

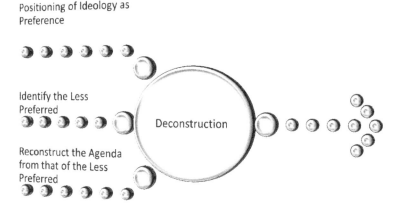

Identify the Less
Preferred

Reconstruct the Agenda
from that of the Less
Preferred

Figure 3.8 Three pronged nature of deconstruction mechanism

a set of anonymous models, who are strategically Hispanics, Red Indians and other races in the United States. A Caucasian White with other races on the same platform against a universal background, and all wearing the American brand's jeans and modern progressive clothes, visually depict that they are all sharing the lifestyle of Moss. The projected ideology is celebration of multiculturalism. The women-men representations are equally interesting. Women wear their hair short, are muscular and aggressive in their postures, while men have long hair and are effeminate and reticent in their poses. The projected ideology is gender role reversal.[18]

Of course, we understand that the coolness and the progressive liberalisation that the commercial projects is to attract the Gen X, the adolescent community that rebels against stereotypes. But what is Gen X being fed with? The deconstructionist shows otherwise. Is it multicultural with a Hispanic imitating Kate Moss's lifestyle? The other races are not celebrating their cultural identities. Rather, Schroeder insinuates that the poster is attempting to standardise difference, and the uniformity is nothing but the replication of the pattern of visual dimensions of Kate Moss, the Caucasian White artefact of the developed economy. Now look at the woman-man role reversal as depicted in Table 3.1. May the reader deconstruct?

Table 3.1 The progressive
stereotype

(Wo)man	Man
Muscular	Effeminate
Aggressive	Reticent
Short hair	Long hair

Now compare Table 3.1 with that of 3.2.

Table 3.2 The patriarchal
stereotype

Man	(Wo)man
Muscular	Effeminate
Aggressive	Reticent
Short hair	Long hair

There is no difference between the tables, because the attributes still preferred in the name of cultural progression are the stereotyped attributes of the male gender. The benchmark is still the man. The system has not changed. Women are now considered an important labour force for a system that needs more economic output! So, we have slogans: "Women can walk shoulder to shoulder with men." The adolescent generation, in the name of coolness, is being fed into the same patriarchal system, which has to be reproduced through them. Similarly, looking at the revamped television commercial of the washing powder *Nirma*, apparently the fair gender may rejoice at the machoistic gesture sported by the women represented as helping men in getting the vehicle stuck in a puddle to move out. But the deeper deconstructive procedure, if applied to this film, sends the message loud and clear that to get superlative status in society, women need to act like men, which, needless to say, combats the agenda of gender parity by showing all the more the disparity in the social approval system which is still predominately masculine in its calibration. Whereas, the competing washing powder *Wheel*, in its commercial, by showing a superstar, Salman Khan, essaying a role of a husband exercising his judgment in the selection of a washing powder (stereotypically a woman's job) exhorting his spouse to switch over to *Wheel* and participating with equal fervour in the act of washing clothes attests the quintessential feminism as a powerful force.[19]

Closer to home, let us review one of the finest examples of deconstruction as a tool of argumentation. In the early 1990s, India opened gates to MNCs. *Pepsi* started with the tag line, "*Ye dil maange more*" or "My heart asks for more". *Cola* comes in later and advertises: "Open happiness". *Thums Up* declares, "Taste the thunder". In a crowded market, what could a new soft drink do to differentiate itself from the big gang? *Sprite* came up with a sprightly line, "*Sirf bujhaye pyaas, baaki sab bakwaas*", or "Only quenches thirst, rest is trash". The second part of the clause deconstructs the ideological stands of each and every member of the big *Cola* gang. In fact, *Sprite*'s visual communication strategy is deconstruction at its best. It has a nerd winning a girl by whisking her away from the stereotypical hero, stating that wit and not "coolness" is the winning strategy. Or wit is the new coolness. Almost all episodes of *Sprite* use deconstruction as their communication strategy.

Deconstruction is destroying the apparent layer of construction and unearthing a new meaning in an act of communication. You can use it to create an entirely new dimension for your audience by discovering something which is camouflaged. This asset of our style shield thus opens a vista of view if used as a communication technique to show what is *potentially* hidden and to revamp the audience's focus by giving it a surprise overhaul.

So go, surprise the audience.

• Asset 6: Foot in Door

Imagine an Indian housewife preparing lunch. She is late; her children and husband will be back anytime soon. She is irritated. There is a doorbell. She opens the door. "Ariel Madame," says the quintessential salesman. Perhaps the most difficult job on the Indian soil is the salesman's job. The housewife, already irritated, is not looking forward to this interruption. She asks him to go. He refuses, he cajoles, he begs, he persuades: "This is a better powder! I will lose my job; this is the last on the list." He is immovable and determined. She cannot stand this interlude anymore. She unceremoniously bangs the door against his face. It just so happens as the door shuts, the salesman interjects the swinging door with his foot. The door is unable to shut completely, as his foot obstructs the closure. There is a tiny opening left, still!

From the salesman's woes, let's move to the crowded BEST buses in the Indian capital. A traveller clings on to another, hanging from the gate of the moving bus. The passengers shout, "No place. Get off." The conductor warns, "You'll get hurt; we are taking no more." He still hangs on as the bus gathers speed. Gradually, a miracle happens. A bus that is packed with passengers, and has no place for even an ant, suddenly "creates" space for this unwanted traveller, who is slowly and steadily pushed in and accommodated in an already overcrowded bus.

Your child hates milk. But s/he has to drink it. The glass is big. You choose to be smart. You bargain: "Drink two sips, and then you can go and play." The child falls for it. Two sips looks to be a feasible small task. S/he starts sipping, and you start narrating a story. You stop midway. The child requests, "What happens next?" You continue as the child goes on sipping, and finally both the milk in the big glass and the story get consumed.

All these episodes teach us a very important lesson – the lesson of "making way". You might have a big project in mind. But with a hostile audience, you cannot start with the huge plan immediately. You need to lead them to the final lap. So, break your project into its pilot project points and start with them. Start with baby steps, with an audience who do not know where these steps are leading them to. But with each step, work hard, make it engrossing, such that the audience craves for more, or get each step to gradually build credibility into your line of thought until you finally reach your destination. This is the salesman's technique of "making way". Freedman and Fraser[20] have already popularised the foot in door technique as a psychological method of getting people to agree to you the second time because of their obligation to have agreed to you before, though the first request was humbler compared to the second. Read their iconic "Compliance without Pressure: The Foot-in-the-Door Technique" in the 1966 issue of the *Journal of Personality and Social Psychology*.

One of the frequently asked questions (FAQs) in an entrepreneurial course is how do you sell to big companies. *Success* magazine tells you that foot in door is the way to reach the big sharks. Look for smaller subsets of big companies, for starters. Instead of *GE*, try the *Fleet Services* division of *GE Capital Solutions*, for instance.[21]

What do you gain? The name of more potential decision makers. Instead of telling your prospects the complete range of products that you have (remember they are busy, tired and full) do your homework well and choose a small problem your prospect has been facing for so long.[22] See that you know how to solve it. Thus, land your first contract, even if a tiny one, and work on it. The point being made again and again is to break the company into their smaller units and target any one of them; break your portfolio into one small focused service matching the focused but small problem your prospect faces, and project that. Work towards getting small contracts at small levels and build your way up the ladder. Now you know what it means to be an entrepreneur.

If SRK is thinking of launching his son in B-Town in the next five years (notwithstanding his rebuttal that his son needs to finish his graduation[23]), he is already administering the foot in door strategy. The continuous updates of his son's teenage life, Instagram pictures, Twitter talks amongst his fraternity gushing over his son's looks and how they would love to launch him (ace director, Karan Johar says he is ready[24]) "makes way" into the audience memory, which if built meticulously over the next year or more becomes a full-fledged launching pad for Aryan Khan. You have already started accepting him!

From a star son's launch to breaking through big companies, this very familiar asset of our selling apparatus has also helped tax reform bills to be passed in the United States in the 1980s and 1990s. Particularly the 1981 US reformed tax had the following debate work around it:

> reformed tax with a 28% top rate would silence (though it certainly would not win over) the capital formation crowd, it was reasoned, the traditional allies of tax reform might be able to form a coalition with low-rate supply-siders that would be large enough to pass a bill. This was the foot in the door for tax reform.[25]

It will be difficult to not find an example in this "compliance without force" technique in any field as such. It is too integral to human psychology to be overlooked and to not have been, even unknowingly, applied and practiced.

- Asset 7: Door in Face

When you want something, ask for more. This technique helps in formulating a relativity index which you can use to show your demand in a modest vein. A simple analogy exemplifies this technique very well. We often have experience of bargaining with street vendors. These street vendors knowingly escalate prices of their items to an exorbitant degree, anticipating that the customer would not pay him the quoted amount. This escalation gives him this relativity index. When the customer starts bargaining, the vendor starts slowly moving down the bargaining matrix, thus leading the customer to feel elated with her new-found power. And finally when he agrees to sell her a 1000-rupee item for just 660 INR, she is elated since she thinks she has clinched the deal with her bargaining prowess. But actually it is the seller who emerges triumphant in the bargaining duel, because the actual cost of the item may have been just 400 INR. He deliberately started with a higher amount, forestalling well in advance that the customer will initiate the price war. He generates a pseudo feeling of triumph in the customer and leads the deal into his desirable range. On the other hand, the buyer can also begin with a low price and slowly raise it to mislead the seller.

The same technique may be replicated by a communicator when s/he is "bargaining" with the subordinate to do a certain work. S/he can give more work knowing well in advance that the subordinate will voice her rebellion. Then s/he can come down to the actual quantum work apportioned for the subordinate by creating a relativity index of a larger work account which can make the actual work request look moderate.

A professor can use this technique by asking students to attend two extra sessions of her course just to make one extra session demand appear modest. The modesty works psychologically because it is *also* human nature that when you say "no" to a big demand, you feel kinder to the next small demand. Social psychologists like Robert B. Cialdini and his co-authors studied this "guilt" quotient in their article "Reciprocal Concessions Procedure for Inducing Compliance: The Door-in-the-Face Technique", this time appearing in the 1975 issue of the same journal that published Freedman and Fraser's work.[26] Both "non-coercive compliance" techniques in foot in door and door in face play with the BIG versus SMALL adjustment index. They both make use of the "small" as a relative calibration. The latter uses "BIG IS BETTER" to position the "small" as lucrative compared to the more direct "SMALL IS BETTER" in the former, such that the dwarfing of your demand in the latter enhances its receptivity by deliberately building a giant framework to calibrate.

- Asset 8: Consistency Reminder

Your job may be done if you use the coercion of the consistency technique. If you link what you are demanding from your supervisory manager with what s/he had communicated earlier you will create pressure. If your manager opines that s/he values creativity and if your idea is repudiated by her for being implausible because it is new, you can always get back to your manager by reminding her of the approbation s/he had granted to creativity and innovation in her erstwhile communications. Since now s/he will be under pressure to maintain "consistency" with her own past pronouncements, the supervisor might say "yes" to you. In this way you make it difficult for the other party to say "no". Thus you can get a "yes" by making "no" a tricky proposition. We baptise the practitioner of Munter's technique as the Innocent Bully.

As mentioned in the "Walk the Talk" chapter, an interviewee is as powerful as the interviewer when it comes to the pressure of circulating benefits. The interview game has changed. It is time you bully the interviewer. The exercise entails a simple act of perusing the vision and mission statements of the companies interviewing you. Let us look at the vision and mission statements of three corporations – Infosys, HSBC and McKinsey (see Script 3.15).

Now as an interviewee, you are being asked the million dollar question by the *Infosys* recruitment team, "Why should we hire you?" You can say many things, but a small instance stating how you take it upon yourself to inquire after your customer once the product or service is disseminated so as to keep track of the credibility of the functionality of your organisation's products and services, exemplifies your work ethos. You will garner eyeballs. You know why. The "following-up" criterion is not the front-runner on the Vision and Mission page of the website. It is hidden in the write-up as a subset of the main point! That shows you read, and get into depth. It also depicts your foot in door prowess! And you remind the organisation to which you apply that your work

Script 3.15 Corporate vision/mission of Infosys, HSBC and McKinsey

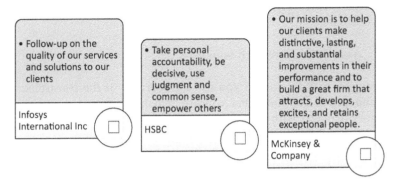

Infosys International Inc
- Follow-up on the quality of our services and solutions to our clients

HSBC
- Take personal accountability, be decisive, use judgment and common sense, empower others

McKinsey & Company
- Our mission is to help our clients make distinctive, lasting, and substantial improvements in their performance and to build a great firm that attracts, develops, excites, and retains exceptional people.

Sources: "Vision and Mission," Infosys International Inc. Accessed on 14 May 2016 <www.infosysinternational.com/visionmission.aspx>.

"Our Vision and Values," HSBC. Accessed on 14 May 2016 <www.hsbc.com.tr/eng/about_HSBC/our_vision_and_values/>.

"Our Mission and Values," McKinsey & Company. Accessed on 14 May 2016 <www.mckinsey.com/about-us/what-we-do/our-mission-and-values>.

ethics is consistent with theirs. None of this is overtly done. You hardly quote. You suggest by saying nothing at all. Consistency reminder is all about saying so much by saying nothing at all, and hence the **innocent bully**. Are we being consistent with the 1990s generation of management students' affection for Ronan Keating and *Notting Hill*, or do we need to say it all? Interview skills are very much akin to Keating's iconic soundtrack – "You say it best when you say nothing at all." The hiring agent needs to "feel" your consistency with them, and it is only your ethos that can play a big role in this rather pragmatic but equally sentimental corporate affair.

As an interviewee, I declare to the hiring team of *HSBC* that my hero is Prof. Satish Dhawan (not a name that corporates will hanker after; not the typical Bill Gates, and not HSBC names). Why? You've led them to ask you what you want to answer. When India's satellite launch vehicle programme of the late 1970s boomeranged, headed by Dr. Abdul Kalam (the rocket system plunged into the Bay of Bengal and not into its destined orbit), the chairman of the Indian Space Research Organisation, Prof. Dhawan declared in the press conference (called solely by him) that this venture was his responsibility. He apologised for the programme's failure. Dr. Kalam always mentioned this episode because he was the project director, and the failure was his responsibility. But Prof. Dhawan showed supreme leadership qualities, Dr. Kalam says in many of his interviews. And the next year witnessed the success of the project, with Prof. Dhawan calling on Kalam to hold the conference.[27] I am not talking about *HSBC*, nor am I quoting the sub-point in their website about "personal accountability", but this story will "consistently remind" the recruitment panel of *HSBC* their own value systems they stand for. This is innocent bullying of sorts.

If you are being interviewed by *McKinsey*, and if you state that one of your strengths lies in skills you have developed, exceptional skills (assuming you can prove them) in assisting clients in their endeavour to upgrade their performance, it will be difficult for your employer not to give weight to your assertion given the website proclamation of the same set of values. This tool of consisting cohesion of your merits with the mission of the company can develop a powerful coercive impact on the receiver of your message. In this way, consistency creates its own matrix, within which placement of the espousal of your idea can ensure its encomium and approval.

Hereafter, we as the modern Hephaistos of managerial communication present our final countdown to successful "make the way to walk the talk" techniques in strategic communication for managerial, administrative and corporate settings. We know Thetis' shield did not protect Achilles from his destiny. But our shield is also an awareness of the realities of corporate dead ends that we as managers have to encounter and live through. We have to play the game – maybe a losing game, but then no game is a game if there is no chance. If you are playing it, then the circular reasoning assures us that there is always a chance! On that note, the persuasive game needs the following to do a *checkmate*.

As a short recap, see Table 3.3 to have an eagle's eye view on the assets for the selling apparatus of persuasion.

This persuasive asset kit, like the communication tool kit, is also the product of seminal interdisciplinary domains. Table 3.4 is a tribute to the history of ideas that the Selling Apparatus is indebted to.

Table 3.3 Assets for the selling apparatus

Assets	Terminologies
Balance theory: break the Achilles' heel in the audience opinion, where audience's credibility anchors are the Achilles' heels	• Cross-examination • Achilles' heel • Fallacy of common sense
Problematisation: confuse the audience with rhizomatic interpretations of their grand-narratives	• Harvey Dent Technique • Mono-rhetoric • Grand-narrative • Poly-rhetoric • Rhizomatic narratives • Multi-perspectives • Subjunctive Mood • 2 + 2 = 4 • Catch-22
Problem-solution structure: hype the problem	• Performative act
Inoculation: disarm opponent by using opponent's point of view	• Enemy virus • Two-sided cons/pros format • Eliminating options format • Pre-empt opposition
Deconstruction: expose the underlying economic agenda of ideological pinnings	• Theory of perspectives • Less preferred • Ideology • Identity construction
Foot in door: start with small requests and with consequent follow-ups lead the audience to the final big goal	• Small is big • Pilot project points • Non-coercive compliance
Door in face: formulate relativity index which you can use to show your demand in a modest vein	• Big is better • Inducing compliance
Consistency reminder: go through your narrative and remind the audience of theirs, because yours is consistent with theirs	• Innocent bully

Table 3.4 Theoretical backgrounds of the selling apparatus assets

Domain	Thinker	Year	Text	Term	Communication technique derived
Law	Co-opted by Mary Munter	Late 20th century	Guide to Managerial Communication: Effective Business Writing and Speaking	Cross-examination Fallacy of Common sense	Balance theory
Sophist Philosophy	Protagoras	5th century BC	– – – –	Rhetoric	Problematisation
Critical Humanities	Jean-Francois Lyotard	1979	The Postmodern Condition: A Report on Knowledge	Grand-narratives Plural narratives	
Hypertext in social media studies	– – – –	– – – –	– – – –	Rhizomatic narratives	
Performative studies	Judith Butler	1997	Excitable Speech: A Politics of the Performative	Theory of performativity	Problem-solution structure
Medicine	Co-opted by Mary Munter	Late 20th century	Guide to Managerial Communication	Immunity Vaccination	Inoculation
Physics	Einstein	20th century	– – – –	Special Relativity Theory	Frame of reference
philosophy	Jacques Derrida	1967	Of Grammatology	Post-structural school of thinking	Deconstruction
Social psychology	J. Freedman and S. Fraser	1966	"Compliance without Pressure: The Foot-in-the-Door Technique" in Journal of Personality and Social Psychology	Compliance without pressure	Foot in door
Social psychology	Robert B. Cialdini et al	1975	"Reciprocal Concessions Procedure for Inducing Compliance: The Door-in-the-Face Technique" in Journal of Personality and Social Psychology	Inducing compliance	Door in face
Interview skills	Mary Munter	Late 20th century	Guide to Managerial Communication	– –	Consistency reminder

Notes

1 We are talking about arguing that which cannot be argued. That is the challenge. That is why we call such situations the Catch-22 situation. Yet, your job is to argue; how do you do it? How do you argue the unarguable? Achilles' heel metaphorically means a weakness. A weakness that you cannot do away with. Yet, you have this daunting task of doing exactly the impossible. And the strategic way of doing it then would be to show the weakness in the other side, that is, find their Achilles' heel. And as modern Hephaistos, we are trying to do that. Protect you by (UN) protecting the audience, because we cannot actually repair the heel. The corporate communicator is like Hephaistos because s/he is asked to make a shield for a person, who anyway is destined to die, because s/he has a defined weakness. Most of the times, the job of the communicator in a situation of conflict is like Hephaistos'. The idea is that weaknesses are integral. Notwithstanding that, what is it that I can do? Communication is also about covering up. The agenda is not necessarily to be honest and admit to the weaknesses that exist. If my major concern is about removing the Achilles' heel, then I am not a communicator; I am God, because the heel is, we think, a metaphor for destiny. But Communication is a skills subject, and skills are about managing destinies. It is in that context we pitch communicators as Hephaistos, that is, we all know that in this difficult situation we are developing agency for communicators to help them win a losing game. Hence, we call it "Persuasion". The idea is to make the audience's point of view weak, and if one can first do that, one can then think of positioning one's point of view more appropriately.
2 Ibid.
3 Ibid.
4 Jean-François Lyotard. *The Postmodern Condition: A Report on Knowledge*. Manchester University Press, 1984.
5 Ibid.
6 Ibid.
7 Ibid.
8 Judith Butler, *Excitable Speech: A Politics of the Performative*. New York: Psychology Press, 1997.
9 All dialogues have been self-translated from "Delhi Belly: Aamir Khan's warning," YouTube video, uploaded on 17 June 2011. Accessed on 10 May 2016 <www.youtube.com/watch?v=JKk76qLFY68>.
10 William Shakespeare. *Julius Caesar*. Ed. Samuel Thurber. Boston: Allyn and Bacon, 1919. Shakespeare Online 26 Feb. 2013 <www.shakespeare-online.com/plays/julius_3_2.html>.
11 Apoorva Bharadwaj. "Shakespeare on leadership, communication and management: Implications for cross-cultural business contexts." *Journal of Creative Communication* IX.2 (2014): 161–184.
12 Peter W. Cardon. *Business Communication: Developing Leaders for a Networked World*. New York: McGraw-Hill, 2015.
13 Pragyan Rath, "The Shield of Rhetoric." *Aesthetic Problems in Literary Ekphrasis*. M. Phil Dissertation, Central Institute of English and

Foreign Languages (CIEFL) [now English and Foreign Languages University] Hyderabad, 2005.

14 "Excerpts." [Claude Lévi-Strauss, "A Writing Lesson," *Tristes Tropiques*. 1955. New York: Criterion, 1961. 290–293]. 11 May 2016. <www.english.illinois.edu/-people-/faculty/debaron/482/482readings/levystrausswriting.htm>.

15 Jacques Derrida, *Of Grammatology*. 1967. Trans. Gayatri Chakravorty Spivak. Baltimore: John Hopkins University Press, 1997.

16 Self-made for illustration of point.

17 Jonathan Schroeder, "Critical Visual Analysis." *Handbook of Qualitative Research Methods in Marketing*. Cheltenham: Edward Elgar, 2006. 303–321.

18 Image accessed on 23 May 2016 <https://s-media-cache-ak0.pinimg.com/736x/d2/da/68/d2da682b2f89d11fab89945df3f41092.jpg>.

19 Pragyan Rath and Apoorva Bharadwaj, "Deconstructing Symbolic Ideology in Contemporary Communication Strategy in Advertising: The Case of Nirma and Wheel." *IIMB Management Review* 26 (2014): 17–27.

20 J. Freedman and S. Fraser, "Compliance Without Pressure: The Foot-in-the-Door Technique," *Journal of Personality and Social Psychology* 4 (1966): 195–202.

21 "Selling to Big companies: Strategies to break through." *Success* 2 February 2009. 13 May 2016 <www.success.com/mobile/article/selling-to-big-companies>.

22 Ibid.

23 "SRK wants kids Aryan, Suhana to first finish studies then enter Bollywood." *The Indian Express* 22 April 2016. 13 May 2016 <http://indianexpress.com/article/entertainment/bollywood/shah-rukh-khan-wants-kids-aryan-suhana-to-first-finish-studies-then-enter-bolly-wood-2765393/>.

24 Prashant Singh, "No one else can launch Aryan Khan: Karan Johar." *Hindustan Times* 27 December 2015. 13 May 2016 <www.hindustantimes.com/bollywood/no-one-else-can-launch-aryan-khan-karan-johar/story-kLVBkn4sBpv9E1qXK074cO.html>.

25 Joseph J. Minarik, *Making America's Budget Policy: From the 1980s to the 1990s*. Armonk: M. E. Sharpe, 1990. 161.

26 Robert B. Cialdini, Joyce E. Vincent, Stephen K. Lewis, Jose Catalan, Diane Wheeler and Betty Lee Darby, "Reciprocal concessions procedure for inducing compliance: The door-in-the-face technique." *Journal of Personality and Social Psychology* 31.2 (1975): 206–215.

27 " 'Former President APJ Abdul Kalam: 'A Leader Should Know How to Manage Failure'," Knowledge@Wharton. 3 April 2008. 14 May 2016 <http://knowledge.wharton.upenn.edu/article/former-president-apj-abdul-kalam-a-leader-should-know-how-to-manage-failure/>.

Chapter 4

You've got mail
Strategy in style

Now that we know the toolkit as well as the shield in strategic communication, let us focus on the various kinds/types of occasions in which managerial communication manifests itself. Broadly speaking, the most prevalent, familiar, daily and even inevitable occasions of managerial communication happen to be

(a) Business messages and
(b) Business reports/proposals/plans.

Let us start with our analysis of the role of persuasion in probably the most familiar of all occasions of messaging, communicating and managing in corporate sector, more so in contemporary times of the social media – mails. Letters have been the age old tools of communication. With the bandwagoning of the World Wide Web and even smartphones, the nature of messaging is continuously undergoing mutation with shrinking of language from "as soon as possible" to ASAP; with interference of symbols amidst orthodox and conservative words; or even with the interface of casual and formal versions of the global language – English, and its many cultural variants (Hinglish, for instance, in India). In this complex flux, we as researchers of managerial communication would like to reintroduce the stylistics of business messages, not so much in terms of their technical formats, but more in terms of their underlying strategies that camouflage their profit agendas in the display of corporate communication etiquette in typical managerial situations. Our investigation is into the "why" – why the camouflage, why the diplomacy or even why the etiquette?

Written forms of communication can be dangerous. It is so because any form of writing becomes an archive, an unresolvable and uncontestable evidence, an undisputable document and history of a managerial event. In future then, we need to be extremely cautious about what we write on behalf of the communicatee, and even more for the well-being of the organisation we work for; after all, we are employees of an organisation, and we can never overlook the legal consequences of *archived* managerial communication.

There would be innumerable situations with innumerable methods of handling them. But, if we take into consideration an eagle's view of corporate messages, we can count the types on our fingers. We list for the benefit of our readers a unique taxonomy of business messages, based on an exercise in cataloguing various kinds of messages evolving through the response to typical kinds of managerial situations. The taxonomy then is more in terms of the written stylistics as strategic responses to particular managerial situations. To put it more conveniently, classification of messages that we offer is more a classification of managerial situations for which those messages have been developed. The following *then* is our taxonomy of corporate business messages; in other words, the typology of managerial situations that require letters, emails, short messages, or any other form of written messages, popularly grouped under the macro-corporate term "business messages".

Table 4.1 Corporate taxonomy of business messages

Types of managerial occasion	Types of business message
You receive a product/service that is unsatisfactory. You know you have legal authority to display dissatisfaction.	Claim
Your organisation has been sent a claim message, and you have to accept.	Apology or "yes" to claim
Your organisation has been sent a claim, request, recommendation, but you cannot entertain.	Refusal to claim, request, recommendation
You communicate to your employees, team.	(a) You give them what they want – good news or the popular news (b) You have to break the bad news – the unpopular news
You have to get your way through.	Persuasive messages

Source: All figures, boxes and tables are by authors, unless otherwise mentioned

Claim message

When do we write claim messages? When we know we have a right to. We are all aware of provisions of guarantees and warranties. Hence, the confidence to claim! Yet, there are some styles to follow even in confident occasions. Let us analyse the following fictional corporate incident similar to many such familiar occurrences in real time.

Caselet 4.1 On *NetStar*

> The web development company *NetStar Technologies* developed an e-commerce web portal for a customer called *Online-Bazar.com*. After launch of the online commerce portal, the following complaint/feedback was given by the customer to the web development service provider.

Script 4.1 Scripting claim message

> To: Riya Banerjee <riya@netstarl.com>
>
> From: Ramanika Khanna <ramanika@onlinebazar.com>
>
> Subject: Problem in Web Application Software in Mozilla Firefox.
>
> Ms. Banerjee,
>
> Please address the non-functioning of the web application software in Mozilla Firefox web browser as soon as possible.
>
> It is our usual practice to have a preliminary testing of our newly developed portal and to get subsequent feedback from our end users (suppliers and customers of *OnlineBazar.com*) before the formal launch of the website. In the process, we have been informed that our portal is not loading and opening in Mozilla Firefox web browser, whereas the portal is opening and loading correctly in all other browsers like Google Chrome, Safari, Internet Explorer, Microsoft Edge, etc.
>
> You have been designing and developing software programs for us for the last six years. We had a good experience of working with you. We hope this time you will be able to fix the

website for us at the earliest, so that the customer experience of our portal on Mozilla is as good as on other browsers.

Thanks,

Ramanika Khanna,

OnlineBazar.com

Commentary on Script 4.1   On claim

Perhaps the simplest level of strategising is required here. Yet a claim message stands out to a certain degree in complexity in the taxonomy. The nature of the managerial activity is that of nitpick, an accusation. Yet, the managerial complexity is more about how to complain, particularly to an organisation with whom you have had good relations ("for the last six years"). You need to maintain the relationship, but you also need to CLAIM! The stylisation involves direct but polite complaining in the form of a request ("please address"). The etiquette, however, has deeper agendas. How do you politely complain, yet maintain goodwill? We have a format which we coin as the **Context Creation Strategy**. Complain, register the flaw but do not blame the organisation; blame a procedure within the system.

Let us reinvestigate the message through the lens of our Context Creation Strategy.

Every message has three segments to it – the beginning, the middle and the end. And an email has a subject line. The format below exhibits the abstract design derived from Script 4.1.

Formatting context creation strategy in a claim message

Subject Line: Specify direct need

Introduction Paragraph: Polite emphasis of main idea (request)

Body:

- How fault was discovered (through internal organisational process)
- Evidence (if any) attached

Conclusion: Reinforce immediate need, but on a positive note (goodwill)

Ramanika does not blame Riya and her organisation for a faulty product. She creates a context that helps her "describe the problem" rather than "complain". And the context is, interestingly, a systemic one. Her company runs a preliminary software test with the help of her online users immediately after every purchase, and while running the test, the online users **discovered** that the portal was not opening on the Mozilla browser. This is context creation. It is important to note that the subject line, the introductory line and the ending are crisp, short and to the point, and direct, but with a liberal dose of "please". It is the body of the message that holds the key to strategy for this nature of a message. The idea is that a claim message by virtue of being a claim does hit the nail on its head. So, a written document ready for its archived corporate history, with its polite and intelligent reference to the problem, is more than enough.

Strategy for claim message

> **Systemic Discovery:** Complain, register the flaw but do not blame the organisation; leave it to a systemic context.

Apology or "Yes" to claim

The truth is that no organisation will be happy to receive a claim message. A claim message is a direct accusation at the organisational ethos, because a claim points out flaws in the service/product the organisation values, stands for and is proud of. Hence, a claim is a psychological setback to organisational reputation, brand and market image. Moreover, what if the circumstance and situation is such that the claim withstands the test of doubt, organisational image cleansing activities and out-of-court settlement practices? In sum, what if the claim is irrefutable? The consequence is potentially severe.

We are human, and organisations are collective human endeavours. We need to refer back to our strategy toolkit and revisit the goodwill parameter. On one hand, goodwill is all about a relationship track record. On the other, it is also about strategic positioning of failures, vulnerabilities and weaknesses. And the latter is exactly what we need to fall back upon in an unavoidable situation of saying "yes" to a claim. How do we say "sorry" and yet retain the angry and unhappy client, diminish the word-of-mouth negativity,

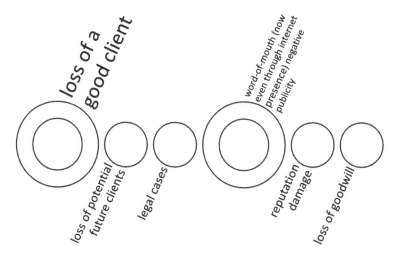

Figure 4.1 Damage due to claim

preserve future clients, avoid legal attacks, retain reputation as trustworthy producers of good quality and, overall, maintain the goodwill track record that one has worked so much for. Take a look at the following instance:

Script 4.2 Scripting apology to a claim

To: Ramanika Khanna <ramanika@onlinebazar.com>

From: Riya Banerjee <riya@netstar.com>

Subject: Experts on the way; Portal running successfully on Mozilla Firefox

Ms. Khanna,

We will send our experts to fine-tune the software on Mozilla Firefox this coming Monday. They will also help instruct your suppliers and customers to follow guidelines on the use of Mozilla browser like using latest updates, clearing cache, etc. to enable them use this portal without any hassles.

We are thankful to you to have helped us address this grave issue in the nick of time. Before deploying and launching any

Web portal, *NetStar Technologies* follows a standard User Acceptance Testing (UAT) process of Software Development Lifecycle (SDLC), which also involves testing the portal on different web browsers for compatibility, performance, navigation and user experience. The portal was tested successfully to be running on Mozilla Firefox. A snapshot of same is attached for your satisfaction.

This is also a great time to introduce our next level software product for a faster web browser experience. Our experts will be happy to provide you with more information on our software development future X project. We look forward to many more years of productive business with you.

Regards,

Ramanika Khanna,

NetStar Technologies

Commentary on Script 4.2 On apology

We must remember the contradictory salient points when we apologise:

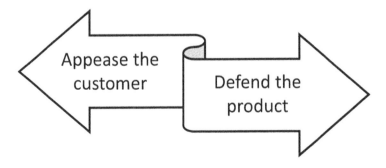

Figure 4.2 Contradiction in apology

The client needs to be appeased, because the client is an agent of transmission of the virtues of our product or service. Ironically, the one golden rule that we can never forget as employees of our organisation, even while being apologetic to the client, is our ethical organisational affinities. We cannot admit on pen and paper that our product is faulty, or at least directly confirm that our product or service is flawed. We can be sorry for the inconvenience caused, but not inconvenience the organisation by letting it get embroiled in a legal hassle. Hence, the context creation strategy has a further shade applied to its strategic agenda, a shade that has to achieve a paradoxical complexity – appease yet defend. The impossible is managed and in a sophisticated manner through three smart moves. We call it the **ADD** format: Appease, Defend, Defocus.

Appease   **Defend**   **Defocus**

Appease	Defend	Defocus
Ego benefit to an angry client	Defend through systemic procedure	Defocus the attention from the faulty product/ service by limelighting a new product

Figure 4.3 ADD format for apology

We can evaluate in Figure 4.3 the estimated proportion for each attempt.

Formatting context creation strategy in an apology to a claim

Subject Line: Specify direct action

Introduction Paragraph: Mention main idea with a concrete action plan

Body:

(a) Thank for fault finding
(b) State how that helped you in time
(c) Defend now (explanation and assurance of company's process for quality)

Conclusion: Regain possible lost goodwill by offering personalised assistance or new product/service.

The most important thing that we need to keep in mind when apologising to a claim is the action plan. After all, the client demands the product/service. So there is no time to waste with an unnecessary, lengthy apology. Rather, give the client what s/he wants – a better version of the required product/service. So, the subject line should be a direct confirmation that the client deserves ("experts on the way"). As is the case with the subject line, the introductory part should also have the confirmation ("experts on the way") as well as a viable action plan ("coming Monday"), all directly and clearly assembled. That is all that the clients really want to know – so give it to them, and do not waste time apologising in the first sentence itself.

The rest of the message is prepared in a manner such that its archiving does not add to the history of blunders but to a track record that demonstrates how tackling with blunders from time to time has made the organisation sustain itself successfully. As is the case with the claim message, the strategy here too is played out in the body of the message. Convert the grievance into a boon, and hence the client gets the best ego benefit that you can ever give and that also to the client who is an accuser ("we are thankful to you to have helped us address this grave issue in the nick of time"). It is as if the accusation has saved your organisation from grave danger. Once the ego benefit is delivered do the needful for your company record now – defend your product/service through context creation again (User Acceptance Testing [UAT] process of Software Development Life-cycle [SDLC]). You can add evidence if you can provide it ("snapshots attached"). Beyond mention of the standard procedures, do not waste time elaborating on the issue. Hence, the main focus while scripting these letters is on the technique of Defocus. How? Through the conclusion, cross-promote any new service/product that you want to showcase, as is the case here with software development future X project. Thus, the following format establishes a triple etiquette through benefit, defend and defocus context creation.

Strategy for "Yes" to claim message

ADD Context Creation Strategy

Appease: The complaint is altered as a saving grace

Defend: Procedural testing was positive

Defocus: Cross-promote another service

"No" to a claim message

We cannot bend organisational rules for every claim message. Yet, how do we refuse? Any refusal has to be carefully authored, and hence compulsorily defocussed. This is a complex situation, because you are not going to appease the client – you are refusing the client. So, a lot is at stake, and yet you have to refuse. The context creation reaches a zenith in complexity, and strategy reaches its peak in application. We have four refusal formats that can be shuffled within various sub cultural complexities. But as structural frameworks, they remain distinct, inexorable and valid as in the following four defocussing instances.

- **Refusal 1:** The curious case of incentives

Let us review one of the common recurring situations in business messages: performance incentives – "I want XYZ amount of money as incentive for my excellent performance." And what if you do not want to oblige, because you cannot? Look at Script 4.3.

Script 4.3 Scripting the curious case of incentives/refusal Sample 1

Dear Ms. Sharma,

You have been one of our worthy employees contributing to the growth of this company for the last five years. As you know, it is a well-known fact why talented employees choose our company.

Every year we carry out the process of performance appraisal deploying certain stipulated yardsticks of gauging the work done, the details of which are known to each and every employee of the organisation. To keep the process of this appraisal fairly transparent, we circulate the schema for the performance appraisal and the incentive system followed for calculating the extra work done and the sterling performance delivered by our employees at the beginning of each financial year. As you know, we follow a rating system which becomes the basis of disbursement of incentives to our employees every year. As your rating was 3.5 on the five-point scale, we are crediting INR 2,53,000 in your salary account on the last working date of this month.

Next year, we will be introducing one more new parameter for incentive assessment which will enable our employees to get extra payment for the overseas errands they undertake for proliferating the business of the company globally. As you have been doing lot of good overseas work for past so many years, you will be delighted to get incentives for your efforts next year which will compensate you handsomely for the new overseas clients you bring for the company.

Sincerely,

Rina D'Souza

Assistant Manager, Global Disc

Enclosures: Policy Details

Commentary on Script 4.3 On refusal

The situation is tricky. There is a demand for incentives ("crediting INR 2,53,000"). Yet, there is a trick hidden in the message, and that trick lies in the number quoted in the letter. The incentive demand must have been *much more* than INR 2,53,000, and that *much more* is being refused. Yet, there is no sign of a refusal in the message, or is that so? The ADD technique manifests itself once again, but with greater *discreteness* through context creation. The Subject Line here would be indirectly significant; a direct refusal cannot be quoted. A neutral heading may be quoted as "incentive reconsidered". But what that actually amounts to is hardly mentioned. Had this been an apology, we know how the Subject

Heading would have looked: a direct happy admission to what the client was looking for.

Strategy for Formatting the subtraction in the ADD format in incentive refusal

Subject Line: Provide subject of message without revealing refusal: neutral message

Introduction Paragraph: Build credibility through ego benefit for client (APPEASE)

Body:

(a) Present objectively with its merits and limits the systemic procedure through an organisational policy sold as audience friendly (DEFENCE)

(b) Indicate refusal by quoting the amount of the incentive, which clearly is the result of an audience friendly organisational appraisal policy

Conclusion: Shift emphasis away from refusal by presenting silver lining sales promotion of the appraisal (DEFOCUS)

When you have to disappoint a client, you may as well begin with ego benefits in direct or circular fashion, depending on what your agenda is; you might want to appease only the client, or you might want to use the client to build credibility for your organisation. This phenomenon of ego benefit to the client, in turn to the product, and even more in turn to the organisation in the introduction, is called the RESALE. And you definitely go for a "resale" *only* when you want to refuse. Thus, the circular benefit from our communication toolkit is presented ("As you know, it is a well-known fact why talented employees choose our company").

The body of the message is significantly strategic, as in most cases with written communications, and more so in refusals. After all, we must be sure we have the right language for the refusal that should not legally and even socially implicate our company. So, just like in a claim, and even in a "yes" to claim, we fall back upon the tried and trusted motif of the systemic or organisational backup – the same context creation is prepared here as well. We take recourse to what we popularly joke as Dummy Excuses:

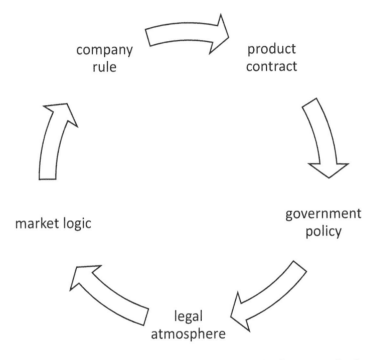

Figure 4.4 Dummy excuses in context creation of defence in refusals

You lay out the systemic procedure in concrete terms, but even within the concrete layout, resale the fund, policy or contract as not merely a limitation, but as client and market friendly. And as a result of that friendly and considerate policy, you are crediting a certain amount that is due to the client. So, monetary enclosure emerges as a product or follow-up of the "worthy" policy, is not pitched as an "appeasement" to a client's demand and is henceforth strategically situated as the concluding line of a dense body and not as a separate line that stands out in the visual space of a message. The latter is both a defence as to why it is what it is, and also a defocus, because there is no statement in the message that positions the credit as an answer to a claim. And the conclusion is another typical "go" at a cross promotional activity, opening doors to future probable incentives, but deep down is the over-used defocus agenda of refusal messages. Thereby, this discrete defocus is an intensified ADD strategy, but with a greater dose of discreteness. Let us call it, ADD discretely, while you are subtracting surreptitiously. In other words, the **Subtraction Strategy**.

Strategy for the curious case of incentives

> The Subtraction Strategy
>
> **Defend**: Resale organisational policy as client friendly
>
> **Defocus**: Add enclosure/credit as outcome of friendly organisational policy, while simultaneously subtracting a chunk that you will not give

- **Refusal 2**: Refusal to a request: passing the buck

A lesser legally worrying version of a corporate message that an organisation faces most of the time is a "request". The difference between a demand for incentive and a request is the possible legal repercussions of a "no" to the former as opposed to the latter. However, a refusal to the request is not without intangible consequences. Goodwill still matters, and turning down a request of help is an affront to a future possible client-relationship. So, how do we approach a refusal to a request? The context creation strategy rises to the occasion again.

The context here is a request to VVVW for competent HR personnel for a new start-up. Let us review Script 4.4.

Script 4.4 Scripting a refusal to a request

> Dear Asha,
>
> You have developed a wonderful organisational process with your innovative start-up. It is an honour for us to be of some assistance to you.
>
> We agree with you that any successful organisational process needs sustenance and entrepreneurial care. And for both, a competent HR personnel is the need of the hour. Although our

organisation on account of its recent relocation policy is short of executives, we are eager to help your worthy organisation.

VVVW is a new organisation that has been developing a foot-in-door approach to HR executive training. They have had recent collaborations with some of the big corporations like BBQ and MTRR, to name a few. Their senior executive personnel would be available at the following number – +91–8854672XXX.

Regards,

Meethal Chopra

VP, coordinator CCC

Commentary on Script 4.4 On refusal

Apart from the regular appeasement and context creation, there is something more to learn from the script here. And that is the *strategy of grammar*. A complex sentence is phrased through clauses, and each clause is a semblance of a simple sentence, an independent sentence or the independent clause that becomes a subordinate clause in a complex sentence. For instance, "I went to the market" is a simple sentence. "It was raining" is also a simple sentence. With the word "while," I join both the simple sentences to form a complex one. In fact, I get two kinds of complex sentences with the phrasing of independent clauses, depending on which clause comes before and/or after which one.

• Sentence 1: "While it was raining, I went to the market."

Or,

• Sentence 2: "While I went to the market, it was raining."

In sentence 1, the activity of going to the market occurs in the second half of the sentence, and hence is the second independent clause.

In the second sentence, the activity of raining occurs in the second half, and is *now* the second independent clause.

A lot depends on the occurrence of a clause in the rear or fore part of a complex sentence; it decides not the precedence of activities, but the position of limelight of meaning, particularly when "conjunctive adverbs" like "while" or "although" are used to join independent clauses. Conjunction is a part of the speech that connects clauses. An adverb adds more to a verb, adjective or even a clause. So, a conjunctive adverb joins two independent clauses, like "while" does. So, in sentence 1, it is the second clause that has more impact on the reader, while the first with the word "while" takes a back seat, as it gets defocussed in the meaning making process.

- Sentence 1: "While it was raining, I went to the market."
  - Independent clause 1: "It was raining"
  - **Independent clause 2: "I went to the market" (limelighted)**
  - Conjunctive adverb: "While"

Similarly, if we interchange the positions of the clauses, as is the case in sentence 2, the activity of raining gets the limelight, as "going to the market" gets defocussed in the first half of the long clause with the conjunctive adverb.

- Sentence 2: "While I went to the market, it was raining."
  - Independent clause 1: "I went to the market"
  - **Independent clause 2: "It was raining" (limelighted)**
  - Conjunctive adverb: "While"

Let us attempt the **conjunctive adverbial strategy** in the refusal to a request. The only conjunctive adverb used in the entire message is "although". It is a complex sentence; the first half has the excuse, the denial, the inability to fulfil the request, while the second clause is all about the help the organisation wants to provide to the client. Thus, the hint of positive assistance in the second independent clause overshadows the negative denial in the first independent clause. Now that help has been promised, it needs to be delivered. So, the concluding part of the message has the reference to any other organisation that *might* help the client with her request. In other words, you *pass the buck* politely and thoughtfully.

Formatting strategy for refusal to request

The conjunctive adverbial format

Defocus: First independent clause in the complex sentence contains the denial, while the second contains a positive promise of support.

> Pass the buck: Concluding part ends with references to other
> organisations which the client *might* try.

The help is an attempt at goodwill.

In place of a conjunctive adverbial strategy, we can also attempt
the **proverbial subjunctive mood** as discussed in the persuasive
shield techniques. Instead of,

> *Although our organisation on account of its recent relocation
> policy is short of executives, we are eager to help your worthy
> organisation,*

we can also write,

> *Had our organisation continued its previous policy of execu-
> tive exchange program me in the face of the current reloca-
> tion policies, we would have definitely provided you with the
> required personnel.*

Thus, subjunctive mood is a grammatical strategy that proposes
a wishful or hypothetical condition, particularly when the conditional affair is not the real state of things, and you want to defocus
the real state of things. So, instead of saying,

> *we cannot provide executives because we have stopped our
> exchange programme and have started a relocation programme,
> on account of which most of our executives are not with us;*

we paint a positive picture stating the conditional affair

> *Had our organisation continued . . .*

- **Refusal 3:** Denial of proposal: Mine is better

There is a claim, a request and also a suggestion. And when the
suggestion is a proposal by your teammate, colleague, company
you have a contract with, a consultancy and even your partner
organisation, it is dicey to refuse. But when you *have* to refuse, then
you *must*. Such kinds of refusal owe their strategies to our already

silhouetted persuasive shield – technique of problematisation. Let us read Script 4.5 to revisit problematisation.

Script 4.5 Scripting denial of proposal

Madhurima,

Consultancy has become a standard norm in corporate practices today, and looking at our financial hurdles, we need to carefully consider your timely proposal for the hiring of one from RST consultancy, which has been doing wonders with many other emerging start-ups like ours.

Hiring a consultant from RST consultancy can be an unpredictably expensive and complicated affair. The expected cost of hiring an RST executive amounts to XXX INR, and even more would be required to sustain one. And we need to remember that we have been facing some financial hurdles in the recent past. Moreover, we do not have a partition culture in our organisation for specialisations. The "jugad" nature of work in our organisation calls for hands-on involvement rather than the deployment of trained and specialised teams for specific jobs. Hence, a financial consultant would mean a reorganisation of the division of labour and a culture of specialisation in our organisation. That would be quite a difficult revamp for the company to handle even before we think of hiring a consultant. In contrast, going for a merger with an experienced start-up like FRS, with us being their executive partners, would not just unburden our recent financial setbacks, but also help us have access to specialised resources without our team falling prey to a stratified organizational structure, thus preserving our unique work culture.

I submit my proposal in the hope that your immense expertise, as always, will help further the unique aspects of our company; aspects the conceptualisations of which have benefited immensely from your innovative ideas. Looking forward to your positive feedback as always.

Best,

Manisha, IRM Executive

Commentary on Script 4.5   On refusal

After an elaborate strategy toolkit and a tenacious persuasive shield, the strategy of problematisation in a scenario of refusing a proposal is more easily detectable. The Subject Heading as is the case with all "no" messages has to be kept neutral, as in "feedback for proposal". We do not know whether the feedback is positive or negative. Hence, the message has to be read. The introductory paragraph has to create the context in which the given proposal is positioned as important and hence needs a "careful consideration". It is a common management gag that any message that begins with "careful consideration" usually ends up in a refusal. Yet, the context needs to be established to develop the courtesy of appreciation of a received proposal. In other words, the context creation strategy works here as a resale of the proposal, which will be denied later (ego benefit to the proposal maker).

The body of the message as is the case with messages in this segment is integral to the strategy that this message needs to carry out. The word "unpredictable" that pops up in the middle of the first opening sentence of the body of the message is significant. It projects the sense that in the process of consideration, there have been discoveries. And in this message the discoveries are in the form of two problems: (a) price and (b) complexity. Thus, the proposal has been beautifully problematised, and each problem "discovered" has been duly discussed, enumerated and justified. Post justification, the writer puts forward her own proposal as a "contrast" to the client's proposal, thereby positioning her own recommendation that can bypass the problems that the client's proposal had. The persuasive shield has already taught us the importance of making way to walk-the-talk (here, write-the-talk). So, the client's proposal has to be problematised well enough to be able to make way for a contrasting proposal, which is most often your own proposal.

The concluding paragraph is a resale of the chosen proposal but as benefitting the client's interests, and thus providing ego benefit to the client all over again. Thus, a predetermined act of problematisation in the context creation strategy is an integral principal that underwrites the message enacting the denial of recommendations. The "in contrast" positioning of your recommendation over the client's recommendation becomes the **In-Contrast Problematisation format**.

Formatting strategy for refusal to recommendation

The in-contrast problematisation strategy

Resale the Client's proposal: State the importance of consideration of the proposal

Discover the context for problems in the proposal

Position your proposal "in contrast"

Inter-office MEMO (within organisation)

We have been concentrating on communicating practices with external stakeholders. But the "yes" and "no" conditions are also reproduced internally. You owe explanations to your employees, teammates or subordinates for every policy/decision change that you are part of. In a broad scenario, there are two kinds of news that you may deliver to your internal stakeholders. One is the popular news that has been waited for – the popular demand which your organisation heads have finally acceded to and approved. The other is the bad news – the unpopular news which your organisation heads have at the cost of the popular demands. So, let us review both the situations through our context creation lens through the popular subcategory of business messages: inter-office MEMO, or the memorandum.

Good news to internal employees – climax to anticlimax

In general corporate parlance, a memorandum has its genesis in legal tools of communication where an official contract, policy or other legal and organisational details are outlined for the knowledge of the direct stakeholders who have to oblige by it. In other words, it is a direction; actually, an information. Yet, there is a trick in delivering information, when the information given is that which would give stakeholders immense joy, because they have been anticipating it, waiting for it, and even because they have been requesting it. Thus, a positive MEMO is also an acceptance of a request, more precisely a collective request, maybe even a collective claim. See Script 4.6 for a joyful MEMO.

Script 4.6 Scripting good news MEMO for "Within Organisation" stakeholders

To: All Employees

From: Mohan Raj Kumar, Administration Department

Date: 10 November 2016

Subject: Saturday off from 1 December 2016

The "Saturday off from work" will be effective as of December 1. As we all agree, having our Saturdays free to us means more "me time", since effectively we are interacting with our clients through five days of the week until late hours. We need time for ourselves so that we return refreshed on Monday.

Personal development of our invaluable employees has always been the priority of our organisation and its HR policies. In the light of the "Saturday off from work" regulation, we have tweaked our HR policies to include some more insightful personal development opportunities to enhance our employees' professional profiles. We introduce these opportunities within our newly launched HR policy – the Employment Academic Scheme. The protocols are listed below for further active participation also effective from December 1.

Employment Academic Scheme

- Two major research papers in related areas of expertise per year
- Four national and two international Management Development programmes in reputed training programmes in expert domains in *only* accredited institutions of training per year
- Foreign language courses, particularly East Asian languages, at primary and secondary level compulsory for international relationship building
- Higher level of software languages' training from accredited training institutions
- National and international conferences highly recommended with complete internal financial support
- One major project on market research in collaboration with our partner clients in a three year evaluation term.

And these protocols are to be followed with ample home organisation support beyond regular work hours.

Please visit the HR website for the complete Employment Academic Scheme protocols and subsequent processes of activations. You are welcome to direct your queries to the senior HR manager Mr. Amitanshu Bahl at 560 within working hours.

Salutation

Commentary on Script 4.6 On good news

When we reviewed the apology mail ("yes" to a claim), we came across the important perspective that the author had to keep in mind while drafting the write-up: to be direct and immediate about the much desired action plan, for the simple reason that you give the client what s/he wants. In this scenario as well, having the weekend off in an organisation that has Saturday as a working day and every other weekday having a late hour culture ("we are interacting with our clients through five days of the week until late hours") is a luxury, a dream, a need, a comfort, a hope for every over-worked employee. If that is what you as an organisational decision maker feels the need to *gift* your people, the gift should be announced immediately. Why prolong their wait? This is exactly the idea behind the way a subject heading and even an introduction gets authored in such messages. Give the good news in action plan format. What is the difference between the two (news and action plan) in terms of impact? A simply inscribed happy resolution "you can have your Saturday off" does convey the potential of what the great news might mean, but does not confirm the exact application in time and space for the applicant. Hence, an action plan is necessary because it confirms the actual practice of the philosophy – Saturday off actually starts to be a reality from the 1st of December, 2016.

However, the introduction just does not stop at the declaration of the action plan, as is the case with apology mails. An acceptance of a request is not necessarily positioned as an apology. There is an additional resale. Why resale a policy, which has already been approved and declared? We resale when there is a potential to refuse, as has been the case with most of the formats for refusals. Here, it is a direct acceptance. Yet, we go for a resale. For the intelligent, those who can read between the lines, the resale is the signal to the impending strategy of even business acceptances. Look at the resale again:

> *As we all agree, having our Saturdays free to us means more "me time", since effectively we are interacting with our clients through five days of the week until late hours. We need time for ourselves, such that we return refreshed on Monday.*

The phrase "as we agree" clearly announces the interested party with the author cleverly not objectifying the party as a separate "other", but assimilating a collective community of which s/he is equally a part of ("we"). It is *almost* like saying, "I agree with you," but need not necessarily *just* mean that. In a resale strategy, when you want to justify a collective request as a reasonable and desirable action, it is so because the "reasonable" and "desirable" request was *not* practiced before. It means that the organisation heads had not thought about this much required need of the employees. Rather, the employees have compelled the authorities to comply. So, saying "as you wanted it," is not as smart and *face saving* as saying "as most of us agree" (see Figure 4.5).

The resale also serves two strategic purposes in an acceptance message.

In the first place, a "buffer" is an important segment of a resale. It is disguised as ego benefit. Rather, ego benefits function as buffers as well. Ego benefit is given because you are making way for *impending* and *unforeseen* information that might turn the apple cart of the authority-employee relationship. Here, the Employment Academic Scheme is the turning point of an otherwise simple acceptance message – the anticlimax, or, maybe, the real climax. The scheme is positioned as a tangible benefit for an employee – employee personality development. On the other, the scheme is also a *penalty* that the employee needs to pay for her demand. Nothing comes free in a corporation. The process of the scheme, though beneficial and visionary, is also time consuming; hence the "after office hours" also indicates the use of the "me time" that has just been *gifted* to you to do as you please. So, "to do as you please" is now a long-term practice of "do as we please" because the authority ("we") has given you that extra time to further accentuate your employee profile not only for your betterment (positioned as ego

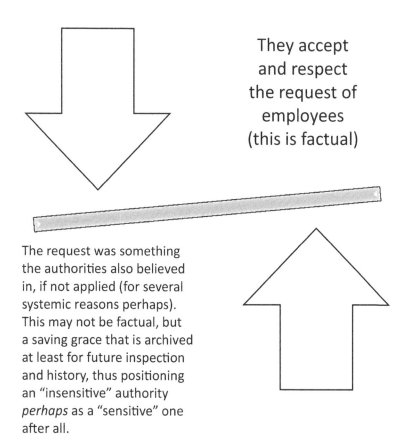

They accept
and respect
the request of
employees
(this is factual)

The request was something the authorities also believed in, if not applied (for several systemic reasons perhaps). This may not be factual, but a saving grace that is archived at least for future inspection and history, thus positioning an "insensitive" authority *perhaps* as a "sensitive" one after all.

Figure 4.5 Face saving conjectures for decision makers compelled to say "yes"

benefit for the employee), but also and evidently for the betterment of the organisation as well (circular reasoning again). Thus, every silver lining also is a limiting silver lining that defocuses the real organisational penalty that you need to pay for the benefit earned through demand. Hence, the best nomenclature of this schematic is the **Limiting Silver Lining format.**

The conclusion then is easy – you offer help, cross-promote or reassure your acceptance. Let us reinstate the Limiting Silver Lining scheme for giving into employee demands.

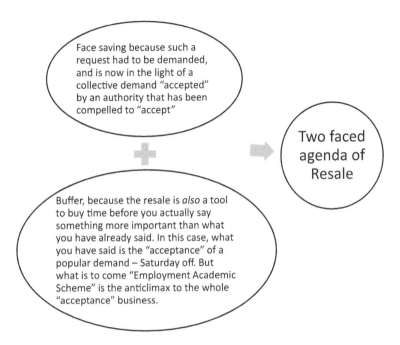

Face saving because such a request had to be demanded, and is now in the light of a collective demand "accepted" by an authority that has been compelled to "accept"

+

Buffer, because the resale is *also* a tool to buy time before you actually say something more important than what you have already said. In this case, what you have said is the "acceptance" of a popular demand – Saturday off. But what is to come "Employment Academic Scheme" is the anticlimax to the whole "acceptance" business.

Two faced agenda of Resale

Figure 4.6 Harvey Dent agenda of resale in acceptance message

Formatting strategy for good news within organisation

The limiting silver lining strategy

Resale the employee proposal through ego benefit apart from direct action plan of the acceptance: collective acceptance "we" and buffer as ego benefit

Defocus Penalty: Limitations in the form of new rules or schemes *but* in the form of employee benefits

Bad news to employees – anticlimax to climax

What happens when you cannot accept the popular demand by your employees; when you have to perform the ugly job of breaking the bad news, the unpleasant information, the dreaded organisational policy? On one hand, the subordinates have to follow the authoritative rules, but on the other, winning the support of subordinates for the compliance of the authoritative rules improves the employee-employer relationship, and hence promotes a healthy organisational culture. In this tricky situation (if we remember our persuasion shields well), problematisation is the shield that we require. Let us look at the following sample for a better understanding of a tricky situation in the context of a bad news MEMO.

Script 4.7 Scripting bad news MEMO for "Within Organisation" stakeholders

> To: All Employees
>
> From: Arvind KV
>
> Date: 14 November 2016
>
> Subject: Proposed plan for employee personality development programme
>
> Personality development is an important aspect of employee growth. And growth needs as much work as leisure periods to manifest itself. As increased market competition requires more enhanced employee grooming for image development at not just a personal level, but also at an organisational level. It is in this capacity that the Saturday off request was a justifiable public demand. It has been for quite some time that we have been contemplating whether to expand weekends into "me time" zones for employees to rejuvenate themselves through their choices of extracurricular activities that daily lengthy work hours are unable to provide, or to develop an employee personality development programme at an organisational level.
>
> "Me time" zones offer a needed weekend break, but self-expenses and limited knowledge might curb the process of knowledge derivation, and the whole idea of the weekend as self-development time zones may not actually materialise into the proposed idea, a visionary basis on which the weekend off request has been contemplated by the employee union.

While "me time" does offer a break, a within-company pro-gramme sponsored beyond salary receipts with a state-of-art provision of a panoramic knowledge access portfolio, along with proficient trainers hired for the sole purpose during the weekend, provides an occasion of informed learning and teach-ing as well as socialising, while maintaining working hours of weekdays with corresponding salary packages. The weekend offs will be induced as a social development programme, with a six-hour in-depth session, and the rest of the time will be set apart for personal weekend goals but in the manner of recrea-tional activities for family participation.

Now let us all work together in our weekend employment development programme for a long-term image makeover of our organisation.

Sincerely,

– – – – –

Commentary on Script 4.7 On bad news

The script is crafted in a manner very similar to the refusal to a pro-posal – the In-Contrast Problematisation Strategy – but with a few tweaks. It would be because these are similar types. The introduc-tion starts with a buffer: "Personality development is an important aspect of employee growth." Then follows the problem statement:

> As estimated, increased market competition requires more enhanced employee grooming for image development at not just a personal level, but also at an organisational level.

So, the entire letter is now authored almost after the manner of a management case study. In other words, a problem is identified, and then alternatives as probable solutions to the managerial problem are recommended. It is more so as if the management authority is thinking aloud with the employees. Interestingly, the dilemma between which recommendations to choose is shared in a transpar-ent manner.

> It has been quite some time that we have been contemplat-ing whether to expand weekends into "me time" zones for

employees to rejuvenate themselves through their choices of extracurricular activities that daily lengthy work hours are unable to provide, or to develop employee personality development programme at an organisational level.

Yet, this *transparency* is the trick, similar to the strategic use of snapshots in advertisements. Snapshots are photographs of "unposed" moments of life, but those "natural" or "unposed" moments are as much strategically directed as those which are posed. Here, the dilemma is presented as a natural and "unposed" culmination of managerial problem solving. Yet, this dilemma is as much a strategic pose. Look at both the alternatives carefully,

(a) *to expand weekends into "me time" zones for employees to rejuvenate themselves through their choices of extracurricular activities that daily lengthy work hours are unable to provide;*
(b) *to develop employee personality development programme at an organisational level.*

Recommendation (a) is the popular demand, the employees' proposal, and (b) is the unpopular alternative, the actual and already decided solution that the author has to break to this crowd. And the rest is easy to guess. The body begins with regular problematisation of (a) and, in contrast, (b) is posed as naturally a more prosperous solution to the problem "estimated" by all. So, continuing with our symbolic nomenclatures, we coin the strategy in a bad news message to our employees as the **snapshot strategy**.

Formatting strategy for bad news within organisation

The Snapshot Strategy

Snapshot: Resale the problem with dilemma between probable solutions (one is the popular demand and the other is the bad news)

Problematise the popular demand

Thus, if we create a taxonomy of managerial situations to which we need to respond through written forms of persuasion, we get the following taxonomy tree – the Context Creation Persuasion Tree.

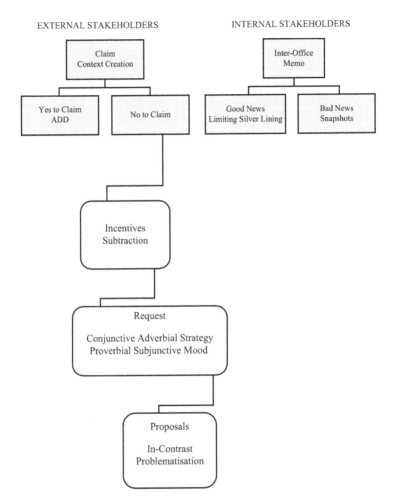

Figure 4.7 Context creation persuasion tree (business messages as per typical managerial situations)

Nuanced taxonomy of business messages

Now let us attempt the Context Creation Persuasion Taxonomy in an imaginative but plausible corporate situation. The difference now from our earlier conceptual drafts is our introduction of nuanced variations of the conceptual taxonomy; we dive deeper into the use of strategy in a more complex situation of client-stakeholder-organisation relationship involved in a more intangible and abstract paradigm of business. Here we develop a more graded ramification of our Context Creation Persuasion framework of business messages, which we term as the nuanced taxonomy of business messages.

Case Study 4.1: A hypothetical business situation for *Dragon Wagon–Painter's Canvas–Save Nature*

We invent a circumstantial parallel to the *Volkswagen* April 2007 poster, depicting a blindfolded elephant tied up and placed inside a spacious room (obviously in the car),[1] with possible outcomes of complex business nuances, posing a fictional description of a business problem with fictional players. We have *Dragon Wagon* instead of *Volkswagen*, *Painter's Canvas* instead of *DDB*, and a big, fictional animal welfare organisation *Save Nature*. The commercial poster is retained, but in our fictional context with the declared replacements.

• **Situation 1**: Claim

As *Save Nature*, there is a lens that you would use to review this poster. In the light of the ensuing issue/s, you need to craft a mail to the advertising agency, addressing your discomfort.

Script 4.8 *Save Nature's* scripting claim

> Subject: Image makeover required for the blindfolded elephant image in the advertisement copy of *Dragon Wagon*
>
> Dear Mr. Q,
>
> Please change the imagery used in your recent *Dragon Wagon* poster exhibiting an elephant that is blindfolded so that it can act as a positive visual stimulus, thereby extricating your company from the controversies related to cruelty to animals.
>
> We can understand that your central selling theme of spatial adequacy led to the germination of the idea of using an

elephant with its mammoth body to accentuate your idea of "big". But here at *Save Nature*, we think that the image carries a huge baggage of negativity which we are sure you would not want your brand to be associated with. The negativity emanates from the sentiments the picture evokes – an elephant incarcerated, blindfolded, with its limbs tied up – which act as visual indicators of brute animal torture. There are diverse ways of promoting the idea of space, and we are sure that a creative director like you can come up with scintillating ways of innovative promotions with images that invoke positive and pleasant emotive outcomes.

Next time when we come across a *Painter's Canvas* poster, we hope to see a pleasant visual pageantry instead of seeing pictures of handcuffed and blindfolded animals.

Looking forward to a positive change,

Save Nature Team

Commentary on Script 4.8 Nuances in claim

The document begins with the central idea that finds placement in the very first line of the message so that it renders the message in a direct and easy-to-understand format by bringing into focus the principal theme of the correspondence. The document does not contain any pejorative words or accusatory language that transgresses the bounds of business communication etiquette, yet it voices the concern felt by *Save Nature* very powerfully by elucidating clearly and objectively the rationale behind the claim that the *Dragon Wagon* poster using an elephant is objectionable.

The message uses both emotional and logical appeal. Emotional appeal is obvious when the message alludes to the plight of the elephant in the image with its eyes blindfolded, limbs tied up, sitting in a pathetic cage separated from the merry company of the herd of its elephant companions. Logical appeal is seen in the ways the communicator argues for salvaging the brand image of *Dragon Wagon* and *Painter's Canvas* by dissociating the image from negative associations that the image potentially evokes ("thereby extricating your company from the controversies related to cruelty to animals"). The message gives ego benefit to the creative director when the author of the message expresses a sanguine confidence in the creative prowess of Mr. Q by stating that he is sure Mr. Q would come up with better promotional innovations that would act as positive stimulants. However, the signing off perhaps says it all, and with no mincing of words: "Next time when we come across a *Painter's Canvas* poster, we hope to see a pleasant visual pageantry instead of seeing pictures of handcuffed and blindfolded animals." This is a **polite threat**!

The polite threat strategy

> Thus, maintaining the etiquette of goodwill credibility, the author crafts a comparable version of Context Creation after a typical claim format, but without the application of systemic discovery here. This is more a deadly combination of logical and emotional appeal, with a strong but almost threatening reinforcement of the unwanted scenario. The context demands the polite threat. Thus, we introduce a variant of the systemic discovery angle of context creation strategy – the polite threat angle.

- **Situation 2**: Apology

As the advertisement agency, you receive an objection letter from *Save Nature*. You read the situation post the *Save Nature* mailed in a certain manner, weigh the issues that finally propel you to agree in the affirmative (to *Save Nature*'s objection). You need to craft an apology mail to *Save Nature* stating your affirmation to their request. Let us review one such attempt.

Script 4.9 *Painter's Canvas* scripting apology

> Subject: Decision to change the advertising imagery in the light of *Save Nature* advice
>
> Dear Mr. President,
>
> We have decided to change the imagery of a blindfolded, handcuffed and incarcerated elephant used for promoting our "spacious" *Dragon Wagon* model.

We thank you for bringing to our notice the negativity associated with the image. While designing our copy we had only decided to use the image of elephant with the idea of accentuating our central selling theme of space, which no other living creature except the big and the beautiful animal like the elephant could have impressed upon our viewers. We thought the image completely justifies the tag line "space for your every need" with its elephantine spatial highlight. But since there is likelihood of people misreading it and deriving meanings of animal incarceration and cruelty, our advertising team decided to recall and revamp this poster.

Our team has already started working on the new poster, and soon you will find *Dragon Wagon* being promoted for its space, ridding itself of the elephantine baggage of negativity.

Thank you once again for raising this issue. We appreciate your sensitivity towards animals of this planet that deserve a life as graceful as the humans.

In future we would welcome collaborations of any joint promotions of *Painter's Canvas* and *Save Nature* which would enhance the visibility of both the brands.

Regards,

R

Commentary on Script 4.9 Nuances in apology

The document provides good news that the plea of *Save Nature* is accepted, and gives the news the well-deserved empathetic space as in the first line of the message to reinforce the positive outcome of the earlier claim. Though it is an apologetic communication affirming the claim, the author is careful in explaining her justification in using the imagery, hinting at the innocuous usage of the animal picture. It echoes the sentiment of *Save Nature* when the message uses the words "big and beautiful" with "elephant", thereby dispelling the notions of animal subjugation associated with the promotional print. It ends with aligning its ideology with *Save Nature* when it reverberates their philosophy by claiming that animals deserve the same life of grace that humans expect for themselves. Since it carries good news, it uses this contact opportunity for initiating the idea of working in collaborations that can mutually profit both the brands. Thus, there is a deliberate reminder of the similarity of ethos for both parties of negotiation; consistency reminder is at work.

Deliberate consistency reminder in apology by *Painter's Canvas*

> Thus, maintaining the etiquette of goodwill credibility, the author crafts a comparable version of the ADD strategy after a typical triple etiquette protocol in an apology or acceptance of claim format. The variation is in the stronger version of appeasement by reverberation of the *Save Nature* ethos as even in the *Painter's Canvas* and *Dragon Wagon* ethos. Thus, the ADD strategy transforms into a pronounced use of the persuasive shield of consistency reminder, defocussing the offence by focusing on the values of *Save Nature* transposed onto the values of *Wagon* and even the agency.

- **Situation 3**: Refusal Styles

You, the advertisement agency, receive an objection letter from *Save Nature*. Notwithstanding the issues, you decide that you can still pursue your process as it were. You need to craft a justification mail to *Save Nature* stating why you would still continue, notwithstanding their objection.

We have four styles of showing our refusal in this very sensitive situation.

Script 4.10 Scripting refusal style A

> Dear President,
>
> We appreciate your concern and sensitivity towards issues of animal welfare, and we are aligned to your ideology but with a different perspective.

Though our commercial shows an elephant that is blind-folded with its limbs tied, the image nowhere shows it being manned by a human being who is torturing it or taming it by violent means. There are times when animals are tied up so that they can be rescued and safely brought to safe havens because at times even animals misread human intentions and rebel against human agents even if they are trying to work for their own good. The motive behind using this image is simple; we want to underline the idea of space, which is our central selling theme and which no other living being can more strongly establish than the big and the beautiful animal like the elephant. We had toyed with the idea of finding other alternatives to present the idea of space, like showing large families getting seated comfortably inside the car or people reclining as the space allows them room for relaxation, but none of these images could have carried the "weight" of the image of an elephant, which captures the idea of space beautifully.

Moreover, we wanted to differentiate our advertisement from the clutter of other commercials that promote auto-mobiles with space. Demonstrating big families or numerous friends getting inside the car and sitting conveniently pre-sent hackneyed images which have been overused by market-ers, and hence an animal like an elephant could have only given us that differentiating edge in the competitive market. Therefore, we request you to consider the given premises of selection of the chosen imagery to understand our need to continue with the same image. We are confident through our various test trails and Facebook and Twitter updates that people appreciate our creative presentation. After all, this image conveys our idea more powerfully than a thousand words can. We will also add a line: a safe space for anyone large.

We would like to share our very ambitious project – the future of space – with future animal series posters for some other automobile contracts. They have been precisely designed for our symbolic allegiance to the wildlife conservation projects undertaken by your esteemed organisation.

Salutation

Script 4.11 Scripting refusal style B

We appreciate your concern and sensitivity towards issues of animal welfare and we assure you of our alliance with these issues.

Though our commercial shows an elephant that is blindfolded with its limbs tied, the image nowhere shows it being manned by a human being who is torturing it or taming it by violent means. There are times when animals are tied up so that they can be rescued and safely brought to safe havens because at times even animals misread human intentions and rebel against human agents even if they are trying to work for their own good. The motive behind using this image is simple; we want to underline the idea of space which is our central selling theme and which no other living being can more strongly establish than the big and the beautiful animal like the elephant.

Though we believe that our intentions and the interpretations derived from the image by the viewers would be innocuous, we can work out some alternatives which can address your concerns as well.

One of the alternatives is to write a disclaimer as a footnote on the image itself, stating that the animal depicted in the picture does not propagate notions of animal captivity and has been just used to convey the idea of space. The disclaimer can further cite that the advertisers in no way would like to promote animal subjugation at the hands of humans. This strategy is in line with the statutory warning issued when the actors in movies are shown smoking stating clearly that the actors do not promote smoking. The images of smoking are not axed or edited; this warning is simply considered enough to alert the viewers. Hence, the communication strategy that works for smoking should work for this animal imagery, if at all you think that it might be misread as propagation of animal incarceration.

While we await a common ground premise for a suitable statutory mandate, we would also like to share our very ambitious project – the future of space – with future animal series posters for some other automobile contracts. They have been precisely designed for our symbolic allegiance to the wildlife conservation projects undertaken by your esteemed organisation.

Salutation

Script 4.12 Scripting refusal style C

We appreciate your concern and sensitivity towards issues of animal welfare and we assure you of our alliance with these issues.

At this early stage of our ambitious commercial contract with *Dragon Wagon*, your timely comments have been insightful. We have carefully considered every nuance of your suggestions and have come to an informed and studied conclusion that we have used the image to conjure up only the idea of the weight of the elephant in the minds of our viewers, and our tagline eliminates any doubt otherwise – "space for your every need".

We thank you once again for writing to us so that we could get the opportunity of sharing opinions with such an esteemed organisation. We take this opportunity to share our very ambitious project – the future of space – with future animal series posters for some other automobile contracts. They have been precisely designed for our symbolic allegiance to the wildlife conservation projects undertaken by you.

Salutation

Script 4.13 Scripting refusal style D

We appreciate your concern and sensitivity towards issues of animal welfare and we assure you of our alliance for the same.

Though our commercial shows an elephant that is blindfolded with its limbs tied, the image is also conspicuously honest about the limits of subjugation that it represents. If it would have been the case of animal subjugation by the humans, you could have found the image bringing into its frame some human figure taming it or even torturing it as well. The image as it stands now has no human element that might hint at the animal harassment done. We wish we could have showcased our idea of space by some other means, but all the other alternatives of accentuating space (showing big families or gangs of friends sitting comfortably in the car) have now become abysmally hackneyed and hence have lost their impact. We are sure that the image of elephant will serve the purpose of reinforcing the image of its weighty grandeur. We are confident that you will appreciate this innovative presentation of a visual which our marketing team has used to promote the central selling theme of the product, *Dragon Wagon*, which is essentially innocuous.

We thank you once again for writing to us so that we could get the opportunity of sharing opinions with such an esteemed organisation. We take this opportunity to share our very ambitious project – the future of space – with future animal series posters for some other automobile contracts. They have been precisely designed for our symbolic allegiance to the wildlife conservation projects undertaken by you.

Commentary on Script 4.10 Styles A, B, C and D

All the four of the scripts convey refusal using our already documented context creation refusal techniques, but with interesting graded variations to suit the sensitive occasion.

Style A follows the subtraction strategy with an ironical addition of a proposed tag line ("We will also add a line: a safe space for anyone large") without accepting the actual claim of *Save Nature*, which is removal of the poster altogether. However, the other interesting aspect of the script is our introduction of the technique of discounting alternatives.[2] You present one by one all options possible and go on to prove that they may have not worked and hence you zeroed in on the current option.

> *We had toyed with the idea of finding other alternatives to . . .*

And as the outcome of discounting options, we get:

> *Therefore, the given premises of selection of the chosen imagery underline our need to continue with the same image.*

Proposing discounting alternatives strategy

You convince the reader that you have exhausted all your options and are left with nothing but the present choice to push your agenda.

Style B follows the typical dimensions of the conjunctive adverbial strategy:

> *Though we believe that our intentions and the interpretations derived from the image by the viewers would be innocuous, we can work out some alternatives which can address your concerns as well.*

And also,

> *While we await a common ground premise for a suitable statutory mandate, we would also like to share our very ambitious project – the future of space – with future animal series posters for some other automobile contracts.*

However, we contribute an additional strategy, this time by providing alternatives. The writer affirms her own perspective and defends it, but at the same time gives alternatives to the reader by means of which the readers' fears are mitigated, and it turns out to be a win-win situation for both of them.

Like,

> *. . . we can work out some alternatives which can address your concerns as well.*

Providing alternatives strategy

> You continue with your current stand but give alternatives to the reader by means of which his or her concerns are put to rest.

Style C uses the technique of neutralising communication by offloading from the verbiage concerned, the negative connotations it carries.

> *We value your concern for animal welfare and the invaluable inputs you have shared with us. At this early stage of our ambitious commercial contract with Dragon Wagon, your timely comments have been insightful. We have carefully considered every nuance of your suggestions and have come to an informed and studied conclusion that we have used the image to conjure up only the idea of the weight of the elephant in the minds of*

our viewers, and our tagline eliminates any doubt otherwise –
"space for your every need".

Neutralising communication strategy

> Use neutral language taking care not to employ any nega-
> tive wording to describe the situation affirming your stand of
> defending your position in the face of stark criticism.

Lastly, Style D uses the proverbial subjunctive mood to convey that "had" situations been different, the actions would
have been too. Thus, it is indirect refusal, yet tactful neutral
communication.

If it would have been the case of animal subjugation by the
humans, you could have found the image bringing into its
frame some human figure taming it or even torturing it as well.

Thus, we develop a MultiLateral Style of Refusal Framework.

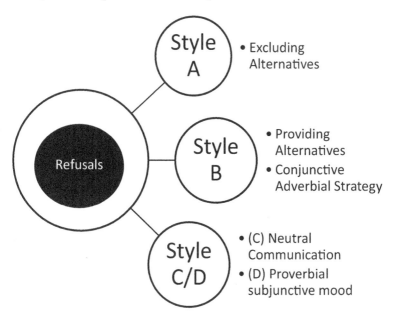

Figure 4.8 Multilateral style of refusal framework

- **Situation 4: Good News**

As the commercial agency, you receive an objection letter from *Save Nature*, which you need not oblige. You craft a mail for your in-house creative team stating your positive decision.

Script 4.14 Scripting good news within organisation

Dear Colleagues,

Congratulations for coming up with an advertisement which not only won accolades from critics by virtue of its creative innovation, but has also won approval from *Save Nature* who had initially taken a stern stance against it.

Save Nature issued us a letter dated 21 July 2016 voicing its criticism on the depiction of an animal in the image of our poster, apparently shown in despicable condition with its eyes blindfolded and its limbs tied up. We wrote back to them expounding how the image of the animal has been aesthetically used to accentuate the enormity of space in a novel way and in no way it propagates animal captivity or subjugation.

They accepted our stand and have decided to call off their protest against our promotions. Hence you can go ahead with your promotional plans.

In the light of this incident, we have also come up with a policy for future poster productions. From now on, we will take consultations from external agencies before finalising our symbolic visuals in order to get a better perspective on our creative art.

Once again I appreciate you all for your creative prowess and look forward to seeing the same kind and level of work which can act as our differentiating strategy of cutting the clutter of routine promotions.

Commentary on Script 4.14

Limiting silver lining strategy is well used with deliberate neutral placement of creative limitation towards the end of the script:

> *In the light of this incident, we have also come up with a policy for future poster productions. From now on, we will take*

consultations from external agencies before finalising our symbolic visuals in order to get a better perspective on our creative art.

- Situation 5: Bad News

As the commercial agency, you receive an objection letter from *Save Nature*, which you have to oblige. You craft a mail for your in-house creative team stating your decision.

Script 4.15 Scripting bad news within organisation

Dear Colleagues,

We appreciate the creativity with which you came up with the print commercial for *Dragon Wagon*. Creative license is a double-edged weapon. In the light of the *Save Nature* concern over the potential misinterpretation of our blind elephant advertisement, we have been in a dilemma whether to continue with our creative license or change our poster to avoid controversy.

The poster powerfully conveys our car's central selling theme of space, thanks to the weighty presence of an elephant in the image. We are proud of our metaphoric presentation. But we all know that *Save Nature* has taken a strong objection on the way the elephant is depicted, which, according to them, is like promoting animal captivity and subjugation. The *Wagon* is a product for the informed and educated consumer segment – the very same segment that caters to environmental concerns through various popular *Save Nature* initiatives. We tried our level best to expel the negative notions they have anticipated as possible forms of public outcry against our poster, but in vain. I, therefore, request you to come up with an alternative commercial that can promote the product with equal efficacy without unnecessarily falling prey to misinterpretations that might be too costly for us to bear. I am sure you will be able to do a great job again.

Painter's Canvas commands a rich tradition of producing advertisements that stand out for their uniqueness, creativity and aesthetic innovation. I look forward to receiving promotional ideas that perpetuate the same tradition of artistic marketing.

Commentary on Script 4.15

The mail gives organisational bad news in an adroit manner. It begins with a softer note exhibiting appreciation before the issuance of bad news. This soft note acts as a cushion mitigating the impact of bad news. Then the problem is stated, along with the dilemma – the desired news ("to continue with our creative license") and the undesired one ("change our poster to avoid controversy").

Then follows the usual problematisation of the desired news to make way for the undesired news, but now as the good news. The snapshot strategy is at play again by profiling the audience segment consuming our posters as well as *Save Nature* concerns as the same audience.

> *The Wagon is a product for the informed and educated consumer segment – the very same segment that caters to environmental concerns through various popular Save Nature initiatives.*

• Situation 6: Positive Controversy

Post the *Save Nature* fracas, you are worried about your future with other clients. You need to craft a mail for your potential client organisation reaffirming why they should work with you.

Script 4.16 Scripting sales persuasive message after positive outcome of past controversy

---

Dear XYZ,

If you are looking for an advertisement agency which can carve a niche market for your unique product launch by virtue of its creative advertising, making your product promotion assume classy dimensions, differentiating it from the routine string of hackneyed promotional messages, then *Painter's Canvas* is the right venue for you.

We have worked for reputed organisations and companies like *PTR*, *NCQ*, the *Big M Lords*, the *Golden Parachute Mines* and even *Dragon Wagon,* among many others. *Clientale* and *Marigold* have been the recent additions from the *Fortune 500* in our ever burgeoning clientele list.

We have not just brought back out-of-memory organisations like *Little Daisy* and *Mother Apple* into global discourse through what leading magazines like *ADaRT* and *AdverterialMessaGE* have termed as "pushing the envelope" invention in strategy; art designers like *MieselP*, *Fashioista* and *Cariel* have even termed our metaphoric inventions, like the now famous blindfolded elephant for *Wagon* and the brutal daisy for *Marigold* among other much discussed contributions in social media, as erudite context creations fetching back in vogue to the premium surrealism of the evergreen cult creator, Salvador Dali, thus gradually paving the way for replacing the more gauche tactics of scandals used in low-brow marketing practices.

The narrow line between surrealism and low brow insensitive gimmicks has led us through debates with social watch dogs, as the now very popularly documented argument with *Save Nature*. But in due course of time, an informed and healthy conversation between us has not merely encouraged our artistic practices, but also helped us in becoming the prized advertising agents for the macro cause of animal welfare by *Save Nature*. This is our first foray into social responsibility posters through tie-ups with corporates like *Wagon* and *Save Nature*, where our blindfolded elephant is retained as the brand logo for both; in the former, the huge spacious car brings back the animal safely from its poached surroundings, and in the latter, it is the spacious car that is big enough for saving big animals suffering at the hands of hunters.

As the CEO of *Squirrel Trail* states, when he received the Best Poster award at the *Martini Global Corporate Communications Awards* in January 2016 while dedicating the award to *Painter's Canvas*, we are an agency that is not only uniquely artistic, conscious and flexible, but even more significantly the trendsetter in the inoculatory aspects of "turning the tides" in corporate communications.

We shake the world, but retain ties, he said, and that is how we serve the corporations and the world by shaking and stirring but retaining our artistic licenses.

Since your organisation is also known for being innovatively enterprising, we feel we must reach out to you for the obvious reasons of like-minded collaborations. Please find attached with this mail the new schemes that we have formulated for the benefit of organisations like yours. We understand your needs, and are eagerly waiting for that golden moment when you would want us to direct your next campaign.

Partner now and get our special price offers for new clients willing to sign up with us.

Painter's Canvas: Painting a New Future for You.

Commentary on Script 4.16　Nuances in sales persuasion messages after overcoming a controversy

We introduce a complex situation in corporate communication: persuading future clients to join you, particularly when you had been mired in public gossip. Any gossip definitely leads to greater public memory, but it also brings with it negative connotations for your organisation. So, how do you still retain your clients, and even more categorically, how do you create future clients? It helps if you managed to sway the controversy to your side: you come out clean. Then a simple straightforward, persuasive sales message may be dispatched to potential clients, but definitely remember to personalise them and not blindly mass reproduce. Let us extract a format from Script 4.16.

Format/proposition for Script 4.16　The surreal confession

Beginning: A problem solution shield works. You need cutting edge public recall – "we are experts in it. Hence, we understand your need and think we can serve you the best." No recall of controversy.

Body: Credibility and Benefit toolkit to be used in abundance. Bandwagon your clientele list, and do not forget to mention the organisation whose name brings back the memory of the controversy. But defocus by cushioning the name amongst many others, and add more additions of new corporations that have joined you recently, after the controversy has died down.

We have worked for reputed organisations and companies like PTR, NCQ, the Big M Lords, the Golden Parachute Mines, and even Dragon Wagon among many others. Clientale and

Marigold have been the recent additions from the Fortune 500 in our ever burgeoning clientele list. We have not just brought back out-of-memory organisations like Little Daisy and Mother Apple into global discourse . . .

Do not praise yourself. It appears defensive and arrogant, particularly after coming out clean in a controversy, even if the losing party is as big and reputed an organisation as *Save Nature*. But you have to establish your win! So circular reasoning or sourcing and referencing praises from credible mouthpieces about exactly those elements of your work that have been responsible for controversial debates seals a strategic deal of defence. We call this the Defocussed Dynamics of Defence and Positioning or the **Surreal Confession**. Big names help defocus the controversy, and big praises from big names reposition your work as significant. But the "subconscious" advertisement of controversy is always there.

(a) *ADaRT and AdverterialMessaGE have termed as "pushing the envelope" invention in strategy*; [you hint that your creative inputs are controversy potential, without saying so], thereby you gradually pushing the envelope of your audience's acceptance of the controversy but now in the intellectual light of pluralistic artistic perspectives because big names legitimise the style.

(b) *. . . art designers like MieselP, Fashioista and Cariel have even termed our metaphoric inventions like the now famous blindfolded elephant for Wagon and the brutal daisy for Marigold among other much discussed contributions in social media, as erudite context creations fetching back in vogue the premium surrealism of the evergreen cult creator, Salvador Dali, thus gradually paving way for replacing the more gauche tactics of scandals used in low brow marketing practices.* [You mention the controversial poster but do **not** highlight it as the **only** singular proposition. Cushion it with a few others to establish that this is your **style** of work, and media discussions have been a continuous ally to your creative ventures. In other words, social discussion has always accompanied your creative outputs. But you beautifully now position your controversial output not as scandalous techniques of communication, but as artistic ventures that are trend setters in the art market because of your deliberate resurrection of the great surrealistic painter Salvador Dali. Anyone who knows surrealism and Dali also knows the intellectual legacy of Modern Art, and similar propositions get legitimised even more.]

(c)   *The narrow line between surrealism and low brow insensitive gim-*
micks has led us through debates with social watch dogs, as has
been the now very popularly documented discussion with Save
Nature [you actually now do mention the controversy, but in neutral terms – "popularly documented discussion"]. *In due course*
of time, an informed and healthy conversation between both of us
has not merely encouraged our artistic practices, but also helped
us in becoming the next prized advertising agents for the macro
cause of animal welfare for Save Nature. This is our first foray
into social responsibility posters through tie-ups with corporates
like Dragon Wagon and Save Nature, where our blindfolded ele-
phant is retained as the brand logo for both; in the former, the
huge spacious car brings back the animal safely from its poached
surroundings; and in the latter, it is the spacious car that is big
enough for saving big animals suffering at the hands of hunters
[You position your win but the "win" is camouflaged because the
losing party is also positioned as the co-creator of this harmony,
thus erasing the competitive victory in a battle of controversy. But
in reality, this is a deliberately disguised documentation of a negotiator's winning stroke at a subconscious level, which can be easily
discerned by an intelligent and insightful audience.]

(d)   *As the CEO of Squirrel Trail states, when he received the Best*
Poster award at the Martini Global Corporate Communica-
tions Awards [double ego benefit], *while dedicating the award*
to Painter's Canvas [circular reasoning], *we are an agency that is*
not only uniquely artistic, conscious and flexible, but even more
significantly the trendsetter in the inoculatory aspects of 'turning
the tides' in corporate communications [positioning our negotiator's skills here, and not merely our artistic skills; after all by
clinching the *Save Nature* deal, we have been an exemplary deal-
making organisation. We have inoculated the social watch dogs,
thus, getting a circular reasoning technique to "subconsciously"
declare *Canvas*'s winning streak in negotiations. Plus, the description of the controversial motif – the blindfolded elephant – is the
final stroke in the "unconscious" discourse on the victory.]

(e)   *We shake the world, but retain ties, he said, and that is how we*
serve the corporations and the world by shaking and stirring but
retaining our artistic licenses. [We do a consistency reminder at the
end, but through a credible mouthpiece again; we make someone
else credibly state our company ethos as a praiseworthy ethos.]

Now, consistently remind the future client that their ethos is not different from yours:

Since your organisation is also known for being innovatively enterprising, we feel we must reach out to you for the obvious reasons of like-minded collaborations.

And, then a resale of new collaborator avenues can be peacefully described.

This is a persuasive sales message, and we call *this* technique of persuasion the Surreal Confession. So here, we are confessing (telling the truth) but strategically manipulating the confession as a subconscious advertisement of our negotiation skills, our victory over *Save Nature* and even the legitimisation of the blindfolded elephant as a credible motif. The confession is too surreal to be understood as a confession; it is more an exaggerated documentation of self-credibility building. We say "exaggerated" because of the sheer effort in the use of expertise and circular reasoning!

- **Situation 7: Negative Controversy**

In the erstwhile episode, we considered a lucky situation of winning the negotiation in the face of controversy. Now let us consider the unlucky situation of losing it.

Script 4.17 Scripting sales persuasive message after negative outcome of past controversy

Dear XYZ,

If you are looking for an advertisement agency which can carve a niche market for your unique product launch by virtue of its creative advertising, making your product promotion assume classy dimensions, differentiating it from the routine string of hackneyed promotional messages, then *Painter's Canvas* is the right venue for you.

We have worked for reputed organisations and companies like *PTR, NCQ,* the *Big M Lords,* the *Golden Parachute Mines,* and even *Dragon Wagon,* among many others. *Clientale* and

Marigold have been the recent additions from the *Fortune 500* in our ever burgeoning clientele list.

We have not just brought back out-of-memory organisations like *Little Daisy* and *Mother Apple* into global discourse through what leading magazines like *ADaRT* and *AdverterialMessaGE* have termed as "pushing the envelope" invention in strategy; art designers like *MieselP*, *Fashioista* and *Cariel* have even termed our metaphoric inventions, like the now famous blindfolded elephant for *Wagon* and the brutal daisy for *Marigold* among other much discussed contributions in social media, as erudite context creations fetching back in vogue the premium surrealism of the evergreen cult creator Salvador Dali, thus gradually paving the way for replacing the more gauche tactics of scandals used in low brow marketing practices.

The narrow line between surrealism and low brow insensitive gimmicks has led us through debates with social watchdogs, but this has only helped us better our art, while doing away with the negative results that our creative imaginations have sometimes led us to. But our recent forays into social responsibility posters through tie-ups with corporates like *Wagon* and *Save Nature* is a testimony that even social watchdogs approve of our artistic talents.

As the CEO of *Squirrel Trail* states, when he received the Best Poster award at the *Martini Global Corporate Communications Awards* in January 2016 while dedicating the award to *Painter's Canvas*, that we are an agency that is not only uniquely artistic, conscious and flexible, but even more significantly the trendsetter in the inoculatory aspects of "turning the tides" in corporate communications.

We shake the world, but retain ties, he said, and that is how we serve the corporations and the world by shaking and stirring but retaining our artistic licenses.

Since your organisation is also known for being innovatively enterprising, we feel we must reach out to you for the obvious reasons of like-minded collaborations. Please find attached with this mail the new schemes that we have formulated for the benefit of organisations like yours. We understand your needs, and are eagerly waiting for that golden moment when you would want us to direct your next campaign.

Partner now and get our special price offers for new clients willing to sign up with us.

Painter's Canvas: Painting a New Future for You.

Format/proposition for Script 4.17: Camouflaged inoculation

Now what happens when *Save Nature* wins, and you have had to affirm to their demands? You need to assert your reputation **even more** with your future potential clients. So, the camouflaged advertisement/surreal confession does work, but with slight modifications. This time, when you are actually expected to openly confess, you don't. Defocus the controversy, and the enemy party now has to be positioned as your association credibility builder as well as your ego benefit deliverer. So, using *Save Nature*, you need to reposition your **surrender** (remember, earlier you never surrendered; you won) as not only a successful business venture, but also as a positive affirmation of your creative style that is so integral to your organisational image in the market. So, instead of a confession (which was easy in the earlier case, because you had won anyway), we reposition your confession as a circular reasoning anecdote (because *Save Nature* becomes our indirect mouthpiece).

The narrow line between surrealism and low brow insensitive gimmicks has led us through debates with social watch dogs but this has only helped us better our art, while doing away with flipsides that our creative imaginations have sometimes led us to [defocus rather than confess]. *Our recent forays into social responsibility posters through tie-ups with corporates like Wagon and Save Nature is a testimony that even social watchdogs approve of our artistic talents.* [There is no mention of the controversial motif; no mention of losing the negotiation with *Save Nature*; but that *Save Nature* has a tie-up with you post this controversy. Using the immense public goodwill of *Save Nature*, you now project that you are into socially responsible poster creations, and thereby obliquely inoculating the social circuit from raising any further ethical concerns questioning your commercial philosophy.]

So, Surrealistic Confession now becomes the Surrealistic Inoculation. Surrealism is an art practice that exaggerates the real object, such that the unconscious or intuitive expressions and intentions get highlighted rather than the scientific dimensions of the representational object. Thus, surrealism is an interesting technique to say the unsayable.

We can now diagrammatically outline a nuanced taxonomy of business messages.

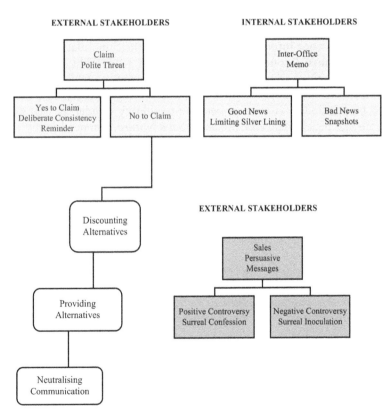

Figure 4.9 Nuanced taxonomy of business messages (business messages as per typical managerial situations)

Thus, we come to the end of the entire taxonomy of the economy of business writing. The chapter comprehensively has encompassed the kaleidoscopic variety of corporate situations which necessitates the adoption of appropriate strategies of communication. An aspiring business writer can treat this chapter as her diary guiding her as to how to hit the keyboard with the right notes to get the right action upshot for her authorial performance. The various models and frameworks formulated can be easily comprehended, implemented and manoeuvred, making the quotidian activity of business writing an orchestrated and outcome-oriented exercise. Hence goes the age-old axiom from the remote past . . .

A pen is mightier than the sword
Kudos to the knack of keyboard . . .

Notes

1 Image accessed on 1 August 2016 <http://1.bp.blogspot.com/-Ke1S-3nSpUMY/Ujqds5H5UBI/AAAAAAAAAF8/pbfBUlZDrNc/s1600/VWKidnapped.jpg>.
2 See "Eliminating Options" from Peter W. Cardon. *Business Communication: Developing Leaders for a Networked World.* New York: McGraw-Hill, 2015.

Chapter 5

Sherlock Holmes in action

Managerial investigations (cases, reports, proposals, plans)

When we think of a "management situation", we mean a crisis that needs attention. The crisis is either immediate or deferred (long term). Hence, the manager has to first develop analytical skills to spot, understand and define a crisis – *why* is it there, *how* is it there, and *if* it is there, *what* will be there in future and what will happen to *whom* in future, as there are many stakeholders (internal and external) involved in any business decision as highlighted by Chapter 4 on business messages. Introspection on managerial communication leads us to the understanding of business messages as carriers of decisions that iron out problems of an organisation. In fact, any act of communication is a carrier of decision, an action that develops into a result, post introspection of organisational problems. And if we do have a decision to take, we forget that there is more complexity involved in positioning a decision. Why? Because *a decision is not a decision unless it is accepted as one*. Until the decision is *not proved as apt*, it remains an attempt at solving issues. In other words, if there is an attempt to solve issues, there must be more than many attempts, and thus, there are "solutions" rather than "a solution". How do we know which is the "right" solution? In this labyrinth of "rights" and "wrongs" that which clearly stands out is the unavoidable outcome – the plurality of solutions. If we work backwards from the position of plurality of solutions, what we get is plurality of problems. And this circularity of pluralities is the crux of rationalising a management situation. How do we understand a problem? Any medical student would have an answer for this.

Back in the nineteenth century a medical expert did find a method to the madness, a method that has, until recently, made great sense to top management institutes. He created a fictional character with the iconic name of Sherlock Holmes, and what he devised for the icon was a splendid weapon of introspection derived from medical case study practice. So, here again, we have a new addition to definitions – a case. What is a case? A medical instructor has her students surround her while s/he discusses a case – a medical situation that grows into an example that you can learn from. You learn the good things; you learn how not to do the bad things; you learn how to avoid mistakes; you learn to know how to deal with mistakes when you do them; in sum, you learn from a case, an example, an instance, an illustration of a situation which has issues, and also efforts to handle the issues. A case can be fictional or real, but either way, you learn from the plethora of activities it produces for posterity. Though no real time situation premeditates lessons for posterity, the moment the situation becomes a case, it does. Experts who discover things to learn and hence things to teach describe a situation as a case. Then headlong, every similar or dissimilar phenomenon is referred to as *that* case! A case then becomes the reference point while making any judgment, analysis or decision on any other situation. This has become the pattern of inquiry in medicine, in investigative fields like crime and law and even in contemporary management scenarios.

How do we study a case? There are two important ingredients that one has to start with in a case study.

(a) Data
(b) Inference

Let us see how we treat data in a case. And to do that, we go back to Arthur Conan Doyle and Holmes and re-read the masterpiece *Silver Blaze*. Pay special attention to the highlighted portions in the extract reproduced here.

Case Study 5.1: Sherlock Holmes

Script 5.1 Some portions from *Silver Blaze* by Arthur Conan Doyle

> Edith Baxter was within *thirty yards of the stables when a man appeared out of the darkness and called to her to stop.* As she stepped into the circle of yellow light thrown by the lantern she saw that *he was a person of gentlemanly bearing, dressed in a gray suit of tweeds, with a cloth cap. He wore gaiters and carried a heavy stick with a knob to it. She was most*

> *impressed, however, by the extreme pallor of his face and by the nervousness of his manner.*
>
> She was frightened by the earnestness of his manner and ran past *him to the window through which she was accustomed to hand the meals. It was already opened, and Hunter was seated at the small table inside.*
>
> His *head had been shattered by a savage blow from some heavy weapon*, and *he was wounded on the thigh, where there was a long, clean cut, inflicted evidently by some very sharp instrument.* It was clear, however, that Straker had defended himself vigorously against his assailants, *for in his right hand he held a small knife, which was clotted with blood up to the handle, while in his left he clasped a red and black silk cravat, which was recognized by the maid as having been worn on the preceding evening by the stranger who had visited the stables.* Hunter, on recovering from his stupor, was also quite *positive as to the ownership of the cravat.* He was equally certain that *the same stranger had, while standing at the window, drugged his curried mutton, and so deprived the stables of their watchman.*

Source: Arthur Conan Doyle, *Silver Blaze*, www.mysterynet.com/holmes/13silverblaze/ (accessed 12 July 2016).

This is a story, and a story is an entire mess. Why do we call it a mess? Because we have to make our kind of sense of this mess; we need *our* story that we have to build from the *given* story. The thing to understand is that there is a problem. A horse is stolen! But who stole the horse? The mystery writers say they follow a trail; they look for clues. A management practitioner will look for data. Data is that small item in the labyrinth of a story that constitutes your building block to *your* argument about *your* story of the given story. For instance, the following is data:

He wore gaiters and carried a heavy stick with a knob to it

It matters to your analysis that he "carried a heavy stick with a knob to it", hence it is data. It is easily data, because it is a recognisable object/ characteristic that can be scouted for and procured and whoever owns it would be the expected suspect. After all, the trainer was found murdered and the stranger who carried the stick was in the vicinity of the site of crime during the night, and the knob is a classic weapon to hit and injure and thereby kill an adversary. Thus, the stick with a knob is a scientific and factual data, or, in legal terms, solid evidence. The solidity of the object makes it an unquestionable data. But every data is not a fact. It is not solid and is not an object. For instance,

> by the extreme pallor of his face and by the nervousness of his manner

Thus, the pallor and the nervousness render a psychological dimension to the data. Qualitatively, the data indicates that the suspect is worried, and that signals his mental state before the crime is committed. He is definitely under stress; so, the evidence of stress says something about what the man could have potentially been planning to do. On the other hand, what an analyst might also fail to note is that no murderer in his sane mind would like to expose or hint at his mental state. But maybe Simpson was an exception. The ambiguous or plural indications are the complex contexts of the psychological data. Hence, we have two kinds of data in any analysis – the quantitative and the qualitative – and both play an equally important role in investigation.

Should there be so many data in the story? How do you make coherent sense of all of them? We need to refer to biology and taxonomy. You will have to classify data into similar families. And how does one classify? The answer is also hinted at by Doyle in the story. We reproduce more lines from the story:

> It is one of those cases where the art of the reasoner should be used rather for the sifting of details than for the acquiring of fresh evidence.

Let us try a similar activity here. We look for data only about the horse from the original script.

Silver Blaze, the horse

- Has a brilliant record at horse racing.
- Is in his fifth year and each time he has brought prizes of the turf to Colonel Ross, his fortunate owner.

- Up to the time of the catastrophe he was the first favourite for the Wessex Cup.
- The betting is three to one on him.
- Enormous sums of money have been laid upon him.
- *Every precaution was taken to guard the favourite.*

The last characteristic is not available in the paragraph that actually describes the horse, and from which we *sift* most of the characteristics listed under Silver Blaze category. Rather, the information *highlighted* is excavated from another paragraph that actually introduces the trainer and the watchdogs of the stable that houses the prized horse. From the original text, we have the two paragraphs adjacent to each, where paragraph 1 has major description on the horse. But the underlined line, which is also a major point on the horse, is available in paragraph 2:

> Paragraph 1: It is obvious, therefore, that there were many people who had the strongest interest in preventing Silver Blaze from being there at the fall of the flag next Tuesday.
>
> Paragraph 2: The fact was, of course, appreciated at King's Pyland, where the colonel's training-stable is situated. *Every precaution was taken to guard the favourite.* The trainer, John Straker, is a retired jockey who rode in Colonel Ross's colours before he became too heavy for the weighing-chair.[1]

This is what we term as *sifting of data*, borrowing the word "sift" from Doyle of course: "It is one of those cases where the art of the reasoner should be used rather for the *sifting* of details than for the acquiring of fresh evidence." You will have to scout across the entire length and breadth of the case and find any solid or psychological data that adds to our understanding of Silver Blaze.

From *sifting*, we move to the next stage of introspection. Data on its own is of no value. What we make of the description of data selected for a particular family of characteristics is significant in case analysis. For instance, if we relook at the Silver Blaze family of data, we can come to a conclusion that there would be many people who would be interested in preventing Silver Blaze from running the contest this time. We call this the *art of inferring*.

Identifying and then *sifting* data into appropriate classifications and deriving meaningful *inferences* are the requirements of setting up a good case background, or more technically the background is now a Situation Analysis. The gospel of Situation Analysis is to rearrange data from the given case than supply additional data from generalised knowledge collated over years of education. As Doyle has already warned in the original text: "do not look for fresh evidence; make use of data given first."

Now that we have completed a rigorous Situation Analysis with various classifications of families of data, we can take the next flight of introspection. Our subsequent job is to identify a problem or problems. Again, we need to refer to medical investigative methods in the form of diagnosis. How do we diagnose an issue? As a first approximation, every managerial situation will have a predominant and commonsensical problem, very visible and easy to approach and identify. As in the case with Silver Blaze, the stranger Simpson is suspected and finally arrested for being the culprit, *only* because he owned the stick with the knob (quantitative data) and he was nervous in the night of the murder (psychological data). But the trick to a good diagnosis lies in the scepticism of the illusion of common sense. Probe deeper and look beyond the obvious. To do that, list another set of data, but this time the data becomes a symptom.

Cold, fever, cough and many other such bodily signals are symptoms of illness. The patient goes to the doctor. The doctor examines the symptoms and conducts a number of experiments, interestingly not to find, but rather to *eliminate* illnesses until he cannot. After all, any one symptom can have many *inferences*, as we saw with our multiple inferences drawn for our psychological data on pallor and nervousness. After all, do culprits show their nervousness? And that could be a strong inference amidst a coterie of inferences that can turn the apple cart against the conclusion that Simpson was the culprit. So, diagnosis works on the *principle of elimination rather than verification*. Let us try to understand the *art of elimination*.

If we had to choose from the range of data in our Situation Analysis, we would perhaps look at one such evidence a bit more closely. The guard for the night, Hunter, was drugged. This is solid, factual evidence. But the interesting *inference* is that no one else was. Hence, the nature of the data is perhaps symptomatic of a larger agenda. It signals foul play. So, the data, evidence or symptom can be put to the test for either verification or elimination.

- *Data/Symptom/Evidence*: Hunter was drugged, but nobody else in the house.

The question for verification/elimination is WHY? The answer would be an attempt first to verify the commonsensical and obvious conjecture – Simpson was the man behind the drug act. For convenience's sake, let us call it Inference 1.

- *Inference 1*: Police and Hunter feel it is Simpson behind the drugging act, since he was the only one standing at the window and could have drugged Hunter's curried mutton. Others, including the trainer, his wife, the maid and the other two lads had curried mutton for dinner that night in the trainer's kitchen and were not drugged.

In effect, Inference 1 is the verification act – you try to verify the symptom against the popular conjecture. This helps lay the foundation of verification – the popular belief does have substantiation for its existence. Most often, it is the case.

However, the probe continues, because we now have to attempt another level of verification. But this level will need our persuasion apparatus to not verify but problematise Inference 1. In the second attempt to verify, we attempt an elimination act, where we search for any other reason for Inference 1 to be the way it is or rather to not be what it appears to be, for the simple reason that through a process of falsification we are attempting to find alternate possibilities or deeper layers of complexities. In sum, Inference 1 is now the new symptom, and the act of falsification is the new act of verification of the new symptom.

- *Inference 2*: "Powdered opium is by no means tasteless. The flavour is not disagreeable, but it is perceptible. Were it mixed with any ordinary dish the eater would undoubtedly detect it and would probably eat no more. A curry was exactly the medium which would disguise this taste." Simpson could not "have caused curry to be served in the trainer's family that night, and it is surely too monstrous a coincidence to suppose that he happened to come along with powdered opium upon the very night when a dish happened to be served which would disguise the flavour."[2] Therefore Simpson may be eliminated from the case. Who can order the kind of dish that can be served?

Thus, a range of levels of inferences and inferences of inferences or process of verifications and falsifications lead to what we would like to call the Working Hypothesis.

- *Working Hypothesis*: "The opium was added after the dish was set aside for the stable-boy, for the others had the same for supper with no ill effects. Which of them, then, had access to that dish without the maid seeing them?"[3] Straker (the trainer) and his wife are the only two people who could have chosen curried mutton for supper that night.

The phrase "working hypothesis" perhaps best represents the spirit of investigation, particularly a managerial investigation. We began this discourse with our concern for "right" solutions and "right" problems. And we had also mentioned that we need to prepare our own story from the given story in the case. In other words, our investigation into a situation is itself a narrative, and we have to build a convincing one at that. The reason behind building a convincing narrative is because we have to convince an external party to accept the solution that we offer as *the* solution to the crisis that we have to manage. As mentioned before, there will be several narratives with several attempts to solve a problem, or problems for that matter. Hence, it becomes a case of verification and falsification of not just *inferences*, but also probable solutions. And even before we come to solutions, we must not forget that our entire investigative narrative is built on the sturdy foundation of the identified problem or problems.

Now we begin again with our initial premise – go back to the problem-solution persuasion shield. In other words, we need to sell the problem, and "sell" we must because a solution is the greatest product/service that a manger has to legitimise to even get it implemented. A team, stakeholders, people in power, and many others have a say in the acceptance of a solution as credible. Hence, in managerial parlance, we never give a solution; we always RECOMMEND. And a recommendation needs considerable substantiation. And even more than substantiation, it needs a powerful narrative of a problem, a problem that worries your organisation tremendously, a problem that so much needs elimination. Therein lies the "selling point" of your narrative about the recommendation: sell the problem, and hence pitch the problem. There are two reasons behind pitching a sellable problem:

(a) Identify an interesting problem – the recommendation is more open to being accepted as the solution. And the premise is that there could be many solutions, and your recommendation has to stand out. So, working backwards is a good idea because your identified problem is perhaps the winning card in the entire persuasion narrative of providing a solution to a problem.

(b) If (a) sounds too manipulative and flimsy to more orthodox thinkers, then let us go back to the world of medicine again. Say, M is suffering from either/or

- Cold
- Cough
- Fever
- Weakness
- Allergy

If your diagnosis manages to eliminate all these symptoms except cold, and you reach the conclusion that M is *only* suffering from a consistent cough with no other related symptoms listed; you may state in your prescription that M is suffering from a local allergy. This is your defined problem. And if this is the identified problem, the probable solutions would be those that can help M recover from local allergy. But the Indian cricketer, Yuvraj Singh, with initial similar symptoms had a very different problem, a problem as serious as lung cancer. This would mean that if not diagnosed correctly, the solution provided may not be effective because the nature of the solution is dependent on the gravity of the problem. In either case – (a) and (b) – problem identification is supremely important in any investigation in any field of knowledge.

There is also always a probability that there could be nuanced variations of an identified problem. The best you can do is conduct a rigorous investigation with layers of repeated verification and falsification of various symptoms and data and reach a general consensus on the nature of the problem. Before arriving at that consensus, the best you can do with the first level of identification of a definite nature of a problem is acknowledging the identification. Hence, we call it the working hypothesis. It is still a working statement because we are going to try many other symptoms and their verification and elimination to arrive at this formal identification of a hint of a problem. We conduct the same method of inquiry on as many symptomatic evidences as possible to arrive at the number of such identifiable hints. The collation of the overall nature of these identifiable hints or working hypotheses is our process of producing a focused problem inference.

Thus, problem inference is a focused narration of all the working hypotheses derived from rigorous levels of verifications and falsifications of claims conjectured from symptoms from the given case. A focused narration plays an important role in positioning a definable problem for the case. This kind of narration further classifies similarities and dissimilarities from the collated working hypotheses, thereby developing a discourse on the dominant nature of a common problem (that you derive) and its corollaries in the form of anomalies that do not fit into the commonality of the problem. Before we get labelled as reductionists, we would position the reduction of a case into a relatable and definite problem as a useful method of inquiry in order to develop actionable recommendation of solutions. Hence a definite problem amidst various other problems needs a convincing positioning.

So, how do we prepare a dominant problem identification from perhaps a variety of working hypotheses? The nature of cases are such that there will be a symptomatic help to reach that problem, because there is a problem or problems. But identification of a problem is important through the art of collation and classification, because problems will have a pattern, even if they appear differently. Hence restructuring the differences within the working hypothesis is the test of an analyst, and one of the finest mechanisms of doing that perhaps comes from Jared Mason Diamond's 1997 bestseller *Guns, Germs, and Steel: The Fates of Human Societies*.[4] His use of the Anna Karenina principle to understand the act of domestication of animals is significant for our derivation of a definite Problem Statement. It is from Leo Tolstoy's famous nineteenth-century novel, *Anna Karenina,* that Diamond borrows the principle. The famous opening line by Tolstoy is important:

> *Happy families are all alike; every unhappy family is unhappy in its own way.*

In a similar parallel, Diamond tries to show how an animal can be domesticated if they fulfil all the criteria of domestication. If in any case any one criterion is not fulfilled, then the animal cannot be domesticated. In a similar fashion, when all the working hypotheses point to that one dominant flavour of the problem, we can safely say we have domesticated the problem. Let us try the domestication-of-problem act with the Silver Blaze case as in Table 5.1.

Table 5.1 Arriving at working hypotheses

Symptoms/facts/ evidence	Inference 1 (verification)	Inference 2 (falsification)	Working hypotheses
Hunter was drugged, but nobody else in the house.	Police and Hunter feel it is Simpson, since he was the only one standing at the window, and could have drugged his curried mutton. Others, including the trainer, his wife, the maid and the other two lads had curried mutton for dinner that night in the trainer's kitchen, and were not drugged.	"Powdered opium is by no means tasteless. The flavour is not disagreeable, but it is perceptible. Were it mixed with any ordinary dish the eater would undoubtedly detect it and would probably eat no more. A curry was exactly the medium which would disguise this taste." Simpson could not "have caused curry to be served in the trainer's family that night, and it is surely too monstrous a coincidence to suppose that he happened to come along with powdered opium upon the very night when a dish happened to be served which would disguise the flavour." Therefore Simpson gets eliminated from the case. Who can order the kind of dish that can be served?	Straker and his wife are the only two people who could have chosen curried mutton for supper that night. "The opium was added after the dish was set aside for the stable-boy, for the others had the same for supper with no ill effects. Which of them, then, had access to that dish without the maid seeing them?"
Prime witnesses accuse Simpson: Hunter and the maid.	Hunter: He was bribed, and he ran after Simpson with his dog, but could not catch him. Maid: She was bribed, and she ran to Hunter to tell him. Simpson could have easily come back, after Hunter was drugged, and stolen the horse.	Nobody thought of the dog as the third witness.	A dog never barks if the person is known: Straker?

Source: All figures, boxes and tables are by authors, unless otherwise mentioned.

Now let us collate our Working Hypotheses for our Problem Inference.

- *Problem Inference*: We may thus suggest that the problem is not Simpson, but Straker, notwithstanding his tried and tested description as per our initial situation analysis. The case temperament now changes. The initial analysis suggested that Hunter was drugged by Simpson. But the drug used – powdered opium – is easily detectable in any food. Curried mutton, however, would cover up the taste of the opium quite conveniently. It is not possible for Simpson to order curried mutton that particular night and then drug Hunter. The food choice could have only been made by the masters, viz., the trainer and his wife. Secondly, the prime witnesses – Hunter and the maid – vehemently identify Simpson; but a third witness has not been taken into account, and that too a strong witness. The witness in question is the dog. The dog was used by Hunter to chase Simpson; then how is it that the dog did not bark in the night, when Simpson must have come back for the horse? A dog would not bark at Straker; he is the master! Thus, from Simpson, the attention now shifts to Straker.

So, in our attempt to identify the dominant pattern consistent through our Working Hypotheses, we get the domesticated Problem Statement.

- *Problem Statement*: The choice of supper and the silence of the hound do not favour the charges against Simpson.

Thus, the Problem Statement is the crisp and final cog in the wheel that leads to our Recommendation:

- *Recommendation*: We request a fresh investigation with Straker as the central point of analysis rather than Simpson, and reanalyse the situation and case facts as per the new find.

This rigorous method of case investigation is more popularly discussed in managerial situations as the analytical report. In either case,

(a) rationalising a case, or
(b) writing an analytical report,

we need to understand the protocol of the process – domestication of the problem – as is illustrated in the following table:

Table 5.2 Protocols for the domestication of the problem framework in an analytical report

Episode of report	Terminology	Strategy
Introduction	Purpose/Objective	Lead the audience to the recommendation
Data analysis	Situation analysis	Sifting of data Art of inference
Diagnosis of problem/s	Problem analysis *Diagnosis* • Symptom • Inference 1 • Inference 2 • Working Hypothesis (WH) *Problem Inference* *Problem Statement*	*Art of Elimination* Verification & Falsification *Working Hypothesis* *Summary* *Domestication of Problem*
Solution	Recommendation	Problem Statement requiring Action

Now let us rewrite Silver Blaze as an analytical report through the domestication of the problem framework

Analytical case report on the Silver Blaze case-verdict

The case as it stands: The horse Silver Blaze has disappeared, the trainer John Straker has been murdered, and the stranger, Fitzroy Simpson, has been arrested for the murder of Straker. The horse is not found.

Objective/Purpose of Report (*Lead the audience to the recommendation*)

To diagnose a problem in Simpson being declared the culprit/ review Simpson's arrest.

Situation analysis

Let us review the situation in details.

(a) *Silver Blaze, the horse* (*sifting of data*)

- Has a brilliant record at horse racing.
- Is in his fifth year and each time he has brought prizes of the turf to Colonel Ross, his fortunate owner.

- Up to the time of the catastrophe he was the first favourite for the Wessex Cup.
- The betting is three to one on him.
- Enormous sums of money have been laid upon him.
- Every precaution was taken to guard the favourite.

Inference (Art of Inference)

As mentioned in the case itself, "it is obvious, therefore, that there were many people who had the strongest interest in preventing Silver Blaze from being there at the fall of the flag next Tuesday."

(b) *John Straker, the trainer*

- He rode in Colonel Ross's colours.
- He served the colonel for five years as jockey.
- He has served seven years as a trainer.
- The case also mentions that he has "always shown himself to be a zealous and honest servant."
- Trainer is "comfortably off."

Inference

Known and tested servant and self-sufficient in finance.

(c) *Protection provided at the stables*

- Trainer qualified, tested and known (see trainer case facts tabulated immediately above in this report).
- Three lads under the trainer. The number is fine for a small establishment, containing only four in all.
- One lad sits up through night, while other two sleep in the loft. (Inference: each one well rested, not over-worked)
- "Sound sleepers".
- "Excellent characters".
- Trainer is "comfortably off".
- No drinking; only water tap.
- A hound is there for driving away strangers.

Inference

Trainer is financially satisfied; alcohol effect removed; precaution tight with human and animal service; employees well rested and tried and tested.

(d) *Eventful Day*

- The maid carried curried mutton for Hunter, the lad on guard. The other two lads had supper in the trainer's house.
- On her way, she was confronted by Simpson, the stranger and suspect under question. He bribed her with a pretty frock in return for a favour, carrying the bribe to Hunter. (Inference: He had inside information about the lads.)
- She runs back to Hunter.
- Simpson meets Hunter, nevertheless, and openly bribes him regarding the horses.
- Hunter unleashed the hound and rushed after him, but in vain.
- Before doing so, he locked the stable door. (Inference: Stable was not open.)
- He sent a message to the trainer and told him what had occurred.
- Trainer was anxious, and after an uneasy time, notwithstanding his wife's pleas, he set about for the stable to see if the horses were fine.

D. i. *Morning*

- Stable door was open.
- Horse and trainer absent.
- Hunter was drugged (later declared powdered opium mixed in mutton curry; others also had partaken that meal, but were fine).
- Two lads had slept soundly (Inference: they were not drugged, and there was no commotion in the vicinity that could have led to the disruption of their sound sleep).
- Quarter of a mile away, in an open space, the trainer's body was found.

D. ii. *Site*

- Shattered head with heavy blow from heavy weapon (Inference: weapon surmised, since not found).
- Wounded on thigh, clean cut "inflicted evidently by some very sharp instrument" (Inference: weapon surmised, since not found).

- Right hand, small knife clotted with blood.
- Left hand, clasped red and silk cravat identified as the stranger's by more than one witness.
- Hunter was "equally certain that the same stranger had, while standing at the window, drugged his curried mutton, and so deprived the stables of their watchman."
- As for the horse, "there were abundant proofs in the mud which lay at the bottom of the fatal hollow that he had been there at the time of the struggle." But after that, he had disappeared.

(e) *Evidence against Simpson*

- "An examination of his betting-book shows that bets to the amount of five thousand pounds had been registered by him against the favourite."
- Silk cravat, which he claimed he had lost, identified as his by both the maid and Hunter, and found clasped in the hands of the dead trainer.
- His stick was a penanglawyer weighted with lead, and very possibly could, by repeated blows, had inflicted the terrible injuries to which the trainer had succumbed.
- Had openly bribed for horses.
- Knows information about the house (Inference: unlikely of a stranger). Moreover, "he is not a stranger to the district. He has twice lodged at Tavistock in the summer." (Inference: he has been shady before).
- Hunter was "equally certain that the same stranger had, while standing at the window, drugged his curried mutton, and so deprived the stables of their watchman". (Inference: no one else was drugged, though they had the same food; so Simpson had the best chances).

Inference: Strong case against him.

Problem analysis

Let us look at the facts a bit more closely. (*We start with symptoms that strongly support the case against Simpson and attempt an inoculation.*) (*Art of Elimination*) (see Table 5.3).

Table 5.3 Arriving at working hypotheses

Symptoms/ facts/ evidence	Inference 1 (Verification)	Inference 2 (Falsification)	Working hypothesis (WH)
Hunter was drugged, but nobody else in the house.	Police and Hunter feel it is Simpson, since he was the only one standing at the window and could have drugged his curried mutton. Others, including the trainer, his wife, the maid and the other two lads had curried mutton for dinner that night in the trainer's kitchen and were not drugged.	"Powdered opium is by no means tasteless. The flavour is not disagreeable, but it is perceptible. Were it mixed with any ordinary dish the eater would undoubtedly detect it and would probably eat no more. A curry was exactly the medium which would disguise this taste." Simpson could not "have caused curry to be served in the trainer's family that night, and it is surely too monstrous a coincidence to suppose that he happened to come along with powdered opium upon the very night when a dish happened to be served which would disguise the flavour." Therefore Simpson becomes eliminated from the case. Who can order the kind of dish that can be served?	Straker and his wife are the only two people who could have chosen curried mutton for supper that night. "The opium was added after the dish was set aside for the stable-boy, for the others had the same for supper with no ill effects. Which of them, then, had access to that dish without the maid seeing them?"
Prime witnesses accuse Simpson: Hunter and the maid.	Hunter: He was bribed, and he ran after Simpson with his dog, but could not catch him. Maid: She was bribed, and she ran to Hunter to tell him. Simpson could have easily come back, after Hunter was drugged, and stolen the horse.	Nobody thought of the dog as the third witness.	A dog never barks if the person is known: Straker?

Problem Inference (WH Summary for domestication of problem)

We may thus suggest that the problem is not Simpson, but Straker, notwithstanding his tried and tested description as per our initial situation analysis. The case temperament now changes. The initial analysis suggested that Hunter was drugged by Simpson. But the drug used, powdered opium, is easily detectable in any food. Curried mutton, however, would cover up the taste of the opium quite conveniently. It is not possible for Simpson to order curried mutton that particular night and then drug Hunter. The food choice could have only been made by the masters, viz., the trainer and his wife. Secondly, the prime witnesses, Hunter and the maid, vehemently identify Simpson; but a third witness has not been taken into account, and that too, is a strong witness. The witness in question is the dog. The dog was used by Hunter to chase Simpson; then why did the dog not bark in the night when Simpson supposedly came back for the horse? A dog would not bark at Straker; he is the master! Thus, from Simpson, the attention now shifts to Straker.

Problem Statement (Problem domesticated)

The choice of supper and the silence of the hound do not favour the charges against Simpson.

Recommendation (Action for domesticated problem)

We request a fresh investigation with Straker as the central point of analysis rather than Simpson, and re analyse the situation and case facts as per the new find.

– – – – – – – – – –

We need to remember a few dos and don'ts in our Domesticating Problem Framework. Thereby, we introduce seven indicators that help write a splendid analytical report.

Seven Indicators of Domesticating Problem Framework in Analytical Reports

1. *Report objective* should be directly or indirectly proportional to the recommendation. You are writing a report to lead the reader to your final proposition.

    • Compare the Objective and Recommendation for the Silver Blaze case.

- Objective: To diagnose a problem in Simpson being declared the culprit/review Simpson's arrest.
- Recommendation: We request for a fresh investigation with Straker as the central point of analysis rather than Simpson, and reanalyse the situation and case facts as per the new find.

2. In the *sifting of data*, the families of data should be such that if the reader does not read the details, the subheadings provide the gist of the case.

   - Look at the following headings of the families of the Silver Blaze analysis, and they say it all in a nutshell.

     - Silver Blaze, the horse
     - John Straker, the trainer
     - Protection provided at the stables
     - Eventful day

       - D. i. Morning
       - D. ii. Site

     - Evidence against Simpson

3. In the listing of symptoms, the need for strategic listing is required. Look out for absences as much as for presences.

   For instance, "that the dog did not bark is symptomatic" is not an easy recognition, and yet is probably the breakthrough data. In effect, this case is popularly discussed as the case of the dog that did not bark. A barking dog is the expected data; that the dog did not bark is the unexpected data.

4. The *problem statement* should be crisp, objective and categorical because the reader will more likely read the problem statement rather than the inference. If s/he is surprised with the statement, s/he might go through the inference.

5. The *recommendation* should just convert the problem statement into an implementable proposition.

   - Compare Problem Statement and Recommendation for the Silver Blaze case.

     - Problem Statement: The choice of supper and the silence of the hound do not favour the charges against Simpson.

- Recommendation: We request for a fresh investigation with Straker as the central point of analysis rather than Simpson, and reanalyse the situation and case facts as per the new find.

6. And above all, remember that the reader will definitely look at three basic headings in any report:

   (a) Objective
   (b) Problem statement
   (c) Recommendation

   So, see to it that (a), (b) and (c) are aligned.

7. Each episode of the report should be self-explanatory, yet aligned to its preceding and following episodes.

-- -- -- -- -- -- --

We tried to derive our analytical report framework from the original implementer of diagnosis – Doyle. But a case is of versatile nature. In this capacity, we introduce the range of meanings of a case from our persuasion shields, particularly the asset called Deconstruction, where we analyse the **text**, the **context** and the **subtext**. How do we differentiate amidst these seemingly similar and often synonymously used terms? Let us understand these variations through a pronounced instance that demonstrates a pronounced communication strategy.

Case Study 5.2: The first promotion of *Satyamev Jayate*, first season

The following reprises the dialogues in the promotion:

Script 5.2 Dialogues from *Satyamev Jayate* – first season, promotion video

Sunday ke din aaram se soeiyega

Saat baje tak, aath baje tak . . .

Nau baje tak . . .

Dus baje tak . . .

Phir to mein aa hi raha hoon

Gyarah baje

Aapko jagaane

(aan meri jaan, meri jaan, Sunday ke Sunday . . .

Translated . . .

Sleep in comfort on a Sunday

Till 7, 8 . . .

9 . . .

10 . . .

I am coming then.

At 11

To wake you up

(humming a popular song: come my darling, my darling,
every Sunday)

Source: Compiled by authors from the promotional video.

The text

The dialogue in the promotion has been provided to us for a diagnosis exercise. Hence, the dialogue in the promo is the "text" that needs to be analysed. A text is nothing but that which is analysed. And to do so, we need to position the document given for introspection in a context. In other words, we have to describe the situation that gave birth to those dialogues, that caused the text to exist, or that even emerge as a document of introspection. The context for the promotional dialogue is as follows:

The context

The superstar Aamir Khan utters the dialogues again, but this time for his successful television reality show – *Satyamev Jayate* [Victory for Truth]. This is the first promotion on television. And this is also the first television serial foray by Aamir Khan and also the first A-listed programme airing at 11 on a Sunday morning rather than the usual prime time, 9 to 10 pm on weekends and even on weekdays. Thus, the context is the background of the text. But, there is more to the context like there is more to the text. What "more to the text" is to the subtext, the "read between the lines", the nuances and the symptoms are to hidden agendas.

The subtext

If we look at the dialogue more closely, we find the following symptoms that are worth asking "why".

(a) The need to build up to the timing of the show – 11 am
(b) The stress on Sunday both in the dialogues as well as the song hummed
(c) The interesting contrast between "to wake you up" and "keep sleeping"

The subtext will make more sense when we elaborate on the context. Aamir doing a television show is not the central motif here. Rather, Aamir adding to the bandwagon of movie stars descending from big to small screen is the context here. It all began with Amitabh Bachchan and his stupendous success with *Kaun Banega Crorepati* [Who will be the Millionaire] that initiated this "small is big" phenomenon. After all, film stars were too big for television, but Mr. Bachchan proved that all wrong. Then Shahrukh Khan entered the business of television, replacing Mr. Bachchan, if not that successfully. But the trend really picked up when Salman Khan successfully conducted *Dus Ka Dum* (Strength of 10) and then blazed through *Big Boss*. Amidst all these success stories, with all his contemporaries having hit the bull's eye, there must be pressure on the perfectionist and intellectual film maker and actor to enter this arena, and if so, to differentiate himself considerably from his colleagues, as he has *majorly* done in the mainstream movie business. As is expected from the marketing genius, his market study would not be any less intriguing. Most of these shows have been losing their novelty because of an overdose of similar formats and all big stars descending from the lofty pedestal of film world to the humble platform of television one after another. Thus, Aamir Khan is joining television when the nation is used to such expectations and even disappointments. Again, the prime time has also become a familiar experience. It would be most probably another show of the same kind in the same time, but with a different superstar. And then the comparison game would begin: who anchored better and whether the TRPs (television rating points) surpassed that of the other competing anchors who are also his competitors in their mainstream field of employment – as is the regular PR (public relations) politics for Hindi cinema superstars. It is in this complex situation that Mr. Khan embarks on a reality show, but with a difference. He comes up with a show on social issues. Now connect this with the dialogue build-up in the promo: "you can continue sleeping till 7, 8, 9, 10 . . . I am anyway coming to wake you up at 11." So, that pun on "wake" is the subtext which a focused investigation will help in developing an elaborate context.

Now, a programme on social awareness is not necessarily the most-massy thing to serve on a competitive platter dominated by glamorous game shows. How to convert this distinguishing factor into a profitable proposition? The product is different, but the product placement is too, and here lies the brilliance of strategy. The timing of the show is strategically different and significant. Look at the build-up of time in the dialogue. So, what is special about 11? There is another play on the significance of the day – "Sunday". If we know our television viewership history, we know the strategy. It was the 1980s and the early 1990s that had an entire India locked up in their homes, glued to their television sets, watching with fervent worship *Ramayana* and *Mahabharata*, the tele-serials that created unprecedented history. Sunday morning thus has the value of nostalgia. And Khan brings back that nostalgia by circumventing the overused contemporary prime-time television blockbusters and fixing his programme time on a Sunday at 11, a time that has lost its prime-time viewership in the contemporary business of television blockbusters.

So, we have a text (the promo dialogue), the subtext (the time, day and the awakening) and the context (the complex background for the whole enterprise). This process of situating the text in a context to develop the potential of the subtexts in the text is called contextualising, or even better, historicising. Thus, Situation Analysis is a process of historicisation!

— — — — — — — — — -

Let us attempt the historicisation exercise on a different text.

Case Study 5.3: Review of Bollywood commercial cinema

Script 5.3 Portions from *Besharam* review as appearing through Press Trust India (PTI) in *India TV.com*

Stars – Ranbir Kapoor, Pallavi Sharda, Rishi Kapoor, Neetu Singh, Jaaved Jafferi

Director – Abhinav Singh Kashyap

Music – Lalit Pandit

Ratings –* 1/2

Action-comedy-drama is one of the popular genres in Indian cinema today, if served with equal responsibility. Abhinav Singh Kashyap, who did a blockbuster directorial debut with *Dabangg*, gave a new dimension to the masala flicks with regional touch. His action sombered [as written in the original text] and one-liners tickled the funny bone. Despite the numerous loopholes in the screenplay, he enjoyed the cinematic liberty and served the purpose of entertainment, which undeniably was a winner.

But that zeal and energy was not maintained in "Besharam".

– – – – –

That's how the story deals further. Unfortunately, along with the non-inventive tale of this flick, the necessary rudiments like dialogues and screenplay fall flat and get no moment to balance themselves.

– – – – –

However, the actor tried hard to paint the blemishes by filling the scenes with his electrifying performance, but his magic didn't work this time.

– – – – –

I'll go with one and a half star for Besharam. The flick doesn't even stand to its title. It should have entertained us blatantly.

Source: "Besharam movie review: Ranbir's worst flick ever," *India TV*. PTI 3 Oct 2013. Accessed 1 Feb 2017 <http://m.indiatvnews.com/entertainment/bollywood/besharam-movie-review-ranbir-rishi-neetu-pallavi-10049.html/page/7>.

Task: Use the review for a historicisation drill in the analytical report format to investigate the debacle of the movie.

An analytical report on the debacle of the movie *Besharam*

The case as it stands: Abhinav Kashyap, who became the game changer in movie-making in recent times with his hugely popular *Dabangg*, failed in a similar genre [masala entertainers] in his second outing, *Besharam*.

Objective/purpose of report

To inquire about the cause of the debacle of the movie *Besharam*, for which shoddy script and poor direction are being blamed. *(We take up the very points of the movie which the reviewer has blamed for its dismal outcome at the box office, to lead the uninitiated reader into a discussion that would eventually problematise those very points of criticism. Here the objective of the report not just defines the scope of its analysis, but also acts as the first crucial step that leads the reader to the final destination. Hence, the objective of the report is the most powerful guiding principle that shapes body corpus of the report. A communication strategist would look at an objective not just as a procedural formality, but also as a tool to position her argument in her premeditated framework.)*

Situation analysis

Let us review the situation in details. *(sifting of data)*

Abhinav Kashyap's contribution to Dabangg

- Abhinav Singh Kashyap, who did a blockbuster directorial debut with *Dabangg,* gave a new dimension to the masala flicks with regional touch.
- His action and one-liners tickled the funny bone.
- Despite the numerous loopholes in the screenplay, he enjoyed the cinematic liberty and served the purpose of entertainment with a winsome upshot.

Problems with Besharam

- The zeal and energy in *Dabangg* was not maintained in *Besharam*.
- Non-inventive tale.
- Necessary rudiments like dialogues and screenplay fall flat and get no moment to balance themselves.
- Such is the momentum carried in 2 hours 20 minutes time, which nowhere thrills you or amuses you.
- The narration is so draggy that the boredom takes a toll after a while, especially in the first half.
- Unnecessary melodrama and uninvited song ventures.
- Abhinav not only skips the chance to develop chemistry between the main actors, but also fails to give a funny yet endearing appeal to Bulbul Chautala (Neetu Singh) and inspector Chulbul Chautala (Rishi Kapoor). The taunting between them, which was supposed to be endearing, seems contrived. While their humour isn't slapstick, the action which occupies the least duration isn't hardcore, one thing which could have been dealt with easily by Kashyap.
- Kashyap doesn't give many combative sequels to Ranbir, which in fact instills in Rishi Kapoor the Sunny Deol zeal.
- Music is another big drawback in this never-engaging flick.
- Pallavi Sharda wasted too much energy on dancing and uttering her dialogues, but just ended up with decent work in place of good work.
- Rishi Kapoor and Neetu Singh try to amuse you with their "mard" debate, corruption and bribe topics but sometimes irritate you.

Plus points in the movie as per the critic (always show conflicting positions from the text in taxonomy categories to show that you are objective and look at both sides of a coin).

- Ranbir tried hard to paint over the blemishes by filling the scenes with his electrifying performance, but his magic didn't work this time.
- Jaaved Jafferi, who isn't portrayed by Kashyap as a big tormentor, is good in whatever limited scenes he gets in.

Problem analysis

Let us look at the inferences drawn from our Situation Analysis to diagnose the problem. (*Historicisation Drill*)

Table 5.4 Historicisation drill

Symptoms/facts/evidence	Inference level I (verification/context creation)	Inference level 2 (elimination/problematisation)	WH (Historicisation/subtext creation)
Non-inventive tale	The story of a boy who steals a car, and then realises that he needs to get the car back from the thief he sold it to because the car belonged to his girlfriend – this is a predictable plot.	The cult status that Dabangg enjoyed was not because of an innovative tale. It was also a hackneyed plot of step brothers fighting, and ultimately uniting into a family. Yes, the main character was shown to be corrupt, yet helped the poor – a stock character still. Rather, the character player's stylised presence had more to do with the success of Dabangg.	The actor concerned has been in the movie business for more than two decades with a massive mass following; but his talents were not used in such genres of movie making till 2009 with Wanted and in 2010 with Dabangg. So, he was the pleasant surprise in the familiar domain. WH: The actor was a significant choice by the movie making team.
The zeal and energy in Dabangg was not maintained in Besharam.	Perhaps true	But the zeal and energy in Dabangg was not created by the script, which was the same old story told so many times; it is the actor's manner of acting the same kind of role with his exaggerated style that made Dabangg famous.	There have been many successful movies that have had their main performers carrying the pressure of the movie through the display of their idiosyncratic stylisations that might have overshadowed content, irrespective of the reviewers holding the movie content in contempt. Yet, much later, those ill-reviewed movies have become cultural cults. For instance, critic Andrew Sarris had said "Carpenter [the director] isn't very gifted with actors, and he doesn't seem to have any feeling at all for

Necessary rudiments like dialogues and screenplay fall flat and get no moment to balance themselves. Moreover, Rishi Kapoor and Neetu Singh try to amuse you with their "mard" debate, corruption and bribe topics but sometimes irritate you.	Perhaps true	Say, dialogues in the movie *Sholay* "kitney aadmi they" ("how many men were there") are simple questions, absolutely flat, hardly memorable dialogues. Yet they are perhaps the most cited in public memory.	motivation or for plot logic. Halloween has a pitiful, amateurish script." But *Halloween* of 1978 went onto add to the "slasher genre" ("Good Movies") (*in-text reference*). It is a well-known fact that the critics slammed *Sholay*, the cult Hindi movie. Particularly the exaggerated stylisation of dialogues through the cult villain – Gabbar Singh. Rajnikant has been famous for his stylish use of goggles. So, Matrix is *also* known for the stylised action sequences, with Keanu Reeves bending in slow motion in the impossible state of the horizontal backward pose, perhaps one of the most imitated stunts even in Indian commercial movies. Take out Salman Khan and his goggles behind his back collar, from *Dabangg*, and the movie loses its attraction. WH: The actor's personality and presentation has a lot to do with innovative expression of a hackneyed plot. Dialogues in themselves in masala entertainment movies cannot click, unless situations and the way they are delivered matter. The "kitney chedd" (how many holes) dialogue, if uttered by a comedian, would perhaps not have its mass appeal as when uttered by a popular actor – in this case, Salman Khan. Shakespeare had his wittiest lines in the garb of low-brow humour delivered by the character called the Fool, not his hero. Here, Salman Khan as the hero plays the Fool and enthralls the audience. WH: Dialogues suiting the personality of the actor or the character accentuates their delivery. Hence it is not enough to author catchy dialogues in the written form.

(Continued)

Table 5.4 (Continued)

Symptoms/facts/evidence	Inference level 1 (verification/context creation)	Inference level 2 (elimination/ problematistion)	WH (Historicisation/subtext creation)
The narration is so draggy that the boredom takes a toll after a while, especially in the first half.	Accepted	How is *Dabangg* immune from it? Yet, one does not feel it.	A critic's opinion is that the screenplay, the dialogues and the narration handle movies. On the other, a consistently present Salman Khan in almost each frame of the two-hour movie (*Dabangg*) had the masses pour in. WH: In the commercial cinema, the pivotal factor that leads to its success is the strength of the actor who should be strong enough to cover up the flaws in the content if any by his powerful presence.
Kashyap should have handled action and humour sequences more adroitly, because in the present form the humour between Neetu Singh and Rishi Kapoor isn't slapstick, and the action which occupies least duration isn't hardcore.	Accepted	When *Dabangg* was released, the actions were touted as comic book style, rough copies of the popular cinema of South India in the first critical assessments in the initial days. The box office numbers and the huge hype following the success created a stream of Hindi movies following similar action styles.	An earlier successful movie is now being considered a precedent for similar movies, ironically, which was critiqued adversely on its release. WH: Success changes the cultural value and intellectual acceptance of a movie.

Where Kashyap succeeded with *Dabangg*, he failed with *Besharam*.

This is true.

But we must understand why. Is it that he just directed a movie very well? Why allow loopholes as cinematic liberty?

The year was 2010. The multiplex culture was reigning; "meaningful" films were being churned out. The masala action genre was out of vogue. Yet Bollywood is remembered for *Sholay*, the quintessential movie of the Hindi film industry, famous for songs, melodrama, one-liners and action, screen superheroes, macho men and villains. Year 2010 saw films like *Guzaarish* (Sanjay Leela Bhansali), *Raavan* (Mani Ratnam) and the like. They did not work, because people were tired of big banners, and their "intellectual" movies. *Dabangg* came in with a new director, a new producer, not a size zero model-heroine, but a yesteryears, superstar's daughter, and a newcomer – not the typical Preetam – A. R. Rahman songs, a comparatively new villain, with the weight of the movie lying completely on the shoulders of an actor who was being written off! And there was a shift from the Punjabi domination to other regional cultures; for example, Uttar Pradesh in *Dabangg*; Jharkhand culture in *Gangs of Wasseypur*; Marathi culture in *Agnipath* and *Singham*; and Rajput culture in *Rowdy Rathore*. By the time *Besharam* released, the trend of plotting the plot in the manner cinematised in these successful flicks was done to death.

WH: The kind of movie released in what kind of trend running at the moment matters.

Problem Inference (Collation of WH into domestication of problem)

We may thus suggest that the problem is not perhaps the screenplay and direction alone, but rather the choice of actor for the genre of movie chosen. A masala flick actor has to have a tremendous goodwill built over years and be of a certain age and stature to win an audience; since the entertainer must have the comfort zone, then what? He gets them to want to come back again and again? Film critic Anupama Chopra puzzles over Salman Khan as an actor, which no critic will do when it comes to Ranbir Kapoor: "He's cinematic comfort food – you go into a theatre to watch him do the same thing over and over again. The story, the setting, the direction, the co-star, they are all irrelevant." Moreover, any genre which is fresh amidst a prominent style that dominates comes in as a breath of fresh air. *Dabangg*, as noted in the problem analysis table, was just that. Today, there have been enough such movies for *Besharam* to have *not* stood out.

There are five major issues to be noted in this analysis:

- All movies need not run because of screenplay and script. Certain genres need certain kinds of actors.
- Goodwill track record and a fan club built over years are important for certain kinds of roles in certain kinds of movies: massy movies.
- Massy movies have been intellectualised post success: Shakespeare, Quentin Tarentino, Wachowski brothers for *Matrix* and Rajnikant have a lot in common! This is postmodern philosophy.
- The critics have typical bias against directors, screenplays and narrations to safeguard actors who are critically acclaimed for previous meaningful movies, and particularly on the verge of becoming new superstars.
- Critical appreciation of actors for the masses is not a well-developed and well-practiced analysis yet in movie appreciation. Rather, it is an evolved form of entertainment racism.

Problem Statement (Domestication of the Problem)

The masala actor needs the critical recognition that masala flicks have been able to get through critical institutionalisation of themselves as a distinct genre.

Recommendation

The movie review system has to develop new parameters extracted from mass consumption of masala movies, already recognised as a different genre, to help valorise a commercial actor's contribution to entertainment, both artistically and commercially.

References

Chopra, Anupama. "Bollywood's Rockstar." 3 September 2011. Accessed 11 November 2013 <www.openthemagazine.com/article/voices/bollywood-s-rockstar>.
"Good Movies With Bad Reviews." Accessed 29 August 2016 <www. huffingtonpost.in/entry/good-movies-bad-reviews_n_6647954#gallery/400246/1>.

Salient features of the historicisation drill in an analytical report

- The verification process is nothing but context creation of the symptom. The context creation is the same procedure that we used for business messages.
- The sub textual creation begins as a narrative process in the elimination segment of the diagnosis.
- We can have several levels of sub textual narration through an intense process of historicisation. In the example on the film review, we have inference level 1 (context creation/verification), inference level 2 (problematisation/elimination), inference level 3 (historicisation) and finally the WH. Thus, the historicisation drill is a layered diagnosis of text, context, subtext, and sub-texts of subtexts and the textual derivations continue, depending upon the intensity of the diagnosis required.
- The historicisation drill involves bandwagoning and expertise building skills. In sum, the context and the subtext involve tools from credibility building toolkits and the benefit distribution apparatus. Hence, historicisation is a massive persuasive narrative.
- When building expertise, the stylisation of documenting the experts and their work follow worldwide institutionalised referencing formats:

    - MLA or the Modern Language Association
    - APA or the American Psychological Association

- Chicago Manual
- Harvard Style Sheet[5]

Though the formats differ in stylisation, the common pattern in all is the reader-friendly connection between the in-text documenting style and the provision of the complete bibliographic details in the specialised section – Reference. For instance, if the in-text documentation of an expert begins with the statement, "Film critic Anupama Chopra says" then the reference section must have all the details of the text that contains the statement made by the critic. So the reference should also begin with the name of the critic, so that it is easy to connect the reference input with the textual input. For instance, the in-text narration has R stating something. The reference will also begin with "R". So the reader who is interested in reading more about what R has said can easily locate her narrative and its whereabouts (publication detail, name of text, page number, website, URL, access date of URL material, website updated date, and so on) by looking for "R" in the reference column. If the author name is unavailable, as is the case with the website titled "Good Movies with Bad Reviews", the "R" is now the name of the text, both in the in-text documentation as well as occurring in the beginning of its own reference details.

- Working hypothesis (HP) is the final inference from the historicisation drill.
- The final domesticated problem is pitched not at an individual level, but at a generic, systemic, organisational or even institutional level. It is not about this particular review, but through the inferences drawn from this review the issue is positioned beyond the given text. Thus, the given text, case and context are symptomatic of a larger systemic issue such that the recommendation is directed to help solve the problem at a macro universal level, and not just at the individual level. This conversion of the micro, the particular, the incidental to the macro, the universal and the omniscient is the test of the analyst so as to view the larger organisational picture. Let us call this conversion of the micro problem into its macro systemic profile, the Patriotic Syndrome. The idea of patriotism comes from the idea of the organisational ethos. We might be individuals, but we are also an integral part of our nation. Similarly, the issue can be an individual issue, but is also an integral part of a larger system.

Hence, the problem statement has to have the larger systemic flavour and the organisational flavour, which is metaphorically equivalent to a nationalistic concern. Since it is an organisational disorder that needs rectification, the problem statement refers to a patriotic concern symbolically – the concern for a system, an organisation, an institution. In the review case, the patriotism was for commercial cinematic system and its subjugation to intellectual critical discourse.

Analytical reports using Harvard business cases

What began as a tradition by the Harvard Business School (HBS) was consumed by the premiere management institutes of the Asian-Indian subcontinent and has thus ushered in the bandwagoning of Harvard business cases in the Asian subcontinent. HBS had a full-time course on its menu called the Written Communication and Analysis Framework, an analytical practice that has had immense currency in the Indian Institutes of Management (particularly Ahmedabad, and also Calcutta) through initial patronage by the likes of S. Sreenivas Rao of IIMA, and collated works of (to name a few)

- Russel Lincoln Ackoff's 1977 *The Art of Problem Solving*
- Charles H. Kepner and Bejamin B. Tregoe's 1965 *The Rational Manager: A Systematic Approach to Problem Solving and Decision Making*
- Thomas C. Raymond's 1964 *Problems in Business Administration: Analysis by the Case Method*

Using the Harvard case bank, along with commentaries on the cases from practising international managerial problem solvers, we come up with our domestication of problem and the patriotic syndrome through our attempt at solving HBR cases. Let us try an analytical report on the HBR case by Joseph Finder – *The CEO's Private Investigation* (see Appendix).[6]

Case Study 5.4:   Cheryl and the need for private investigation at Hammond

Task: An Analytical Report on the Case of the New CEO of Hammond and her Legal Dilemma

Case as it stands

In the face of

(a) regulatory laws,
(b) unethical practices reported by

- external sources (grapevine pronounces bribery allegations on the very successful endeavours of the sales team during the reign of the legendarily successful CEO of Hammond, Jim Rawlings) and
- internal sources (Jackie, the age-old secretary of Jim, reveals the hidden Cayman deal) and
- internal counsel against any corporate investigation that would risk Hammond's image (Bodine, the internal candidate side-lined for the new CEO and Geoffrey, the in-house lawyer);

the following is an analytical report on the legal advice that Cheryl, the new CEO of the firm under consideration, is seeking from Litigation Specialists.

Objective/Statement of Purpose

Whether Cheryl should initiate an investigation at her new firm or not?

Situation Analysis

The following classified information helps us understand the context of the case.

Profile of the legendary erstwhile CEO of Hammond: Jim Rawlings

- Magnanimous settings: bigger office than Mussolini; windows from floor to ceiling with panoramic view of the locality; working fireplace with slate hearth; big and clean desk

  Inference: Establishing the grandeur and ego of the personality – he likes it large and makes sure the world knows about that. Plus, his habit of maintaining a clean desk is all about a choice for a clutter-free arrangement or a diplomatic move of camouflaging what he wants to keep under wraps.

- Club furniture (predominantly masculine)

  Inference: Hence hinting at Jim Rawling's patriarchal propensities or Cheryl's feminist perspective of detecting a patriarchal structure in it.

- Photographs with dignitaries: "skiing with Prince Charles in Klosters; sailing with Gianni Agnelli in Adriatic; schmoozing with King Abdullah at Riyadh Royal Palace".

  Inference: Globetrotter and great social capital displayed (too many people involved and that too dignitaries or a strong nexus)

- Legendary success: Single-handedly transformed a minor producer of airplane shields into one of the leading aerospace companies of the world. Hence, legendary.

- Dying in harness: Notwithstanding sudden death during negotiations for a profitable deal, the five billion worth deal was clinched.

  Inference: He was a profit making machine till the end.

- Telephone not on the desk (hidden in a desk drawer).

  Inference: Everything is not out in the open?

- Rumours of bribery landing foreign contract

  Inference: Not an ethical-friendly ecosystem.

Organisation: Hammond Aerospace

- Legendary CEO, Jim Rawlings, dead.
- New CEO, Cheryl Tobin, from Boeing, interestingly a competing company.
- Was once a small airplane shield producer; now a leading aerospace company.
- New CEO from outside, while the inside candidate, Hank Bodine, Head of Commercial Airplane Division, overlooked by the Board of Directors (BoD).
- Rumours about bribery by sales team of Hammond as secrets of successful clinching of foreign contracts.

Meaningful events as potential sub texts for Cheryl's suspicions

(Intuitive Hints)

- Chairman personally escorts Cheryl to her new room (this could be meaningful, or purely decorous)

- Telephone hidden, and not on the desk (symbolic of a personality that likes to hide???)
- Rumour: Hammond's sales team behind bribery of foreign parties to clinch deals (no smoke without fire? or competitive mud-slinging)
- Photograph of Bodine, Jeffrey and Rawlings as the "three frat brothers": partners in crime or Cheryl over-imagining?

(Hard Facts)

- Internal candidate passed over by Hammond's BoD and external candidate recruited
- Jackie mentioned an un-legitimised wire transfer of millions of dollars from Hammond's accounts to a bank in Grand Cayman (a place not known for any legitimate business dealings with Hammond). This is a fact because it would be too much for a frightened Jackie to lie under the circumstances: when probed, she offered information, while earlier she was stiff and formal. But the Cayman dealing may or may not be ethical infringement just because Jackie was not told about it. Not being told, and Cayman being an outside factor in Hammond's dealings (which a secretary is privy to), however, is potential suspicion.
- Bodine openly suggests that he was passed over by the BoD so that the external entrant as CEO can make changes in the company.
- Cheryl sounds her intention for investigation into bribery rumours to three internal parties: Jackie gives in as informant; Bodine and Geoffrey are against it. Geoffrey's warnings can be taken as prudent advice as well

Cheryl Tobin: The new CEO of Hammond from Boeing

- Does not like Rawlings' advertising of capital. Or is she intimidated?
- Not basking in success for succeeding Rawlings, as realistic about not expecting many well-wishers from the internal organisation, particularly Bodine, who was passed over by the BoD to get her to be the CEO.
- She is either sensitive or suspicious of the following characters:

    - Jackie with her Mrs. Danvers Act:[7] It seems to Cheryl that Jackie, who is still loyal to Rawlings, is using his track record to intimidate Cheryl to present her as a not-so-worthy replacement.

- Weighed down by rumours of bribery, she has first-hand experience of legal problems in Boeing for unethical acts, courtesy and the Pentagon episode.

- Cheryl is practical and knows the game of negotiation well:

  - She knows how to twist Jackie from a firm and stiff secretary to an invaluable informant – Jackie has 18 years of experience of working in Hammond.
  - Wants company reputation spotless. This is not just conscience, but also alertness to the round-the-corner financial filings expected, and if any loophole is discovered, Cheryl knows that current regulatory laws would hold company top officials liable, and would amount to a punishable offence and costly legal hassles.
  - In her earlier organisation, Cheryl was known to be the ice-maiden – one who is thick-skinned – plus her gut feelings cannot be sidelined because she has climbed the charts through guts and brains. You cannot underestimate gut feelings of potential leaders, even if you don't consider them as first class evidence. But as pointers, possible! Plus, Hammond's BoD would not hire just about anyone as the new CEO of a leading company, led profitably (perhaps dubiously in the face of recent regulatory laws) by a charismatic and successful Rawlings.

Competitors/Enemies/Sound Advisors/Frenemies/Informants

(a) Jackie Terrell: secretary

- Potential storehouse of information, as she was Rawlings' secretary for 18 years.
- Initial conversations had a Mrs. Danvers act – it was all about what Jim was or used to do.
- Easy to break the Danvers personality, however, and get her into confidence: Cheryl got her to speaking about the Cayman transmission.
- Only one who provides a possible proof of bribery.
- When Cheryl is later worried post negative assistance from Bodine and Geoffrey, it is Jackie who appears sympathetic, since she inquires after Cheryl with "tenderness".

(b) Hank Bodine: the inside contender to CEO post

- Inquisitive: He himself enters Cheryl's cabin to inquire about changes she intends to make.
- Tough nut to crack – Cheryl's advances are tactfully handled; Cheryl's doubts are neither ascertained nor discounted.
- Counsels against investigation – the disadvantage of company and share prices is thrust upon Cheryl's conscience.

(c) Geoffrey Latimer: in-house lawyer

- Counsels against investigation on following lines:
  - Regulatory environment brutal as top officials get held for any nefarious activities within their organisation.
  - Company's control taken out of Cheryl's hand – she would be the namesake CEO.
  - Cheryl might be misinterpreted to have intentions to discredit her very popular predecessor, and hence lose trust from senior management.

(d) Chairman from the Board of Directors (BoD)

- Overlooked (as a team or otherwise) the internal candidate, Hank Bodine, and recruited Cheryl Tobin from a competing company, Boeing, as the successor of Jim Rawlings, the extremely famous and celebrity CEO of Hammond.
- Personally escorted Cheryl to her new room when she was introduced to her office during courtship (mere customary or strategic?).

Regulatory Bodies

- Foreign Corrupt Practices Act or FCPT: Initiated in 1977. It prohibits bribery as a means to obtain foreign contracts.
- Sarbanes-Oxley Act: Initiated in 2002. It increases personal accountability of corporate directors.

Against investigation: counsel/warning from Bodine/ Geoffrey plus Cheryl's personal experience at Boeing

- Company share price will be affected.
- Investigation cannot be kept secret, as forensic document examiners will be asking questions and looking through various

documents. This will amount to front page news in leading papers (*Wall Street Journal* mentioned by Geoffrey).

- If senior managers are informed:

  - Chances of their becoming cautious is very high because

    (1) the regulatory environment has become very active of late,
    (2) courts have been holding directors personally responsible for corporate malpractices that are known to them, but not acted upon and
    (3) millions of dollars of fees would be required to be scooped up by the company for legal defences for each of the directors.

  - Chances of them taking over decision-making powers from the CEO is equally high, which might result in

    (1) their taking over control out of the director's hand; the CEO becomes just namesake, and
    (2) their misreading Cheryl's investigation inclinations as moves to discredit her popular predecessor (which might result in her losing the favour of senior management).

For investigation: in favour of Cheryl's doubts/fears/ strategy for change

- As Geoffrey has warned, Cheryl is liable to be punished for any knowledge of malpractice in the organisation.
- Quarterly filings are awaiting and Cheryl knows about the Sarbanes-Oxley Act.
- Her memory of the Boeing incident is significant – the Pentagon contract, where the CFO had to resign and even go to prison. It was only a great legal team that could save Boeing from criminal charges.
- This is her way of making her mark (leadership).

Problem diagnosis

Symptom

Cheryl is disturbed by rumours of bribery and wants to initiate a probe to get to know the truth.

Inference 1:

As a first approximation, she would want to be ethical. But being ethical need not be the conscience factor alone. If we problematise that, and our situation analysis provides enough material to do so, we get the following:

(a) The quarterly filings are around the corner, and that is the reason for fear as well, particularly after Cheryl gets warnings (from Geoffrey) of the regulatory environment and its grasp on top officials of companies that avail corporate investigations. The FCPA and the Sarbanes are enough to get Cheryl charged with criminal offences if she is in the know-how of any malpractice in her organisation, and, subsequently, the company has to spend millions and billions on court proceedings.

(b) Apart from Jackie, both Bodine and Geoffrey (internal members) are strongly against investigation, and their warnings are for the company's reputation as well as Cheryl's from the point of view of regulatory bodies, internal distrust resulting from misinterpretation of Cheryl's intentions, and colossal legal, financial and image damage to the company. This is enough to scare any new CEO.

Working Hypothesis 1: Cheryl has to safeguard her future as well as the company's.

Inference 2:

(a) Cheryl did not consider the rumours when she was offered the job. And she was aware of these rumours even then. Thus, we can take this for certain that she knows she is getting into an organisation with possible malpractices.

(b) She has been known as an ice-maiden in her earlier organisation, because she makes tough decisions. So, she is potential CEO material who can handle adversities, or has a sense of it. Plus, would a leading company's BoD recruit an ordinary candidate to be the succeeding CEO post a successful man like Rawlings?

(c) She is aware of regulatory bodies before advice comes from Geoffrey, because of the Pentagon case in Boeing. She knows that a brilliant legal team had managed to save them from criminal charges, and still can, if required. Interestingly, she does call an outsider for suggestion.

(d) From the beginning there are symptoms of her wanting to change the settings of her office which are dominated by Rawlings so far, including the masculine furniture. Whether that is intimidation or the independent assertion of Cheryl as the new boss with a new culture might be interesting to think of. The rumours give her that silver lining to mark her stamp in a new organisation on ethical grounds: She wants a spotless company, and she makes sure she sounds it to three people – the secretary, Bodine and Geoffrey – before calling an outsider, enough to get tongues wagging about her. This might be her way of wanting to be as big as or bigger than her predecessor.

(e) The BoD's move to hire Cheryl and not appoint in-house hand, Bodine, is a strong hint, particularly, when Bodine himself comes charging into Cheryl's room, to inquire about the changes she intends to incorporate, suggesting outright the BoD's strategy behind the decision. Perhaps a need for culture change?

Working Hypothesis 2: She wants to start a fresh culture (ethics) as mark of her leadership.

Symptom:

Cheryl, dejected with in-house lack of support for her investigation (with the exception of Jackie), calls an outsider for help.

Inference 1:

(a) She tries to gather support for her cause, but fails. Hence, she calls an outsider.

(b) There is no process or mechanism internal to the organisation, in the shape of CSR committees, to whom she can appeal for help or consultancy in such moments. In short, there do not seem to be any in-house regulatory bodies to hear such complaints.

(c) We may argue here that the Chairman can be seen in a favourable light because the decision to choose her as the new CEO was the BoD's decision, and he himself has accompanied Cheryl to her new room, to show her round. Yet, Cheryl does not confide in him; she chooses to call an outsider. This could be because she does not know who to trust, particularly after

Geoffrey's suggestions that the Board would take over her leadership mantle.

Working Hypothesis 3: There is a lack of process or mechanism within the organisation or the BoD which can help listen and aid management in such dilemmas/crisis.

Working hypotheses

Let us review the working hypotheses again:
    If we look at our derivations, we find

(a) Even if it is fear driven or self-preservation driven, Cheryl has to think of a process to safeguard herself and, hence, the company.
(b) She might sincerely mean ethics. Even for that, a mechanism has to be initiated.
(c) Even if it is about self-identity and one-upmanship, to start a culture of ethics, Cheryl has to initiate a process within the organisation.

All the above derivations clearly point to the final one:

(d) There is definitely missing a much needed process or mechanism within the organisation or through the BoD which can help listen and aid management in such dilemmas.

Thus, from the above we conclude that the major problem for Cheryl is not the crisis, but the need to have a mechanism or process to handle or manage similar crises henceforth.

Problem Statement: There is a need in Hammond for an internal mechanism from which a process of corporate governance can be initiated, whenever an ethical crisis is due.

Recommendation: To initiate an internal mechanism of corporate governance that can offer consultations on ethical issues in Hammond.

    Thus, the recommendation goes beyond Cheryl and her private dilemma. Rather, the recommendation is more a patriotic concern for Hammond – the need for a mechanism of corporate governance in Hammond.

Recommendations as proposals

A good manager is someone who solves problems. Once a problem is identified, the next stage is about providing a solution. As mentioned before, the problem has to be sold successfully to sell the solution. When we talk about *selling* solutions, we talk about *proposing* solutions. Thus, the other variant of analytical reports is the business proposal. If the analytical report is more about the diagnosis of the problem, the proposal is more about recommending solutions. If the analytical report is more about Problem Analysis, the proposal is more about Decision Analysis. If the analytical report is more about the historicisation drill, the proposal is more about the recommendation of the patriotic concern. The historicisation drill creates the context for the germination of the patriotic concern. The recommendation drill builds the narrative of the patriotic concern. Thus, a Business Proposal is more about the sustenance of the patriotic concern, unlike analytical reports which create the concern. So, how do we sustain a patriotic concern in a coherent fashion? Sustaining Patriotism is then our new framework. Let us rework our way through Cheryl from the Problem Statement again.

The Decision Analysis begins with the Problem Statement because the idea is to now decide what we have to do, and not really find why we have to do what we have to do. "Why" has been decided. Hence, the Decision Objective is the new objective of the narrative. Compare Decision Objective with the Problem Statement.

Problem Statement: There is a need in Hammond for an internal mechanism from which a process of corporate governance can be initiated, whenever an ethical crisis is due.

Decision Objective will *now* be: Establish good management processes to attain good corporate governance.

Now the entire report (proposal) is written from the point of view of the Decision Objective, and not from the original Objective of the report.

Report Objective: Whether Cheryl should initiate an investigation at her new firm or not.

Now that the objective is set, how do we go about finding Nemo[8] (the solution, obviously). We go back to the Anna principle again. Diamond illustrates how zebras cannot be domesticated because they do not fulfil one of the six **benchmarks** required to successfully domesticate animals.

- Not fastidious eaters: adjust to available food like dogs and cats that feed on human waste.
- Reach maturity quickly: elephants take 15 years to become adults.
- Breed in captivity: Antelopes do not appreciate crowded enclosures; cheetahs prefer extravagant courtships.
- Docile by nature: Zebras are like horses, but more aggressive.
- Not panic and flee: deer have a flighty nature.
- Conform to social hierarchy: cats do not like it.

Taxonomy is the secret to a good Situation Analysis. The historicisation drill is the beauty of Problem Diagnosis. Benchmark is the fulcrum of a good Decision Analysis. Why? For the basic strategy of persuasion. If I need to sell my proposal to a team, I sell the problem, but I also sell the multifaceted advantages of my proposal. The argument against my case would be that when I can state the advantages of my proposal, then why not set my proposal against a set of benchmarks? The strategy then is to convert advantages or issues into benchmarks. When I present my proposal as advantageously qualifying against the benchmarks set to evaluate the strength of my proposition, the display of evaluative processes strengthens the value of my proposal in the eyes of the team who would be judging my proposition on its merit.

If I say "the zebra will not be a lucrative animal to domesticate, even if it has all the qualities of a horse, because it is too aggressive", it makes a point.

But if I say "for domestication of the right animal, we need (a), (b), (c), (d) and (e) qualities, or the lack of these result in problem creation", I thereby create a concrete matrix for a solution.

In other words, I create a trap, but it is camouflaged as evaluative. So now, I can propose: "do not choose zebra for domestication because it might fulfil (a), (b) and maybe (c), but definitely not (d) and perhaps with great labour, (e)".

We leave it to our readers to choose the merit of both methods: the direct disadvantage/advantage method or the benchmarking matrix method. In sum, the benchmark, the standard, the parameter, the criterion, the yardstick of evaluation is *more* important when characterising a proposal as good or bad. The tact lies in developing a performative evaluative matrix than merely stating the proposal with its merits or demerits. The matrix is performative because we create the criteria that the proposal apparently satisfies. But the reader reads the criteria as the "given" gospel of evaluation, and thereby witnesses the performance of an objective evaluation as an act taking place right in front of their eyes. The performance of the evaluation renders objectivity to the narrative.

For the Cheryl case, we have the following benchmarking matrix:

- Company's reputation and future (macro and system level)
- CEO's reputation and future (micro and individual level)

Apart from covering the organisational as well as the individual level concerns, the parameter matrix is also clever because it co-opts the antagonist's point of view: Latimer has already warned Cheryl that if she does go for an investigation, the chosen criteria encapsulate the demerits of a rash decision. We have converted Latimer's warnings into evaluative parameters, thus inoculating Latimer and his kind from further objection. Thus, an inoculating benchmark matrix is even more impactful.

Hint 1: Choose the antagonistic symptoms as the benchmark of evaluation.

Now, either you can be satisfied by showing how a zebra is not the best option for domestication, or show how a zebra, a cat, a cheetah, an elephant and many others fare in the benchmarking matrix, and in the process of the performative evaluation zero down upon the most undomesticable or the most domesticable of the lot. If this is too manipulative, then, in an ethical sense, let the best deliver. And the "best" can only be defined through a comparative process.

We also need a competitive matrix as well. And a competitive matrix needs options, alternatives to be tried against benchmarks. The attempt is to perform the idiom "let the best option win", and the best option is the one that fulfils the benchmark matrix the best.

Management evaluation processes have historically popularised the SWOT analysis – strengths, weaknesses, opportunities and threats. We add to SWOT the performative evaluation matrix, wherein the proposer "performs" the evaluation of each option against each criterion through the SWOT matrix. It needs deft handling of the persuasion apparatus to problematise, deconstruct and inoculate the various options against the benchmarks to decipher the "best" alternative as the rightful proposal of solution to the recorded problem.

In the case of Cheryl, we record the following alternatives in the Competitive Matrix:

- Hire external agency on the sly.
- Give a clear message about the intention to investigate any wrong-doing – that would help Cheryl choose her friends from her enemies into her management team.
- Report to the Chairman (BoD) first instead of the external agency.
- Stop digging for dirt. Too much time and effort gets consumed in an investigation, when a new CEO of a leading company has many other important things to do on a daily basis, particularly when she succeeds a popular one.

Hint 2: Alternatives suggest that you have thought through plural angles; hence, choose opposing and diverse options.

Now, you can perform the evaluation of each alternative by judging each against both the benchmarks. Say, alternative 3 is proved the most lucrative. That becomes the proposal.

Case Study 5.5: Decision analysis on the Cheryl case

Problem Statement:

There is a need in Hammond for an internal mechanism from which a process of corporate governance can be initiated, whenever an ethical crisis is due.

Decision Analysis *(Sustaining Patriotism)*

Decision Objective: Establish good management process to attain good corporate governance *(directly proportional to the Problem Statement)*

Criteria: *(Benchmarking Matrix: Use inoculation by using potential adversaries' opinions)*

- Company's reputation and future *(the most obvious criterion and the first parameter that any premise of counter-argument would put forward, as was the case with Bodine. After all, company comes first.)*
- CEO's reputation and future *(Taking off from Geoffrey's propositions, this would be the next best parameter to consider, if one has to stop a CEO from investigation, or push a CEO to investigate.)*

Options/Alternatives *(competitive matrix)*

In the given circumstances, there are four possible alternatives that Cheryl can be advised to do:

- Call an external agency for internal investigation on the sly. There is no smoke without fire.
- Give a clear message about the intention to investigate any wrong-doing – that would help Cheryl choose her friends from her enemies into her management team.
- Report to the Chairman (BoD) first instead of the external agency, as he did appear friendly.
- Stop digging for dirt. Too much time and effort gets consumed in an investigation when a new CEO of a leading company has many other important things to do on a daily basis, particularly when she succeeds a popular one.

(We have chosen opposing action points for objectivity and plurality.)

Evaluation of Options against Criteria *(performative evaluative matrix)*

Alternative 1: Hire external agency on the sly

Criterion 1: Company's reputation

Why not to? (pros)	But if you don't? (cons)
Very difficult to keep an investigation on the sly. External party will ask questions, look into documents, word might spread. Once spread, it would be front page news, and immediate impact would be on the company's reputation and share prices. Hewlett Packard and Merck with Vioxx have been strong examples of consequences of corporate investigations. Moreover, if an investigation does happen and reveals nothing at the end, still the image of a company that has gone through corporate investigation has a stigma.	The regulatory laws are brutal, and if filings are made, and later fraud is discovered, legal implications would be worse with criminal charges on top management as well. So, reputation harm would be inevitable. And cost in subsequent legal procedures would be harrowing, and legal battles would spread over long periods. Thus, money and reputation are at stake for a long time.

Alternative 1: Hire external agency on the sly

Criterion 2: Cheryl's reputation

If you do? (pros)	But why not to? (cons)
If proved right, she saves senior management from legal woes, and can position her account as in favour of management. 25% of the times, (as suggested by litigation specialists), no proof of violation is evidenced. Only a report is generated that can be produced should government investigators interfere; most of the times, it is shelved and displayed only if the client is interested in making it public. So Cheryl can play along these lines. She can keep it quiet, and through help of ready informants like Jackie and maybe some more, she can ask for audit transactions a year back. A new CEO asking for last year's audits is not out of the box and not out of place.	If CEO keeps to herself, expenditures for investigation would start to mount – someone will notice and the BoD will know. The BoD will be against her for not letting them in. Senior management might discredit her intentions that she intends to discredit the popular former CEO, as prudently advised by Geoffrey.

If you do? (pros)	But why not to? (cons)
	However, further problematisation reveals... Checking phone records, government transactions and relying completely on Jackie (she was quickly transformed into an informant, and can be done perhaps for another party as well, though her tenderness does show a likeable quality) may not enable the investigation to be on the sly. Any disclosure can pose the question as to why she did not take the BoD into confidence. Particularly more so because she was recruited by the BoD, who passed over an internal candidate, and her wish to go for a secret investigation could have been aided by the BoD.

We can be sure of at least two outcomes if Cheryl goes for personal investigation. Company reputation is at harm, and an internal rift between the CEO and the BoD in particular is likely. But what comes across also is the plight of the company and top management if fraudulent activities are discovered with quarterly filings on the way, rumours on the brink and Sarbanes currently very strong.

Alternative 2: Give a clear message about the intention to investigate any wrong-doing – that would help Cheryl choose her friends from her enemies into her management team.

Criterion 1: Company's reputation

If she does . . . (pros)	However . . . (cons)
Due to lack of any well-established CSR committee, Cheryl will have to contact the internal audit organisation. The message would be clear about the kind of company culture Hammond supports. The culture that subsumes effort spent on	With such a positive culture, the initial teething problem in the market may not be that "teething" after all: Company shares and reputation damage, at least for the near future, are guaranteed.

If she does ... (pros)	However ... (cons)
checking loopholes, speaking out without fear, even if anonymous, would then become the talking point of Hammond, and a positive talking point, notwithstanding the corporate investigation, and even if no fire is discovered behind the smoke.	
Maybe, the BoD had decided upon an external candidate for the CEO's post to precisely bring about this ethical corporate culture in an otherwise successful company but fraught with bribery rumours. And rumours, if founded on solid grounds, might attract the ire of regulatory bodies, and the rest is history.	**But...**
A mechanism would be initiated to handle such a crisis in the future. The inner Board structure of the company is not known. Usually a publically traded US Company, like Lockheed Martin for instance, would have the CEO call a special officer like the Vice President of Ethics, who would directly contact the Board's Ethics and CR Committee. Hammond does not have one, or is not evident from the case reading, and might think it's high time to have one. Such a body under the three-frat-brothers was not a viable proposition, since Rawlings was responsible for establishing Hammond as a great company precisely using methods that have given rise to rumours of bribery.	If regulatory bodies are taken into consideration (currently CSR is increasingly becoming more than a fad; it is becoming legal), rumours of wrong-doing become fodder for government body interference and that would amount to reputation damage anyway. A strong ethical culture initiated from within the organisation would be a much more strategic face saver in the brink of rumours and possible legal interferences.

Alternative 2: Give a clear message about the intention to investigate any wrong-doing that would help Cheryl choose her friends from her enemies into her management team

Criterion 2: Cheryl's reputation

If she does . . . (pros)	However . . . (cons)
This is a crisis, but the good luck of a crisis is the revelation of the true nature of employees. Cheryl will know whom to keep in her management team.	She will have to face enemies and bad wishes from many internal management officials, particularly if the investigation turns a dud; it would cost her personal relationships with company personnel.
Moreover, Hammond's corporate culture initiated under Cheryl will be her mark on the company.	

Hence, if Cheryl openly declares her intention for investigation, *the major point to be noticed* is the defining moment of Hammond's exhibition of its corporate culture and governance, notwithstanding inevitable internal and external fallouts.

Alternative 3: Report to the Chairman (BoD) first instead of external agency

Criterion 1: Company's reputation

If she does . . . (pros)	(cons)
Bodine already openly suggested the reason for getting Cheryl into the organisation: change.	–
The Chairman, himself, accompanied Cheryl into her office as an introduction.	–
That Cheryl was offered the CEO position by the BoD of the very successful Hammond Company, notwithstanding a successful in-house executive of the hard-hitting and very profitable sales team, the commercial head, Bodine, is thought-provoking.	–
The rumours about Hammond and bribery cannot be privy to only Cheryl; the BoD would be aware of it. Hence, an external CEO may be interpreted as a strategic move from the Hammond Board.	–
The corporate change that Cheryl could bring about would be difficult under the preceding dynamic, powerful and popular Rawlings and the "three frat brothers": a stance evident by the lack of internal CSR body when Cheryl is looking for help.	–

Alternative 3: Report to the Chairman (BoD) first instead of external agency

Criterion 2: Cheryl's reputation

If she does . . . (pros)	However . . . (cons)
The regulatory bodies are becoming stronger by the day in the business world. If Cheryl plays the lone ranger, and later the BoD finds out, when they had been supportive and the recruiters themselves, they would be mighty upset, even if the case turns in favour of the senior management. Hence, support from at least one or a few of the BoD members is beneficial.	If the chairperson resents, then Cheryl will not be able to go forward with the investigation, which she initially could have on her own on the sly.
Lone ranger would mean rather than have her mark, she begins a tradition of upmanship and in-house friction. Again, the support of the chairman would bolster the value of her intentions. Remember, Bodine already expects changes.	The facts are not strong enough for a full-fledged investigation; they are doubts. If she is not sure, what will she tell the chairperson? Doubts? Hearsay?
The change that perhaps the chairperson wants through Cheryl gets initiated, and thus a corporate governance culture becomes the turning point for Hammond under the regulatory eye of the CEO and the Board.	

Thus, if Cheryl takes the Chairperson into confidence rather than play a lone ranger, the obvious benefit is the legitimation of a corporate governance culture within the organisation. Any move supported by top management silences detractors faster and with more emphasis. But if the chairperson resents the move, then what would be the repercussions.

Alternative 4: Stop digging for dirt. Too much time and effort gets consumed in an investigation when a new CEO of a leading company has many other important things to do, on a daily basis, particularly when she succeeds a popular one.

Criterion 1: Company's reputation

If Cheryl stops digging for dirt ... (pros)	cons
Things continue as they are, unless, thanks to rumours, government agencies decide to investigate.	– –

Alternative 4: Stop digging for dirt. Too much time and effort gets consumed in an investigation, when a new CEO of a leading company has many other important things to do, on a daily basis, particularly when she succeeds a popular one.

Criterion 2: Cheryl's reputation and future

Pros	Cons
	She has already sounded off Bodine and Geoffrey (two of the remaining three frat brothers). If she backs, she shows her lack of distinguishing leadership abilities. The adversaries will gain momentum over her with the idea that she can be overpowered.
	She would be living with doubts, particularly with her fear of the Sarbanes when the yearly filings are done.

Thus, stop digging for dirt is perhaps not the most ideal option for Cheryl if she has to live in doubt and fear, or if it makes her powerless in front of her adversaries in the company.

Proposal Inference *(the sister version of problem inference – you basically summarise the SWOT and domesticate the proposal)*

On considering the pros and cons of the alternatives against the criteria, we conclude that Cheryl should be advised to go for alternative 3, that is, instead of playing the lone ranger, she should sound the Chairperson on her suspicions of bribery. She would have the advantage of Option 1 and/or 2, and also avoid the disadvantage of Option 4. How is that? Option 1 is to go for an investigation, but on the sly. Under the light of our argument – that she has no facts, only doubts – she can always persuade the Chairperson for a preliminary investigation within the organisation, a report that can be kept at bay and produced only if required. But, our problem diagnosis revealed that it is not the crisis, but the management of the crisis that matters. Hence, Option 2, or making her intention public, becomes important. We have argued that with the Chairperson's backing (and if the Chairperson wants it open), the adversary problem is better controlled. Option 4 is about not digging into the dirt because Cheryl has many other activities to do as the new CEO. This is precisely why we favour our proposition of confiding in the Chairperson so that a mechanism to investigate the doubts can be set off within the organisation that allows Cheryl breathing space for her other daily activities as the new CEO of Hammond. Moreover, with the backing of the Chairman, Cheryl can initiate a CSR mechanism in the company, thus fulfilling her desire to distinguish her leadership calibre, signalling a healthy corporate culture in Hammond and getting legally armed for the Sarbanes, if and when required.

Recommendation *(sister version of Problem Statement; crisp and clear)*

Cheryl must report to the Chairman (BoD) first instead of an external agency, and not play the lone ranger. This would legitimise an initiation of a corporate governance procedure or mechanism with participation of the senior management officials and hence foster good governance culture and goodwill amidst stakeholders.

We are done with the Problem Diagnosis and the Decision Analysis aspects of an Analytical Report, and now we have to develop the Action Plan for the Proposal. If the report analyses a problem to define a recommendation, the proposal evaluates the recommendation, and the plan extensively describes the recommendation through concrete action steps, famously known as Action Plans (if we remember our Business Messages well, particularly the need for Action Plan in Apology contexts). The plan should be so described that anyone can execute the proposal. Depending on the nature of the recommendation – through foot in door, door on face, consistency reminder or through direct listing of actionable steps – the proposal is described. It is what the notation is – a plan; an executable master plan of the proposal.

– – – – – – – – – – –

Case Study 5.6: Action plan on the Cheryl case

Action Plan

The problem statement is that Hammond is lacking in corporate governance. The recommendation is that Cheryl should communicate her fears to the Chairperson, rather than play a lone ranger. So, the step that Cheryl should now take is to persuade the Chairperson to constitute an internal corporate governance mechanism on the pretext of a preliminary investigation of bribery rumours.

Cheryl's persuasive communication should be drafted accordingly with the following points:

(a) Are there facts strong enough for investigation? No. Under such circumstances, the obvious thing would be to look up for the role of ethics officer in the Board structure. There does not seem to be one.

(b) Next, Cheryl should research on the following examinations, of which outcomes should be the initiation point of conversation between Cheryl and the Chairperson:

   (1) Does Hammond support an anti-bribery compliance programme?
   (2) Does the BoD have an established procedure for such crises?
   (3) Have there been previous investigations? If yes, how were they conducted and what lessons were learnt?

It is likely that the Chairman should consider these points, particularly if there have not been measures of the kind in the board structure of Hammond.

If the Chairperson resents . . . (prepare backup plan)

(a) Cheryl can counter-argue by citing the Sarbanes Act and imminent quarterly filings, the need for establishment of a corporate governance committee/process as the first initiation towards the corporate culture.

(b) That the decision of investigation is aligned with the agenda of the senior management, and would lead to establishment of its goodwill.

(c) Particularly, bandwagoning is required for persuasion at senior management levels. In the same year, under FCPA bribery cases, Baker Hughes paid a $44 million settlement; Vetco Gray was fined $26 million.

(d) Also emphasise upon the success of voluntary disclosures – the best way to avoid criminal charges. In fact, 17/20 enforcement actions commenced because of voluntary disclosures. In 2006, Schnitzer Steel used the voluntary disclosure approach to avoid criminal prosecution.

Once the Chairperson agrees . . .

(e) Option for voluntary disclosure should affect the development of the structure and conduct of the internal audits and compliance programmes.

(f) Periodic ongoing training by experienced legal counsel for directors and senior management would be essential to prepare for more such crises in future. Such training would acquaint the senior management not just about laws and regulations, but also about ways to avoid criminal procedures, if situations come to that.

Contingency Plan *(always remember the back-up plan)*

If the Chairperson resents, then Cheryl should go back to Option 1, that is, conduct a preliminary investigation on her own with her external legal expert. She has Jackie with her, and can find similar recruits who can help the external officer conduct the investigation in privacy. The report can be prepared and shelved until required. In case of Sarbanes or the other, Cheryl can use the report to safeguard herself.

Thus, a complete report/case review is a meticulous combination of problem diagnosis, recommendation/proposal and executable action plan.

– – – – – – – –

Table 5.5 The report framework

- Framework of Objectives
  - Report Objective
  - Problem Statement
  - Decision Objective
  - Recommendation
  - Action Plan
  - Contingency Plan
- Framework of Analyses
  - Situation Analysis (sifting of data)
  - Problem Analysis (problem domestication)
  - Decision Analysis (sustaining patriotism)
- Terminologies in Analyses
  - Situation Analysis
- Taxonomy
- Problem Diagnosis
  - Verification
  - Elimination/Falsification

- Historicisation Drill
- Working Hypotheses
- Problem Domestication

- Decision Analysis

- Benchmark Matrix
- Performance Evaluation Matrix
- Domestication of Proposal

We attach for the benefit of career builders going through this work some instances of Business Proposals/Plans in their more individualistic forms. We position this format as a persuasive financial proposition for venture capitalists in particular.

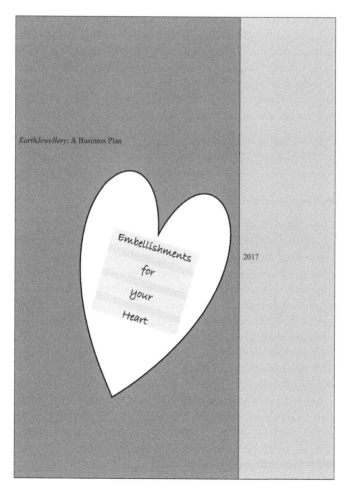

Business Plan

A business plan is a tool wielded by an entrepreneur for alluring monetary funding from venture capitalists for the ambitious expansion of his incipient business. The endeavour made is to sell one's business concept as an innovative idea that can churn out profits.

Case Study 5.7: How to attract venture capitalists for *EarthJewellery*

Script 5.4 *EarthJewellery* case

A woman entrepreneur has opened a kiosk for artificial designer jewellery and fashion accessories in a big shopping mall with the brand name of *EarthJewellery*. She has an innovative idea of selling customised jewellery as per the requirements of her clients by offering them a free fashion consultancy. She is a qualified fashion jewellery designer and has a vision to convert this nascent kiosk into a full-fledged studio. To transmute this vision into a reality she needs financing from some venture capitalists.

The ensuing business plan exemplifies drafting a blueprint of a business idea for selling it to a financier.

Executive summary

EarthJewellery is a new company offering its business in the format of a kiosk which assembles different earth metal pieces to create customised designs for earrings, necklaces, chokers and rings for customers accessorising their wardrobe. Though the concept of junk jewellery is not novel in the market, the market void exists in terms of lack of customised design options as conceptualised by the customers. *EarthJewellery* presents this experience of creating one's own designs with the help of its expert professionals who would show catalogues to the customers of various designs and colours available, and assist customers in choosing the patterns they want.

EarthJewellery is a company of sole proprietorship. Sheena Kochar is the owner of it. She has established the company outlet of *EarthJewellery* recently in April 2015 inside South City Mall, Kolkata.

Though there are many business establishments selling junk jewellery, most of them are focussing on selling ready-made designs with a plethora of hackneyed replicas in patterns and colours.

This company is likely to survive this stiff competition by virtue of the merits listed below:

- The jewellery is completely handmade and displays intricate designs.
- Each design is unique and is not duplicated. It is like wearing a boutique piece, the only one of its kind.
- The jewellery is skin-friendly and non-allergic with medicinal value, the feature conspicuous by its absence in other jewellery marketed in such big malls.
- None of the jewellery stores located in South City Mall make customised customer-ordered designs or offer fashion consultancy.

The sole owner of this company outlet kiosk is Sheena Kochar. She has over 10 years of experience in designing and crafting jewellery. She graduated in jewellery design from the National Institute of Arts & Fashion, New Delhi, which is a NAAC-accredited institute. Though Sheena Kochar will handle the entire business herself for a year or so, she plans to hire two artisans-cum-sales representatives. She will take care of procuring supplies, warehousing the material and keeping the inventory.

The business concept

EarthJewellery is a new company offering its business in the format of a kiosk which assembles different earth metal pieces to create custom-ised designs for earrings, necklaces, chokers and rings for customers who are fond of accessorising their wardrobe. Though the concept of junk jewellery is not novel in the market, the market void exists in terms of lack of customised design options as conceptualised by the customers. *EarthJewellery* presents this experience of creating one's own designs with the help of its expert professionals who would show catalogues to the customers of various designs and colours available, and assist customers in choosing the patterns they want. Since the creation will essentially be an assemblage of variegated metal pieces and stones, it won't take much time – as soon as the customer finalises the design, the jewellery will be ready in just 15–20 minutes of time.

Though gold, silver and diamond jewellery are still in demand, but owing to the advent of the trend of designer dresses, there is a huge demand for junk metal jewellery which can give you a funky, classy and soiree look at affordable prices exactly matching the tints of your dress. This fad for junk jewellery has gained momentum to such an extent that now apparel manufacturers showcase their dresses paired up with customised jewellery that befits the accessory requirement of the dress to give the customer an experience of a complete makeover.

Since the business is of artificial jewellery, which involves small items, it does not need elaborate operations plans.

In the first year of its operation, Sheena will handle the financing part of the business on her own, but as the business expands she would need external funding for its expansion. Moreover, as she has an ambition of carving out a pan-India presence, funding from venture capitalists will be required for this expansion. She does not envisage huge profit margins at the outset and hopes to reach a break-even point at the end of this year. If the business starts churning out profit from next year, she is interested in converting her kiosk into a studio, opening up her own chain of company outlets in all the metropolitan cities in the first phase of expansion. If the response is good, second tier cities will also be targeted.

Company description

EarthJewellery is a company of sole proprietorship. Sheena Kochar is the owner of it. She has established the company outlet of *EarthJewellery* recently in April 2015 inside South City Mall, Kolkata as shop no. G 11 located on the ground floor in front of Wills Lifestyle, a strategic location with high visibility among customers who are aficionados of high-end fashion trends. It showcases completely handmade and eco-friendly terracotta jewellery made of crafts which have medicinal value, and are skin friendly as well as non-allergic. The material is baked at 1000 degrees centigrade and is cast in unique, trendy and traditional designs displaying soothing and scintillating colours. The gamut of product range covers a wide variety of jewellery comprising neck pieces, earrings, bracelets, anklets and rings. This kiosk also accepts orders from boutiques for customised designs with matching colours that complement their dresses. The unique selling proposition of this business is the offer of free consultation to customers. We have also developed a mobile application that updates the customers regarding changing fashion scenarios, as the fashion industry is highly volatile. The target end consumers of the products would be professional and socially active women.

The business hours of the kiosk would be 11.00 am to 9.00 pm, and it would be open seven days a week.

EarthJewellery products and services

The kiosk will house a wide variety of metals – at least 10 different varieties in 50 diverse shades with varying tints. We have, right now, two fashion jewellery designers who have worked in big factory outlets in the past and have rich experience designing jewellery as per the taste of a customer. The kiosk, which is, at present, housed in South City Mall, Prince Anwar Shah Road, Kolkata has the potential to develop a franchise with its chain of multiple kiosks located all over India. We will eventually try to tap the online market too, employing e-commerce tools.

We would also house junk jewellery for kids and jewellery for gifting which men can buy for their female companions.

The business objectives

The salient business objectives for this kiosk include the following:

- To create customised designs for jewellery targeting especially young college-going girls and working women in the age range of 20 to 35 years.
- To innovate fusion designs by producing patterned jewellery that complements both Western and ethnic female attire.
- To focus on the use of earth metals to launch jewellery which has a neo-tribal look for women who yearn to experiment with their looks.
- To collaborate with leading apparel fashion designers for getting updated consultations on the emerging trends in the Indian fashion industry.
- To become an all-India fashion label in the next five years.

Market strategy

The store is located in front of Wills Lifestyle store in South City Mall on the ground floor. It is a very strategic location with high visibility right in front of the main entrance of the mall. Since the store is flanked with other stores selling high-end fashion apparel, it is likely to become a cynosure for customers looking for jewellery to team up with their fashionable costumes. It also has in its vicinity a store for kids' apparel, the Little Betty Blue. Though this store also domiciles some artificial junk jewellery for kids, its range is limited. Hence, *EarthJewellery* will carry some junk jewellery for small girls in the range of 5 to 13 years too.

Though there are many business establishments selling junk jewellery, most of them are focussing on selling readymade designs with a plethora of hackneyed replicas in patterns and colours. The store has flamboyant interiors which is likely to grab eyeballs. Sales personnel are attired in attractive uniforms displaying the name and logo of the kiosk to create an upscale image. We are also planning to place big hoardings of our studio throughout the mall and on roads in areas that are well known for their affluent residencies. In addition to these moves, we will team up with some apparel stores which will prominently display our posters, thereby guiding customers to find companion pieces for their couture in our stores. Since the unique selling proposition of our store is customised designs and free fashion consultancy, our hoardings will flash our promotional taglines reading "fashioning your creativity".

We have an access to a large database of mobile numbers in areas like Alipore, which is primarily a high-class businessperson locality in Rajarhat Salt Lake, where many NRIs reside when they come to India for a brief sojourn. These will be the places where young women would be interested in the kind of fashion jewellery we exhibit and would look for pieces which have no cloned verisimilitude in general jewellery markets and hence are exclusively boutique-bred. We will send our promotional messages to these mobile numbers with images of our latest designs with some first time buyer discounts.

There are many exclusive jewellery sites located in the basement of South City mall which have an already established business stature. But this business is likely to survive this stiff competition by virtue of the merits listed below:

- The jewellery is completely handmade and displays intricate designs.
- Each design is unique and is not duplicated. It is like wearing a boutique piece, the only one of its kind.
- The jewellery is skin-friendly and non-allergic with medicinal value, the feature conspicuous by its absence in other jewellery marketed in such big malls.
- None of these stores make customised customer-ordered designs.
- None of them offer fashion consultancy.

With these aforementioned new offerings we hope to create a niche for our label in the fashion market.

We also would team up with some leading boutiques in the city to procure space for displaying our craft since these boutiques are frequented mostly by women who value innovation in fashion and can afford it.

Customer feedback will be mandatory at the time of billing. To incentivise customer feedback, we will offer a 10% discount on the next billing on a minimum purchase of 2000 INR. This feedback will help us mint new organic designs which will stand out in the market as peerless art.

Operations plan – inventory management

Since the business is of artificial jewellery which involves small items, it does not need elaborate operations plans. All the material will be procured by Sheena, who has contacts with many artisans in Jaipur, and the stock would be stored at Sheena's residence. She will move this stock to her store as per the requirement, and her trained staff would assemble this craft-material to make customised jewellery as ordered by the customers. Some designs will be made in consonance with the latest fashion trends and will be displayed in the studio for sale. Sheena will handle all the inventory management.

Financial projections

In the first year of its operation, Sheena will handle the financing part of the business on her own; but as the business expands she would need external funding for its expansion. Moreover, as she has an ambition of carving out a pan-India presence, funding from venture capitalists will be required for this expansion. The jewellery price range starts from 1000/- per piece and goes up to 5000/- per piece, depending on the material used and the intricacy of its handmade craftsmanship. It targets upper-middle-class to rich-class women. She does not envisage huge profit margins at the outset and hopes to reach a break-even point at the end of this year. If the business starts churning out profit from next year, she is interested in converting her kiosk into a studio, opening up her own chain of company outlets in all the metropolitan cities in the first phase of expansion. If the response is good, second tier cities will also be targeted. In the future we also plan to enhance our product range by including flamboyant clutches matching the costume jewellery.

To begin with, we concentrate on Kolkata as it has 61% population of women, which account for a huge customer base for our products. Out of this 61%, 50% of women are working with large purchasing power, which serves as an indicator of a good forecast for our business. Bengali community is mostly sophisticated – Bengalis are good connoisseurs of art. In the South, there is a fetish for gold, but Bengalis try to experiment with their styles as many of them are associated with theatre or some kind of socio-cultural activity.

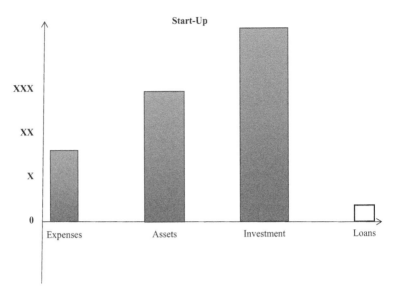

Figure 5.1 Start-up description

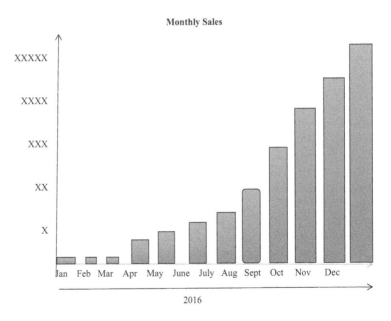

Figure 5.2 Monthly sales description

Management personnel

The sole owner of this company outlet kiosk is Sheena Kochar. She has over ten years of experience in designing and crafting jewellery. She graduated in jewellery design from the National Institute of Arts & Fashion, New Delhi, which is a NAAC-accredited institute. After graduating, she worked with several well-known companies in jewellery design in different parts of India. It was in Jaipur that she met Samaira Mahatani who specialises in terracotta jewellery. She worked with her for two years in Jaipur as a business partner and then decided to open her own outlet in Kolkata as a sole proprietor.

Though Sheena Kochar will handle the entire business herself for a year or so, she plans to hire two artisans-cum-sales representatives who are dexterous in the realm of jewellery design by dint of their work experience and formal degrees in jewellery designing courses. She will take care of procuring supplies, warehousing the material and keeping the inventory. Since Sheena does not have background of accountancy, she will hire an accountant qualified in bookkeeping for handing cash flows and other financial transactions.

Appendices

- Images of latest jewellery designs
- Images of store
- Financial information

The framework for the business plan – the octagon matrix for venture capitalists

So, what we need to extract from the attempted exercise is how to package an entire Action Plan into an attractive Business Plan for venture capitalists. We also call it the Octagon Matrix Strategy that has a threefold mission:

- The motive – to captivate capital investment,
- Agenda – to give a holistic view of a business evolution from infancy to maturity and
- Executive summary – to present the entire body text in just one-eighth of its total verbal volume so that the busy venture

capitalists can get a quick overview of the entire plan. To author it in an interesting way so that the reader is tempted to read the entire text.

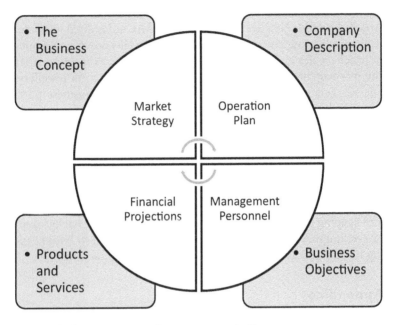

Figure 5.3 Octagon matrix for venture capitalists

The Octagon Matrix has an outer layer and an inner layer. The outer layer has the more qualitative, visionary and philosophical aspects of the project. We call them the Grand Narratives.

Grand narratives of the Octagon Matrix

(1) **Business Concept** – to describe how your business offering stands a sanguine chance of capturing the market by discovering a void hitherto not ravaged by business masterminds.

(2) **Company Description** – to describe the company: when it was established, when it became operational, who is the owner, where it is located, what is the current status of its business proliferation. It should prove that the business concept is no longer a fancy idea and has already materialised in its infancy

and thus can easily evolve into a prosperous venture with some funding support.

(3) **Products and Services** – to catalogue the specific products and services that the company outlet offers.

(4) **Business Objectives** – to delineate the vision for the business which promises a resplendent future. The objectives are written in bulleted points so that it gives the vision an actionable look.

The inner layer has more of the four mainstream management quarters, like marketing, finance, operations and human resource. They are the material projections of the outer Grand Narratives! We call them the Venture Capital Segment of the Octagon Matrix.

Venture capital segment of the Octagon Matrix

(1) **Market Strategy** – to position your business in such a way that you can convince the financier that your business can cut through the competitive clutter and carve a niche for itself. One should be clear about who would be one's target consumers and what specific plans s/he has to reach out to these target consumers, keeping in perspective their psycho-demographic profiling. To showcase new ways of promoting business that is likely to entice customers to invest their money into your products and services. An attempt is made to demonstrate that your business is unique. This is the most important section of a business plan.

(2) **Operation Plan** – to outline inventory management and the operations plan to show how stocks will be procured, warehoused and moved for sale and who would be at the helm of affairs.

(3) **Financial Projections** – to demonstrate that you have done your number work well. You can forecast a certain tentative profit range and in the immediate future can at least recoup the expenditure made. Present fiscal details in the form of tables, charts and graphs so that the financier is convinced that her money will not be lost.

(4) **Management Personnel** – to build credibility by giving credentials of the people manning the company: how they are qualified by virtue of their formal training from reputed institutes and their work experience, and/or by dint of their internship or partnership with well-known names of their business field.

In a similar manner, let us now try an independent Business Proposal as an attractive form of persuasion for *EarthJewellery*.

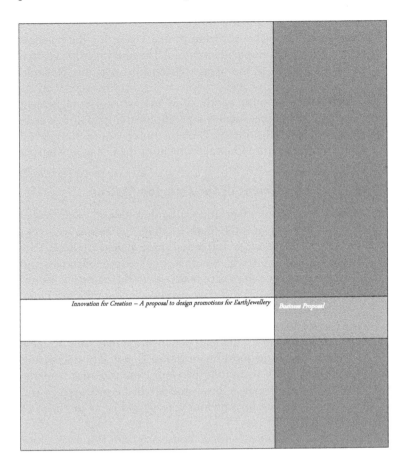

Innovation for Creation – A proposal to design promotions for EarthJewellery   *Business Proposal*

A business proposal is a special genre of analytical report prepared to present products, plans, projects, services or ideas for sale. The objective of writing business proposals is to get new orders, new customers or new business partners. A proposal may take the form of a bid on a contract or a business offer to a government authority or another company/organisation. It is basically a persuasive communication designing the résumé of your company to attract new business. A proposal suggests a plan of action for the reader's benefit.

Case Study 5.8: How to propose a business partnership with *EarthJewellery*

Script 5.5 *EarthJewellery* (Continued)

> As a sequel to the business plan on the jewellery enterprise, let us take up the case of a marketing company called *Biz & Gliz* which is willing to undertake the job of promoting a new fashion brand like *EarthJewellery* first at a local level and then at a national level.

The following is the business proposal by *Biz & Glitz* submitted to *EarthJewellery* seeking a business alliance as a compatible marketing partner.

Executive summary

Biz & Glitz is an advertising agency which would like to work with you on designing promotions for your *EarthJewellery* creations. We are a ten-year-old company with a track record of many successful promotional campaigns, particularly in the fashion industry. Our proposed objective is to publicise the creative craftsmanship of *EarthJewellery* in a way that accentuates the innovation it brings to the fashion jewellery market, pitching it as a unique business and service provider breaking the clutter of a highly competitive and volatile vogue market.

The following is the list of some of the prominent marketing pushups we propose to undertake for you:

- Designing artistic billboards
- Designing print ads and newspaper inserts
- Organising events
- Mapping digital marketing
- Advertising on local cable networks
- Networking with prominent boutiques, to name a few

We have extremely qualified management graduates with a major in marketing and work experience in the range of five to ten years.

Some of them are natives of Kolkata and understand the culture and the taste of the Kolkatans. We have employed people with management diplomas with an experience in marketing in the fashion industry.

Since it is a new business we understand that the economics of marketing is a major issue, hence we provide a marketing package in an affordable range which other companies do not provide. We also would apprise you about tools of evaluation by which you can calibrate the usefulness of our marketing strategies, so that you can understand whether you are getting the desired returns on your investment.

Introduction

Biz & Glitz is an advertising agency which would like to work with you on designing promotions for your *EarthJewellery* creations. Recently we came across a hoarding promoting your label. We really liked your concept of offering customised jewellery designs and offering fashion consultancy which are veritable new offerings in this business. We thought we could do good promotional work for you, and hence, we decided to present this proposal.

We are a ten-year-old company with a track record of many successful promotional campaigns, particularly in the fashion industry. We have done a lot of comparable work in fashion advertising as listed in our appendix. We got national recognition for our performance when we received the prestigious Best Label for Fashion Advertising trophy in the recent NDTV Corporate Marketing Awards, 2015.

The proposal submitted presents the following sections: a clear statement of need which tries to capture your exact requirements, and a project description where we detail out as to how we will lay out our promotional plans for your brand. We will also plot a timeline for various promotional activities and suggest ways in which you can evaluate our output.

In the section on project management we will introduce you to people who would work for you with their qualifications and experience. This section will be followed by a write-up on the budget, thus presenting the financials involved. Finally, we have a section on organisational information where we tell you about our company.

In the appendix you can see a list of the clients with their contact details for whom we have been working. Some samples are also attached of the promotional work we have done for others along with the snippets of the work we can do for you.

Statement of need

To publicise the creative craftsmanship of *EarthJewellery* in a way that accentuates the innovation it brings to the fashion jewellery market, pitching it as a unique business and service provider breaking the clutter of a highly competitive and volatile vogue market.

Project description

Promotion is particularly important for a business like yours since there is stiff competition in the realm of your product. There are many business outlets that offer analogous products which might cannibalise your market. It is important for you to stand out not just because you need to survive, but also because you deserve to stand out since very few businesses like yours must be offering custom-made designs complemented with free fashion consultancy. This message should reach out to your target market.

The objective of this proposal is to devise a marketing plan customised to the special needs of a nascent but innovative fashion brand. We specifically specialise in formulating marketing strategies for businesses that bring new offerings to the table. For example, we have worked with *Tulip*, a fashion label in Delhi that had the unique distinction of making trendy footwear with acupressure therapy advantages. In the first year of its operation it could not draw much business. It is then that they approached us. We worked out many marketing strategies for them, which spiked their sales the next year, and now they are a very well established business house with its operations expanding to ten major cities of the country. Anika Khanna, the owner of this business, is one of the distinguished members of our client list which is provided in the appendix section of this proposal. Her contact details are provided. You can talk to her as a reference and get first-hand feedback of the kind of work we are capable of doing here.

We have worked with several first-time businesswomen like you and have helped them take their businesses to a whole new level.

We propose to do the following for your business:

- Design artistic billboards that attract attention by offering a great palette of colours in abstract designs echoing the creations of Paul Klee with catchy taglines like *fashioning fashion for fabulous females*, for example. These billboards will be displayed in all the prominent malls of Kolkata.
- Alluring print ads for the Calcutta Times, particularly during festival season, displaying a contemporary Tollywood actress who is a glamour icon for young women.
- Printing newspaper inserts for English newspapers like *The Telegraph* and *The Times of India* (as we are targeting English-speaking, upper-class women).
- Organising events in malls, giving prizes like the soiree cynosure prizes for women, displaying a perfect combination of couture and the companion matching fashion jewellery.
- Launching a Facebook page.
- Planning email/SMS campaigns.
- Distributing pamphlets at the entrance of the major malls of the city.
- Arranging kiosks during festive occasions in upscale residential complexes.
- Advertising on local cable networks.
- Networking with prominent boutiques of the city to showcase our creations custom-made for some of their designer apparels.

We have also devised to calibrate our impact factor. These are some of the evaluation methods you can use to rate us.

How can you rate us?

- On your feedback forms include one question which will interrogate them about the whereabouts of the information they got about your business.
- You can compare the sales figures before and after this marketing alliance.
- You can check on Facebook Twitter accounts as your feedback meters mapping the customer responses.

Project management

We have extremely qualified management graduates with a major in marketing and work experience in the range of five to ten years.

Some of them are natives of Kolkata and understand the culture and the taste of the Kolkatans. They know what persuasion tactics work with people. In our workforce we are proud to claim that the gender ratio is not skewed. We have 50% female managers who would be well-suited for your job since they are young and enterprising. They will bring to the table new ideas to promote the kind of products you sell, as your products target female customers. If you wish, we can arrange your appointment with Ms. Monica Halder, who has particularly received encomium for her marketing prowess from our clients. She will give a presentation on the innovative marketing we practice. Ms. Rituparna Sen is another star performer of our team who has experience in promoting jewellery products. She has worked for *Malabar Gold* and *Tanishq* outlets in Kolkata. Both these managers have PGPDBM with a major in Marketing from the Global Institute of Management, Lucknow, which is one of the top ten management institutes in India.

Budget

Given below is the budget to cover the expenses of all these promotional activities.

Table 5.6 Budget details

Promotional activity	Expenses involved
Creative hoardings for major residential/shopping areas of Kolkata	XXX
Print ads in major newspapers in wide circulation in Kolkata	XXX
Event management	XXX
Digital marketing	XXX
Advertising on local TV channels	XXX
Miscellaneous	XXX

Since it is a new business, we understand that the economics of marketing is a major issue, hence we provide a marketing package in an affordable range which other companies do not provide. We also would apprise you about the tools of evaluation by which you can calibrate the success of our marketing strategies, so that you can understand whether you are getting the desired return on your investment.

Organisation information (qualifications)

Our company started its operations in the year 2000. The company was set-up by two senior management professionals who had worked for almost ten years in marketing positions in reputed companies based in Mumbai, which is the showbiz capital of our country. We began by identifying our niche functionality by doing marketing jobs for business establishments which are predominantly in the fashion industry. This helped us in understanding the requirements of this industry more profoundly, so that we could give specialised marketing offers to players in the fashion industry. With this vision in mind, we employed people with management diplomas with an experience in marketing in the fashion industry. All our marketing professionals are from renowned government/ private management institutes of the country with at least three years of work experience. We have attached our company brochure with this proposal. In the brochure you can see our clientele. We have given contact details of all our major clients in case you want to get feedback regarding the quality of our work output. We are also enclosing some samples of the promotional job we have done for some upcoming fashion brands in cities like Delhi and Mumbai. Also find attached testimonials by marketing experts and excerpts from our client feedback to know us better.

Conclusion

Biz & Glitz is the right marketing partner for *EarthJewellery*. Given our specialisation in the fashion industry, we can offer you perfect solutions to your marketing needs. Please contact Rilekha Mehra at rilekhamehra@gmail.com to get the visibility, viability and vision for promoting your pioneering brand as a premium fashion segment.

Appendix

- Company Brochure
- Budget statement
- Sample of the Company Work
- Expert/Client Testimonials

Framework for business proposal

The following framework may be derived from the given business proposal as a guideline for new proposal writers.

Title – Should be concise, preferably ten words. Take the "Who" and "How" question exercise that the title should address. Should be easy to remember, since these titles will be used for identification. Avoid titles commencing with "A Study of . . ." or "An Examination of . . . ."; use descriptive adjective-noun combinations.

Executive Summary – Should contain the following heads:

- Problem – A brief statement of the problem or need your agency has recognised and is prepared to address (one or two paragraphs).
- Solution – Short description of the project, including the work plan, how and where it will operate, for how long and who will staff it (one or two paragraphs).
- Funding Requirements – Explanation of the amount of grant money required for the project and what your plans are for funding it in the future (one paragraph).
- Organisation and its Expertise – Brief statement of the name, history, purpose and activities of your agency, emphasising its capacity to carry out this proposal (one paragraph).

Introduction – Introduce yourself along with your company. Give a reason for writing up the proposal and create a quick credibility statement to build trust for your brand. Additionally offer a preview guiding the reader to peruse the structural evolution of your proposal. Thus an introduction should:

- Indicate that the document to follow is a proposal.
- Refer to some previous contact with the recipient of the proposal or your source of information about the project.
- Find one brief motivating statement that will encourage the recipient to read on and to consider doing the project.
- Give an overview of the contents of the proposal.

Statement of Need – Identify, state and describe the problem or need the reader is facing. Convince her that you understand her need precisely and hence represent a perfect business companion to offer a solution customised to her unique need. Thus spot the need-void and propose to fill up this void. Sell yourself by proving that you are the right party to comprehend the problem, and offer customised solutions to survive the competition offered by other vying product/service providers in your arena. If pertinent, mention difficulties that may be encountered and consider how you propose to overcome them. Your purpose is often stated in infinitive form. Thus, a statement of need should

- Give the background that had led to the emergence of the need or the problem demonstrating your particular view of the problem.
- Present the facts and evidence that support the need for the project.

Project Description – Prove with specifics how you can offer the best solution to the given problem. Give action points and map your entire work plan with graphed timelines. This is the site to prove your specialisation by describing/providing excerpts of your erstwhile work for comparable clients in analogous situations. It has five subsections:

- Objectives
- Methods
- Staffing/Administration
- Evaluation
- Sustainability

This then becomes the locus of the evaluation to assess the results of the project.

Project Management – Give the chronological graph of the work plan with the curriculum vitae of the management personnel manning it. Sell your team by giving their credentials to prove that they are the best human resource to work for your prospective client who is reading your proposal, citing their names and other details for building credibility.

Budget – Give budgetary details. Provide graphs/charts to demonstrate that you have planned the economics of the marketing with all its nitty-gritties. Establish the fiscal sustainability of the proposal. Give the timeline for payments to be made with detailed expenditure breakups to substantiate the suitability of the capital you demand as your fee.

Organization Information – Attach the brochure of your company which is visually attractive, containing all the details of the expanse of the business you command. Prepare it as the résumé of your company to fetch the coveted recruitment with your prospective client.

Conclusion – This is your last selling stroke. End with reinforcing your position as the best solution provider in the given market, outlining your unique selling proposition.

Appendix – Give a sample of your work, client lists and other documents that can bolster your credibility.

Case Study 5.9:   On Southland Bakery

Let us try cracking another Harvard case, this time Ben Gerson's *Taking the Cake* (see Appendix).[9] While doing so, we also add another feature of case analysis, which is audience profiling of the executive team to which the proposal is pitched for recommendation. The audience profiling might be necessary to help the persuader to know how to pitch *dummy* alternatives. And when do we pitch *dummy* alternatives? When we want to *lead* a low-interest audience to our side of the problem. And to do that, we need to refer back to our persuasion shield – give them what they want to get what you want from them. We call this the Dummy Alternative Framework of Analytical Report/Proposal/Plan.

Situation Analysis

*   Major Characters and their profiles

Table 5.7 Profiling characters

Characters	Background	Track record
Alex Kezenas	Glad-handing plaintiff's lawyer	Persuaded a rural jury to assess actual and punitive damages against the Old Cherokee Tobacco Company totaling up to $12.1 million.

(Continued)

Table 5.7 (Continued)

Characters	Background	Track record
Peter Schimdt	Erstwhile counsel to the subcommittee on food and drugs	Did damage control of the bankruptcy of *Aunt Emmy*, a Tennessee pie company.
Richie Snell	Southland Baking Company's director of government affairs	
Ed Malanga	CEO, Southland	Instrumental in promoting Peter Schimdt as Southlands' VP & General Counsel post his saving *Aunt Emmy*. Complacent and confident; gives no importance to advertising.
Mrs. Newland	President, MOOK	Architect of menace in the making.
Ray Slocum	Representative, New Hampshire Republic	
Larry Fischer	Chicago Democrat	
Lou Salvador	Vice-President, Southland Company	Shows intense interest in competitors' product innovation.
Fred Rangle	Southland's chief scientist	Believes that only taste works (derives inference from experience).
Mary Cairnoss	Southland's dietician	
Millie Lepore	Southland's chief dietician	Played a significant role in formulating the original version of the *Mellobar*, Southland's best-selling product, which always came down on the side of nutrition.

- Lawsuit menace
    - Even baseless suit is a headache and money for a company.
    - MOOK's president's recommendation: Mandate warning labels on all foods containing sugars and saturated fats

and ban advertising of all such products on children's TV programmes.

- With health menace suits there is little chance of survival.
- Courts become policy makers when Congress doesn't.
- Companies failing to warn consumers can be tried in court (corporate social responsibility is no longer voluntary but mandatory).
- Earlier only cigarette packs warned – now fats are analogous to tobacco in this matter.
- The concept of safe cigarettes could be sued by courts as argumentation fallacies; point to be noted by food companies following the strategy of producing safer versions of their erstwhile fat laden products.
- Safe cigarettes and improved chizzlewits proved failures.
- Tobacco regulation prohibits marketing to minor, and most of Southland's major consumers are kids.
- Trans fats equated to tobacco – artefacts of manufacturing process not considered as food.
- Law in general holds manufacturers as experts.
- Defective product claim, the most likely lawsuit point.
- Trial lawyer in West Virginia filed suit against Southland.

- Political moves

  - House subcommittee on Food & Drug holding hearings on child obesity and fat content of baked goods.
  - Membership status of cabinets – political opinion leaders on health issues

    - How subcommittee on Food & Drug membership had incumbency prevailing for last ten years – no new ideas harvested.
    - Subcommittee had testimony of (a) scientists, (b) educators and (c) consumer advocates.

- Southland's track record of acquisitions – major blunders of business decision-Making

  - *Aunt Emmy*, a Tennessee Pie company, went bankrupt. Required Southland's legal expert to restore profitability.

- Problematising food companies' stance of "a part of a balanced diet" stricture – arguments against fast food companies:

- Defence by fast food companies – fast food is a part of balanced diet and hence cannot become sole food substitute.

    - The MOOK president's act of problematising this stand by the following arguments:

        o   Balanced diet is not possible owing to current lifestyle.
        o   Working parents have no time to stop to buy vegetables and protein; they get back home too late to cook.
        o   Public schools have vending machines dispensing easy fast food.
        o   Public schools house fast food franchises and allow fast food advertising on TV monitors that are donated by fast food companies.
        o   Obesity is a greater threat than alcohol and tobacco; can trigger heart diseases and cancer.
        o   Diet is a habit which develops from childhood; hence, obese children become obese adults.

- Arguments in favour of fast food companies

    - The United States is not a "mommy state"; it is a nation of free citizens where information is available in abundance and there is a great degree of transparency in disseminating information.
    - Since 1990, listing the levels of calories, fat, cholesterol and sodium mandated by the Food and Drug Administration; in 2006 stating the levels of trans fats mandated – offering enough protection for a nation of free citizens.

- Support "for" and "against" fast food

Table 5.8 Report on fast food reception

Support for fat food	Support against fat food
New Hampshire Republic	MOOK
Chicago democrat, Larry Fischer, apprehensive of the inevitability of warning mandate	Precedents – Cherokee Tobacco case/ Packaged food company case

- Cultural DNA

    Southeast and Middle Atlantic states evinced strong predilection for fast food. In the United States, obesity is a national problem – 20% of the population is obese (61% up since 1991); widespread problem – obesity no longer remains a personal issue but has become a national agenda, a national problem particularly affecting children.

- Southland – company history and market

  - Is the third largest cookie company in the United States.
  - Has a strong foothold in second and third tier towns (obviously populated by people not very intellectually agile to bother about health implications of fast food consumption).
  - Produces *Mellobar*, its best-selling product – outdated yet continuing to sell, has transitioned from breakfast food to snack. Thus Southland comes out as a company which is still resting on past laurels, having done nothing to tip over the nutritional claims of its products.
  - Records current sales as promising – 11% up from last year's figures.

- Southland's vulnerability profile

  - The nutritional claims of *Mellobar*, the bestselling product of Southland, disappeared from its wrapper.
  - Healthy brands cropping up with honey instead of sugar, with canola or palm oil, which have not been hydrogenated, used as healthy ingredients. Collectively these brands are eating up Southland's market share.
  - Major competitors like *Sweetena*, which is the biggest competitor of *Mellobar*, gradually are offering healthier versions of their products by reducing their fat content by 50%.
  - Slotting fee though has gone up; the profit of Southland is more than that of the last year, which presents a contradictory fact.
  - Southland had put up a test trial of healthier product innovation but failed. The outcome was only "tasty is trendy".
  - Saturated fat – any change in formulation processes is risky because (a) it drives up the costs and (b) it drives away loyal customers who cannot pay premium prices – since these are second and third tier city customers. This fact presents strong economic evidence against any change directed.
  - Trans fats have zero nutritional value and this presents scientific evidence. Both economic and scientific evidence are

antithetical, which makes the problem faced by Southland more complex.

- Environmental issue is one more stumbling block since Malaysia, which is the palm oil plantation destination, is liable to attacks by environmental evangelists for deforestation undertaken to give way to palm oil plantations.
- Southland's decision to stress flavour is a design choice that accentuates sales at the expense of health.

Problem Analysis

Explanation I for Case Study 5.9

Let us understand the Problem Analysis as a structural pyramid shaped endeavour. A Problem Statement is the final tiptop of the triangle, built on two layers of Problem Inference (middle of the pyramid) and Problem Diagnosis process (Bottom of the Pyramid).

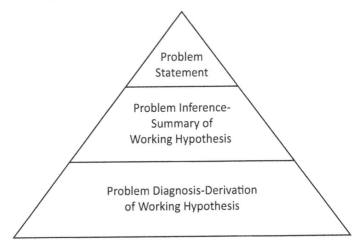

Figure 5.4 Problem processing pyramid

Problem Processing Pyramid – Entails a three-step process for exploring the problem camouflaged in the complexity of the synthetic information available in the case, starting with diagnosing a problem by advancing working hypotheses, deriving problem inferences by summarising those hypotheses and lastly by encasing the problem precisely in one crisp mathematical statement that guides the progression of the analysis.

Problem diagnosis

Symptom 1 – Market menace

(1) Small brands together bundled up as collective menace; (2) Biggest competitor, *Sweetena*

Case in point – Market is nimble and not static. The current phase is of product innovation triggered by lawsuits. Only Southland is a food company resting on past laurels.

Problematisation – *Mellobar* still continues when its biggest competitor, *Sweetena*, is changing. Though Southland proposes through its failed Chizzlewit experiment that taste is predominant, cases of diet Soda and sugar free chewing gums in the 1980s and 1990s were successful in pioneering diet nutrition in the United States. Soda and chewing gum belong to the same genre as snacks – "sinful products".[10] These changes were not pre-empted but were reactionary in nature.

Working hypothesis 1 – Need for a company to recast market reactions into a positive product innovation

Symptom 2 – Legal menace

Cherokee, packaged food, MOOK and the recent Southland lawsuit from Virginia – Law as the company policy maker.

Case in point – Manufacturers are now positioned by lawmakers as experts, and hence they have now become more accountable and vulnerable. In this context, trans fats are no more natural food products but are now branded as an evil produced by processes legitimised by manufacturing processes. On the other hand, cases like that of *Kraft Food* demonstrate that once you succumb to legal coercion you set up a precedent which triggers a chain reaction.

Small coteries of public health crusaders and activists are becoming strong policy decision makers in organisations in matters pertaining to ethical propriety.

Problemtaisation: However, even healthy is not wealthy.

(a) Any ingredient, even if low fat, can be problematised (low fat content triggering tendency to eat more). Even the use of so-called "healthy" palm oil can raise cholesterol levels.
(b) The availability of healthy ingredients like palm oil is fraught with uncertainties since palm oil plantations are increasingly under the scanner for environmental concerns.

Working hypothesis 2 – Need for a company to understand that succumbing to any legal pressure is like inaugurating a tradition of cumulative cascading compliance through coercion which eventually can cripple its autonomy as a corporate entity.

Symptom 3 – Convenience of using tobacco as analogy

• Safe cigarettes, like chizzlewits experiment, failed miserably.
• Legally, the concept of safe cigarettes becomes a logical fallacy since it entails confession of selling unsafe products earlier; point to be noted by food companies following the strategy of producing safer versions of their erstwhile fat-laden products.

Case in point: Big tobacco settlement forbid marketing products that may have some issues related to health of minors, which further aggravates the problem of Southland since major consumers of Southland's products are kids. Moreover, trans fats have been positioned as a health menace like tobacco and hence have the potential to undergo the same stringent strictures. Earlier cigarette companies were forced to put warnings on cigarette packs and now the fat foods will meet the same fate.

Problematisation – Analogy to tobacco is magnifying the problem. Thus, if trans fats are positioned as evil – on equal footing as tobacco – it will be bracketed with "sinful products", culminating into an exponential increase in taxation that will fill up government coffers. On the other hand, food experts can position "health-conscious ingredients" like low fat palm oil which are being touted as a healthy replacement of trans fats as equally deleterious to health.

Working hypothesis 3 – Food industry is becoming easy bait to the taxation lobby.

Symptom 4 – Second/third tier consumers' vulnerabilities

(1) Brand positioning – Southland commands second and third tier markets in Southeast as well as the Middle Atlantic states.

(2) These consumers demonstrate the cultural habit of relishing food which is steeped in fat.

(3) For product innovation and spearheading new trends these markets cannot act as sites of change – places like New York or California can only afford to be the pioneers; but, unfortunately, these places do not have a strong hold of Southland presence.

Problematisation – Notwithstanding the immutable loyalty of the consumer segment of Southland, the very fact that products like *Sweetena*, *Debbie's Blondes*, *Greg's Passion Cakes* and *Pacific Maca-Mania Bits* are able to invade the market space of Southland shows that markets can show amazingly unexpected agility, and businesses have to be nimble to address such volatilities.

Since long-term loyalty, though apparently an epitome of strength, can, in fact, recast itself as a market menace, which when stretched beyond a certain limit can be disrupted very easily. Southland cannot afford to ignore this **elastic theory** and stay complacent with its current business revenues. Hence, any brand with a long-term legacy of loyal consumers should come out with its own defence against this disruptive technology to enhance its longevity in the market.

Working hypothesis 4 – To counter forces of possible disruptive technologies, Southland should not dismiss product innovation which hitherto has been the signature hallmark of its business agenda owing to the long-term stability of its market.

Symptom 5 – Southland's vulnerability profile (see Situation Analysis)

Table 5.9 Pros and cons

Plus points	Negative points
1. Contrary to health awareness premonitions, Southland's profit margins are commendably high.	1. Possibility of legal menace is high since nutrition information vanished from the wrapper of its best-selling product, *Mellobar*.
2. Trial experiment with healthier version of *Chizzlewits* failed with its loyal consumers.	2. Market menace also inflates owing to incursion of healthier products like *Sweetena* etc. into its stronghold space.
3. In the event of healthy product innovation, the possible hazards are (a) price escalation, (b) environmental issues and (c) potential loss of loyal consumers.	3. Design choice could be misunderstood as accentuating sales at the expense of health.

Explanation 2 for Case Study 5.9

Problematisation – What we can derive from this analysis are three hypothetical conditions of crisis.

(a) When the counterforces are clearly stronger than your defence, we call this **"no-choice scenario"** which limits your legroom for initiating strategic changes.
(b) When defence is stronger than counterforces, ignorance of disruptive forces is the clear choice. Let us call this a **"my choice"** scenario.
(c) Catch-22 situation is the third scenario when neither defence nor counterforces are significant or both are equally significant. This is the most fecund situation for a corporate since it provides more flexibility for strategising one's business designs. Let us call this a **"best-choice"** scenario.

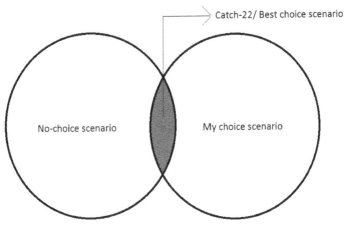

Figure 5.5 Crisis classification Venn diagram

Working hypothesis 5 – Southland, fortunately, is in a sanguine Catch-22 scenario which awards it greater breadth for manoeuvring its corporate strategies for profitable outcomes.

Problem Inference – From the foregone problem diagnosis we can arrive at the following postulates:

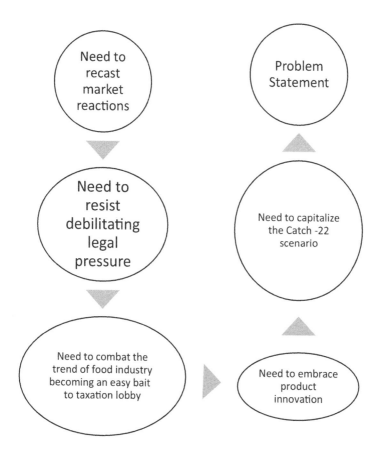

Figure 5.6 Arriving at problem statement

Problem Statement – How to capitalize the Catch-22 scenario by aligning its indigenous corporate autonomy with the political forces of the legal lobby.

Explanation 3 for Case Study 5.9

Patriotic concern reinforced

The Problem Processing Pyramid along with the Crisis Classification Venn diagram reinforce the Patriotic Concern, but via a differential diagnosis, which repudiates the singular insulated approach of looking at a problem in its raw form in its isolated silo; in this case, presence or absence of trans fat. It looks at the multi stratified systems (food industry, legal lobby and consumers) operating in polemical dialogues in a rhizomatic pattern and deriving a problem at the systemic level as an insightful entrepreneur. What is added to this Patriotic Concern exercise is the profiling of the nature of crisis. It is first important for the entrepreneur to know whether s/he is in a "my choice" zone or not, to even think of entrepreneurship.

Decision analysis

Decision Objective – To align Southland's indigenous business designs with the political forces of the legal lobby.

Explanation 4 for Case Study 5.9

Explanation – Decision Objective should transmute the abstract Problem Statement into a concrete target which has to be manifested into an action-oriented goal.

Benchmark

- Criterion 1 – Litigation
- Criterion 2 – Market share

Explanation 5 for Case Study 5.9

Explanation – From the Decision Objective it is clear that Southland has to address two-pronged concerns of mounting legal pressure and the volatility of an agile market. Hence as logical corollary, the Benchmarking Matrix formula for this to be used is simply to refashion these abstract concerns by assigning neutral values to them so that they can act as objective evaluative denominators. These evaluative criteria should not be loaded – they should be capable of attracting positive as well as negative values when the process of assessment of the recommendations is done.

And now comes the most important part of this persuasion endeavour: the Recommendation. How do we influence these many judgement makers to accept my solution? We contend the attempt lies in the alignment of the crisis type and the audience type. We have discussed the Crisis Classification Venn diagram (CCVD). Aligned to CCVD, we have an equally invigorating audience profiling, or even more aptly the profiling of a Devil's Advocate. And to satisfy each type of influencer in my team who takes a call on my proposal, I construct options or alternatives aligned to the probable audience type. In sum, we have come up with four kinds of solutions customised for four kinds of responses pre-empted.

(1) Prudent Inaction:[11]

Continue as is; for audience type – complacent, risk-averse, safe playing.

(2) Entrepreneurial Action – Take lucrative risky decisions; for audience type – enterprising, rebellious, iconoclastic, trendsetter.

(3) Conservative Protection – Preserve or protect the conventional choice by following it; for audience type – trend follower, cautious, traditional, protectionists, believers in bandwagoning.

(4) Red Herring Rejection – Place your recommendation strategically prefaced by other riskier alternatives; for audience type – critic, sceptic, cynic, fault-finder.

Explanation – Solutions are not given but recommended since there is always a team which has the power of audit either to accept or reject it. Hence for wining acceptance, a strategist packages her recommended solution as one of the alternatives in the plethora of "objective" options etched out. The trick lies in first earning rejections for these "objective" options to create a favourable space for your option to step in which now will appear as the "only" viable alternative available in the plural matrix of sundry solutions. To operationalise this strategy, let us revert back to two non-coercive communication techniques of door-in-face and excluding alternatives (refer to Chapter 3).

Explanation 6 for Case Study 5.9

Schematics of Proposing Alternatives

Design a packet of solutions to fit the needs of all audience types. This personality ramification of audience is derived from the kind of responses/reactions which any proposal in a crisis situation will garner following the Crisis Classification Venn Diagram illustrated before.

In a no-choice scenario, where change is impossible to bypass,

(a) the typical response would be an entrepreneurial action. The traits of respondents favouring this option are enterprising, rebellious and iconoclastic.
(b) the team can also elect another polarised reaction of conservative protection which entails deciding to follow the trend. The operators of this option are the ones who are cautious, traditional, protectionists and believers in bandwagoning.

In a my-choice scenario, where the external threat is minimal, the typical response would be prudent inaction. The lineaments of respondents favouring this option are complacent, risk-averse, safe playing.

Catch-22 is essentially a situation of dilemma. But it betokens the best choice scenario for a strategist, since it gives a strategist an opulent opportunity to manoeuvre her solution out of the meandering options available. The strategist will have to definitely tackle two kinds of opponents to whom she would be persuading to buy her decision. One kind would definitely be the protectionist type. But there might be another type or the protectionist category itself can resurface as our fourth type of respondents; namely, the critics. The profile of the critics can be delineated as sceptic, cynical, fault-finders.

One of the aspects of argumentation is to avoid or detect logical fallacies which give semblance of a rational thinking but deep down are saddled with flaws. One of the prime fallacies pointed out by rhetoricians is the fallacy of the red herring. This fallacy works on distraction. The audience is distracted by an argumentator who rakes up an issue allied to the main issue. In this manner, s/he defocusses the main issue to waylay the audience. It is the metaphoric adaptation of the trick used by adept hunters who use a smoked fish called kipper to distract the hounds following a scented trail.

Red Herring Rejection is our allied strategy built on the door-in-face technique (refer to Chapter 3) as well as the defocus technique (refer to Chapter 4). This trick is designed especially to deal with critics. The critics are the audience who are driven by the psychological need of rejection. They need the act of rejection to validate their existence. Hence a dexterous strategist gives them this fodder for rejection so that their existence is validated and subsequently they are ready to consider other options, which otherwise would have been dismissed outrightly.

The Red Herring Rejection involves presentation of a risky option which is a more intense reincarnation of the actual alternative, which is also risky. This is done mainly to set up a favourable contrast, so that when the real option decided by the strategist is positioned, it appears safer.

We get back to Business Message Strategies to develop the scheme of proposing alternatives for case analysis in Table 5.10

Now, let us adopt the Schematics for solving the Southland case, which is a clear case of Catch-22 scenario.

Table 5.10 Schematics of proposing alternatives

Crisis situation	Strategic option	Respondent profile
No-choice	(a) Entrepreneurial Action (b) Conservative Protection	(a) Enterprising, rebellious, iconoclastic (b) Cautious, traditional, trend following, believers in bandwagoning.
My Choice	Prudent Inaction	Complacent, risk-averse, safe playing
Catch-22	(a) Red Herring Rejection (b) Entrepreneurial Action (c) Conservative Protection	Critics, sceptics, cynics, fault-finders

Alternatives *(setting up our competitive matrix)*

There are two options in this case.

• Option 1 – (Entrepreneurial Action)

To diversify the product portfolio by rolling out plural food items not restricted to trans fats but still following the primary "design choice" of accentuating taste at the expense of health.

• Option 2 – (Red Herring Rejection)

2a. To continue the best-selling product *Mellobar* as it is.

2b. To completely recast products on the lines of *Sweetena*. *(Option 2a is the red herring option for rebels in the company; Option 2b is the red herring option for the conservatives.)* See Table 5.11.

It is clear from the afore-illustrated table that Option 1 emerges as the best solution in the given scenario.

Recommendation

Southland Bakery should go for product portfolio diversification with taste-orientation.

Action plan

To put this recommendation into action, let us chart out an action plan for Southland Bakery:

(1) Find alternatives to trans fats. For this hire, revamp the food and nutrition department with the induction of the best food scientists and researchers available in the market.

Table 5.11 Evaluation of options against benchmarks (performative evaluative matrix)

Options	Criterion 1 – Litigation Pros Cons		Criterion 2 – Market Share Pros Cons	
(1) **Product portfolio diversification (taste-oriented)**	Giving appearance of compliance but strengthening the notion of "sin"	Litigators may discern another equivalent of trans fats in these products' ingredients	Long-term upshot – May retain loyal consumers and also may attract new consumers by the act of self-invented competition leading to profitable cannibalisation	Short-term effect – Confusion amongst loyal consumers whether these new products would taste like their favourite Southland snack, *Mellobar*
(2a) To continue as is		Litigation danger	May retain most of its loyal consumers	May lose loyal consumers in the long run (**elastic theory**)
(2b) To recast the products on the lines of its competitor, Sweetena	Safest of all options	May set precedence of servility to external predators	Might pick up sales like *Sweetena*	(a) Trigger confusion with *Sweetena* (b) Might not be a hit with the loyal consumers (c) May lead to loss of autonomy

(2) Sponsor new experiments in developing worthy alternatives to trans fats, which should have the magical output that trans fats generate.

(3) To devise a special team of consumer researchers who can suggest, through rigorous surveys of consumer taste how Southland can go for diversification of the existing product portfolio by producing competitive products in a new unrelated segment. In this process of expansion (which is positioned as positive lucrative self-cannibalisation), Southland can acquire brand equity which would perpetuate the opulent tradition of taste that *Mellobar* had inaugurated eventually becoming the signature hallmark of Southland.

(4) To design an innovative marketing campaign which breaks the antithetical perception of taste versus health by proving and presenting "tasty is healthy" campaign, defocusing health hazards of trans fats and lime lighting taste.

Conclusion

Solving these seven different types of cases, domestic and international, real and fictional, equips a manager with a seven-pronged tool for solving any knotty management problem.

In conclusion . . .

What we call the beginning is often the end.
And to make an end is to make a beginning.
The end is where we start from.
From *T. S. Eliot's Little Gidding*[12]

The volume reaches its climax, commencing its voyage with the foundation of communication management based on the strategies of persuasive communication paving way to the introduction of new techniques of information dissection that empowers the baffled decision maker to choose and undertake the right course of action. Though the work is exhaustive in its treatment with a plethora of cases, examples and episodes from the corporate realm, it is just the primer because there is more to come. This volume would serve the purpose of a key to unlock more erudition packed in scrolls of managerial communication in terms of skills of argumentation, public speaking and sales pitch.

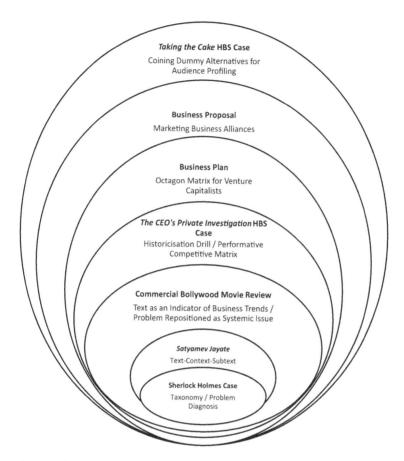

Figure 5.7 Seven pillars of strategic decision-making in complex management case scenarios

As of now, go vocal; get that vivacious, vehement and vociferous voice that translates your verve into volumes of action with

- Strategic Communication Toolkit
- Selling Apparatus Assets
- Nuanced Taxonomy
- Context Creation Persuasion Tree
- Domestication of Problem Framework

- Historicisation Drill
- Performative Competitive Matrix
- Octagon Matrix for Venture Capitalists
- Marketing Business Alliances
- Dummy Alternatives for Audience Profiling

Notes

1 Ibid.
2 Sherlock Holmes later clears the case with those words.
3 Ibid.
4 Jared Mason Diamond. *Guns, Germs, and Steel: The Fates of Human Societies*. New York: Norton, 1997.
5 The various style sheets of references are commonly available on the WWW.
6 We have taken a few points from the teaching commentaries authored by Harry Brandon, founding partner of Smith Brandon International in Washington DC; Christopher E. Kubasik, chief financial officer at Lockheed Martin, Maryland and James B. Comey, general counsel to the same company; Eric A. Klein, working for Katten Muchin Rosenman in Los Angeles; and William J. Teuber, Jr., vice chairman of EMC, based in Hopkinton, for the HBS case *The CEO's Private Investigation*.
7 Mrs. Danvers is the famous character in the legendary novel *Rebecca* by Daphne du Maurier (1938). The character is known for her obsessed act of using the folklore of a deceased character (Rebecca) to intimidate the new character (new second Mrs. Winter), replacing her.
8 *Finding Nemo* (2003) is a famous animated movie that chronicles the journey of the father of the fish *Nemo* searching for his son.
9 We have taken a few points from the teaching commentaries authored by Kenneth B. McClain, independent trial lawyer from Missouri; Laurian J. Unnevehr, professor of agriculture and consumer economics at the University of Illionois; Pam Murtaugh, president of a management consultancy in Madison, Wisconsin; and Richard Berman, executive director of the Centre of Consumer Freedom, Washington DC for the HBS case *Taking the Cake*.
10 As used in and by Jim Collins. *Good to Great: Why Some Companies Make the Leap . . . and Others Don't*. New York: HarperBusiness, 2001.
11 Coined by Professor S. Sreenivas Rao in "Thinking through a Management Situation," Indian Institute of Management Ahmedabad, 1984.
12 *T. S. Eliot's Little Gidding*. 30 March 2017 <www.columbia.edu/itc/history/winter/w3206/edit/tseliotlittlegidding.html>.

Taking the cake

Ben Gerson

Harvard Business Review

www.hbr.org

HBR CASE STUDY

Should Peter tell
CEO Ed Malanga
that Southland
needs to recast its
product lines?

Taking the Cake

by Ben Gerson

Reprint R0403X

Southland Baking Company makes lots of dough—from dough that is drenched in trans fats. Now consumer activists and hungry litigators want to take both away.

Taking the Cake

by Ben Gerson

His house, a handsome Victorian, stood on a low hill in the bedroom community of Bethesda, Maryland. With a pair of good binoculars he could make out, through any of the three dormer windows in his finished attic, the distinctive contours of the Capitol dome. It was one of the minor pleasures of owning this house in this town—at least it had been until last month, when an outsized interpretation of the Governor's Mansion in Williamsburg, Virginia, flaunting four chimneys instead of the historically accurate two, fully materialized next door.

Its owner was a glad-handing plaintiff's lawyer named Alex Kezenas, age 64, who had made a career-crowning killing in 1999. His client was an 18-year-old West Virginia high school shortstop who had developed a fatal case of tongue cancer from habitual use of chewing tobacco. Kezenas had persuaded a rural jury to assess actual and punitive damages against the Old Cherokee Tobacco Company totaling $12.1 million. His contingency fee came to a sixth of that and helped finance the brick obstruction he dwelled in today.

Sitting on the edge of his bed this Sunday morning, gazing distractedly out the window, Peter Schmidt reminded himself that it was Alex's house he minded, not his chosen livelihood, even though he was in no mood for litigators at the moment. A grandstanding New York lawyer had just sued a packaged foods company not unlike Peter's for supposedly making his client fat. The suit seemed laughable. But every lawsuit, he thought, no matter how baseless, was a headache and an expense for the company being sued. Alex was different. Tobacco was a real health menace. More power to Alex.

The phone rang. It was Richie Snell, Southland Baking Company's director of government affairs. "Peter, I have a problem," he said.

HBR's cases, which are fictional, present common managerial dilemmas.

"The House subcommittee on food and drugs is holding hearings tomorrow at 10 AM on child obesity and the fat content of baked goods, and we need to know what's going on. But I've got a sit-down with Senator Fullenwieder at the same hour. Can you go? You know the players even better than I do."

"Of course, Richie," Peter replied, masking his irritation. Surely Richie could have given him a little more warning. The reason he hadn't was probably his customary inattentiveness, although the thought crossed Peter's mind that Richie's intention may have been to maneuver him into saying yes. Before joining Southland's small legal department a decade earlier, Peter had been counsel to the subcommittee. When he left, he thought he'd be spending most of his time at Southland on compliance issues. But two and a half years into his tenure, Aunt Emmy's, a Tennessee pie company in which Southland had recently acquired a majority interest, blew up, and Peter was sent to Murfreesboro to run the place until it emerged from Chapter 11. In short order, Peter had paid its creditors 94 cents on the dollar and restored profitability.

Soon after, CEO Ed Malanga asked Peter to return to Baltimore as Southland's vice president and general counsel, the previous occupant having been dismissed for his due-diligence lapses. Ed had been generous in helping Peter grow into his corporate duties, but he never got over his impatience with the legal department's hairsplitting objections to one or another of Ed's schemes. "Stop thinking like a lawyer!" he'd shout.

Peter's broader corporate duties were evidence that he had indeed learned to stop thinking like a lawyer. "I guess in Ed's eyes I've succeeded," he reflected, with a kind of rueful pride.

A House Divided?

"Hello, Peter."

"Hello, Congressman."

The same exchange occurred several times as Monday's session broke up. The subcommittee's membership had changed very little in almost ten years, thanks to the wonders of incumbency. To Peter's practiced eye, the members had listened with a mixture of amusement and feigned and genuine concern to the testimony of scientists, educators, and consumer advocates. The most vociferous had

been the president of MOOK (Mothers Opposed to Obesity in Kids), a fortyish woman wearing a Chinese-red pantsuit.

"The food companies have a neat phrase for letting themselves off the hook," she announced from the witness table. "They say their products are 'part of a balanced diet.' But who today provides children with the rest of that diet? Not working parents, who don't have time to shop for raw vegetables and healthy protein, and who get home too late to cook them. Could it be the public schools? They're busy turning over their lunchrooms to fast-food franchisees and installing vending machines in their hallways. They even allow food advertising to run on the TV monitors the food companies have donated. Just listing ingredients on the sides of packages isn't going to stop kids from gobbling up their worthless contents. There is only one answer—to mandate warning labels on all foods containing sugars and saturated fats and to ban advertising of all such products on children's TV programs."

She paused to bring a bottle of Evian to her lips. "We know that eating habits get established early. Obese children grow into obese adults. A diet high in saturated fats often results in heart disease. And science is beginning to learn about diet's role in predisposing people to certain kinds of cancers." Citing the work of a Yale medical professor, she concluded: "Obesity alone will kill more people than alcohol and tobacco combined."

"Mrs. Newland," Representative Ray Slocum, a slow-talking New Hampshire Republican, began. "It sounds to me like you're asking us to construct a mommy state, where it's assumed citizens are unable to inform themselves about what's good for them. Since 1990, the Food and Drug Administration has required food companies to list the levels of calories, fat, cholesterol, sodium, and heaven knows what else on their packaging and, starting in 2006, to state the levels of trans fats. That seems to me quite enough protection for a nation of free citizens. I don't understand how you can suggest treating food the same as tobacco."

Later, Peter buttonholed the last committee member to leave the dais, Chicago Democrat Larry Fischer, an old ally. "Level with me, Larry: Where is the sentiment on the committee heading? Do we need to get involved in a big lobbying push? Or should we accept some

Ben Gerson is a senior editor at HBR. He can be reached at bgerson@hbsp. harvard.edu.

kind of warning mandate as inevitable?"

"Peter, as with most issues, you don't have too much to worry about if the public remains more or less indifferent. But you'd know better than I how Southland's customers are spending their food dollars these days."

What's Eating Consumers?

Southland was not a huge operation, but it was a prosperous one. As the third-largest independent cookie company in the United States, it had a strong foothold in second- and third-tier markets in the Southeast as well as the middle Atlantic states. Walk into any grocery store between Hagerstown, Maryland, and Chattanooga, Tennessee, and chances are you'd find three or four Southland SKUs on the shelves. The land of fried chicken and hush puppies liked its snacks and desserts steeped in fat, and Southland saw no reason not to oblige.

But to Lou Salvador, the company's vice president of marketing, sometimes the "southland" seemed a world away from Washington, DC, where he made his home, not to mention New York or California, where trends usually began. Lou took an intense interest in competitors' product innovations. He was the only executive at headquarters to have a television in his office, and it was usually tuned to MTV. But most of Lou's marketing budget went toward trade promotion. Ed Malanga didn't see the point of spending millions on advertising when Southland's product lines were so well established.

Southland's best-selling product was the Mellobar, which was introduced in 1975 as an instant breakfast food, but which over the years had been made smaller and sweeter and now qualified as a snack. In the 1970s, "mellow" was the state of mind people under the age of 30 aspired to achieve, but the name now had a vaguely dated air, and the cookie's original nutritional claims had disappeared from its wrapper.

Peter picked up his office phone and rang Lou. "Would you like to grab some lunch? What do you say we go to that sushi joint over at Harborplace? Oh, I see. All right, then. Rudy's it is."

As soon as Lou's prime rib was placed in front of him, Peter began. "I may be making something out of nothing, but yesterday I sat through a hearing on the Hill about the fat content of food and its connection to health. I couldn't really tell if there was just a codependency thing going on between the do-gooders and the members or if the subcommittee was getting ready to brand our products the latest health hazard. Ray Slocum stood up for us, but he was really the only one. It probably won't amount to anything unless public sentiment starts to turn. But that's what I wanted to ask you about. Are your salespeople getting any signals?"

"Well," Lou said, frowning, "I'd have to say the signals are mixed. So far this quarter, revenues are 11% over last year's, which should allow me to relax. But if you check out the stores that carry us, even a few of the out-of-the-way ones, you see these odd little brands cropping up—Debbie's Blondies, or Greg's Passion Cakes, or Pacific Maca-mania Bits. It's all stuff made with honey instead of sugar or corn syrup and with canola or palm oil that hasn't been hydrogenated. Individually, they don't amount to much. Collectively, though, it must be adding up to some real money. The question is, How do we define success? If it's market share, and it includes these guys, we're losing ground."

"What about the majors?" Peter asked. "Are they noticing?"

"Maybe they're not looking over their shoulder at Pacific Maca-mania Bits, but their research is telling them that people are getting smarter about ingredients and more worried about the connection between eating habits and health. Sweetena is starting to roll out line extensions with half the fat of the original product." Lou was referring to Mellobar's biggest rival, the market leader. "So I guess you could say we're about to be squeezed from both directions. In fact, our margins are already being squeezed—the slotting fees we have to pay for good placement have gone up 17% this year."

Lou turned his attention back to his lunch for a while, then glanced at Peter's worried face. "Listen," he said, "if you really want to know, I've already asked Fred and his outfit to knock off a leaner version of our Chizzlewits. Keep quiet about this, but we're about to test it on a bunch of seven-year-olds. You can come along if you want."

The Cookie Crumbles

On one side of the one-way mirror sat Fred

A grandstanding lawyer had just sued a packaged foods company not unlike Peter's for supposedly making his client fat. The suit seemed laughable.

Rangle, Southland's chief scientist, along with Peter, Lou, one other member of the marketing department, and six Baltimore mothers. On the other side sat six boys and girls, name tags pinned to their shirts, and Mary Cairncross, the Southland dietician who would ply them with Fred's new, improved Chizzlewits. Brittany picked one up and chewed thoughtfully. Caitlin tentatively licked the edge of hers. Brian nibbled a corner and frowned. Kevin broke his into pieces and refused to eat any. Keisha ate the whole thing and burst into tears. And Arthur, scowling, spat a large wad onto the table in front of him and declared, "It looks like a Chizzlewit, but it doesn't taste like one!"

The mothers were embarrassed. Lou was dismayed. Fred, however, looked triumphant. After the mothers were escorted out, Fred addressed Lou. "You think it's the words on the package that moves cookies. It's not. It's taste. People won't eat food they don't like, however good it's supposed to be for them—kids in particular, as we've just seen. Fat carries flavor. You can't get away from it."

The land of fried chicken and hush puppies liked its snacks and desserts steeped in fat, and Southland saw no reason not to oblige.

"I think that's a bit simplistic," Lou replied. "With all due respect, Fred, I'd like to hear Millie's angle on this." Millie Lepore was Southland's chief dietician. "Let's the four of us meet sometime next week—you, Millie, Peter, and me."

Science Versus Nature

Everyone at Southland knew there was no love lost between Millie and Fred. Fred was a believer in better living through chemistry. He was famous for saying "What doesn't kill me makes me stronger." In discussions about what the levels of cholesterol and fats in the company's products should be, Millie, who had played a significant role in formulating the original version of the Mellobar, always came down on the side of nutrition. If Southland's products fell short, it wasn't for lack of trying on Millie's part.

The four of them gathered in Lou's spacious office the following Monday. Lou reached up and doused his MTV. "As you know, Millie," he began, "Peter doesn't usually get involved in questions of product formulation and their impact on marketing and sales. But he's been picking up some worrying signs of increasing regulatory interest in snacks, beverages, and fast foods, so Fred and I are trying to give him

a sense of how much latitude we might have in placating Congress and the FDA."

"We have very little," Fred interrupted. "Everyone's worried about saturated fat, but it is the basis of our products. The pure polyunsaturated vegetable oils Millie would like us to use are expensive and can turn rancid on the shelf. We have a wonderful process that forces hydrogen into liquid oil in the precise amounts needed to produce the flavor intensity and mouth sensation we want in the baked goods we sell. Any change in our processes or formulas risks driving up costs and driving away our most loyal customers. And they're not, Lou, I'd remind you, the kinds of people who can pay premium prices."

Now it was Millie's turn. "Fred, you forgot to mention that partial hydrogenation produces trans fats, which have zero nutritional value. Worse, they elevate LDL levels in the blood while suppressing HDL levels, which could otherwise help the body handle all that 'bad' cholesterol. I've never said this before, but I think it's irresponsible to use trans fats when reasonable alternatives exist."

"Such as?" Fred inquired.

"One hundred percent palm oil, which is already semisolid."

"Did you know that Malaysia, where most of it comes from, has been clearing rain forest to make room for oil-palm plantations? What do you think the activists would do with that little fact?"

"All right. Dried plum powder. The sorbitol, I've heard, holds moisture, and the mastic acid enhances flavor."

"Give me a break."

The meeting broke up before Peter got to say a word.

The New Tobacco

The past week or so had been a detour, albeit an educational one, for Peter. Now legal matters were piling up—an OSHA violation in the Knoxville plant; a trademark infringement by a Miami company; a lease renewal for the Baltimore space. And though he sensed the risk was small, a couple of days earlier he'd asked Naomi Berlin, his in-house litigation counsel, to prepare a legal memorandum on the potential liabilities food companies faced for their products' health effects.

Naomi entered Peter's office and sat down. "Of course I plan to read your memo, Naomi,

"I could imagine a court allowing a class action suit against us to proceed because, in effect, we failed to warn potential customers not to buy our cookies!"

but I've got to figure out our position very soon. Apparently Ray Slocum called Ed to ask him for a campaign contribution, and he mentioned he'd seen me on the Hill last week. Ed figures it had to be a really important hearing to require my presence. I need to call him back, so give me the bottom line. How would regulation affect our liabilities?"

Naomi launched into a summary. "It would set a baseline. If we didn't cross it, which we would not, we'd be in the clear. Naturally, all of our competitors would have to comply as well. Thaxton's got in trouble only because they said their fries were vegetarian when there were traces of beef tallow in the cooking oil. The problem is that courts tend to play policy maker when Congress doesn't. It used to be that a company had a duty to warn only the purchasers of its products about any possible safety hazards. Not any longer. It would be hard to prove that the fat content of some company's cookies is the proximate cause of a particular kid's health problems. But I could imagine a court allowing a class action suit against us to proceed because, in effect, we failed to warn *potential* customers not to buy our cookies!"

"Is there an analogy to tobacco?" Peter asked.

"Well, Congress, as you know, has required cigarette packs to carry warning labels since the 1960s. The duty to warn about fats, if a court should find one, at the moment would fall on us. The cigarette companies tried to develop a safe cigarette, but they were afraid to say so because it would imply their current brands were unsafe. Besides, it tasted terrible. So, by the way, do our new, improved Chizzle-

wits, or so I hear."

Peter groaned as he recalled seven-year-old Arthur spitting out the Chizzlewit he'd chewed.

"Speaking of Chizzlewits," Naomi continued, "the big tobacco settlement forbade marketing to minors, and we know most of our consumers are kids."

"Anything else?" Peter asked.

"Yes. The trans fats in our products seem to present a special case. They're not a food. The FDA refuses to set a daily level for them. They're an artifact of the manufacturing process. Cigarettes carry warnings and are heavily taxed because they aren't good for us. You could say the same thing about trans fats."

Busted

Peter left for Bethesda early that day. The aged pipes in his Victorian required the plumber's attention. As he pulled into the driveway, he saw Alex operating his leaf blower. So that's how retired millionaires fill their weekday afternoons, Peter mused. Alex shut off the noisy machine and walked toward him, looking grave. "Bad break."

"What do you mean, Alex?"

"I just got a call from an old pal. Didn't you hear? About an hour ago, a trial lawyer in West Virginia filed suit against Southland."

Should Peter tell CEO Ed Malanga that Southland needs to recast its product lines?

HBR Case R0403X
To order, call 800-988-0886
or 617-783-7500 or go to www.hbr.org

The CEO's private investigation

Joseph Finder

Harvard Business Review

www.hbrreprints.org

HBR CASE STUDY

Should Cheryl
initiate an
investigation at her
new firm?

The CEO's Private Investigation

by Joseph Finder

Reprint R0710X

If there ever were a time when a chief executive should commission some quiet snooping on her colleagues, this might be it.

HBR CASE STUDY

The CEO's Private Investigation

by Joseph Finder

If Mussolini had been the CEO of a major American corporation, Cheryl Tobin thought, his office wouldn't have been this big.

She stood in the doorway of her new work space, on the 33rd floor of the Hammond Tower in downtown Los Angeles, and took a deep breath. Seven o'clock on her first morning as CEO of Hammond Aerospace. Briefcase in one hand, Starbucks nonfat venti latte in the other.

Go for it, kiddo, she told herself as she exhaled, then resolutely strode over the threshold and across the antique, jewel-toned Serapi rug. She remembered the moment, a couple of weeks ago, when the chairman of the board had solemnly ushered her in here. He'd stood in awestruck silence, presumably to impress her with the majesty and grandeur of the job they were courting her for.

She'd been impressed, all right. But also secretly appalled. It was obscene: easily four times the size of her office at Boeing, where she'd run the largest division. This wasn't exactly her style. A peacock's plumage might impress the peahens, she liked to say, but it was also a flashing neon all-you-can-eat sign for predators.

Floor-to-ceiling windows on two sides, with dazzling panoramic views of Wilshire Boulevard. A private terrace where you could entertain visiting dignitaries. Even a working fireplace with a slate hearth—what was *that* all about?

It was all about the colossal ego of its former occupant, of course. The legendary James Rawlings, the globe-trotting CEO-statesman who'd single-handedly built a minor producer of airplane windshields into one of the world's leading aerospace companies. Jim Rawlings had been a man of immense charisma and iron will, a hard-charging salesman who'd dominated Hammond Aerospace until the

---

HBR's cases, which are fictional, present common managerial dilemmas.

moment, one month ago, when he'd dropped dead from an aneurysm on the sixth hole at Pebble Beach. Right in front of three Japan Airlines execs with whom he'd been negotiating a $5 billion order for thirty H-880 SkyCruisers, the company's new wide-body passenger jet.

Half an hour after they'd carried him away on a gurney, the shaken Japanese executives signed on the dotted line.

Even in death, he seemed so present. His grandiose office had been preserved exactly as he'd left it, a shrine to a cult of personality. They still hadn't taken down the photos on his ego wall: skiing with Prince Charles in Klosters, sailing with Gianni Agnelli in the Adriatic, schmoozing with King Abdullah at the royal palace in Riyadh. The place still reeked of cigar smoke.

She had some serious redecorating to do. For starters, the humidor had to go.

The vast black marble slab of a desk was uncluttered by a single object. Where is the telephone? she wondered. Didn't the guy use a *phone?*

She set her briefcase on the floor, then placed the almost-empty paper cup on the gleaming surface of the desk. It looked almost ironic there, like some Damien Hirst installation.

Now she stood watching the early morning traffic, the Matchbox cars barely visible through the smog. She missed Chicago, didn't much care for Los Angeles, but she could get used to it. Good sushi here, she'd heard.

What the hell have I gotten myself into? Cheryl wondered. No doubt, leading Hammond Aerospace was the opportunity of a lifetime. But at the same time, she was acutely aware that not a few people in this building wouldn't mind terribly if she tripped and fell off her private terrace and took a header onto the asphalt of Wilshire Boulevard, 33 stories down. Not least a guy named Hank Bodine, the head of Hammond's commercial airplane division and the internal candidate for the job she'd just secured. Everyone here had thought he was a shoo-in, himself included.

"Good morning, Ms. Tobin. You're in early."

Startled, Cheryl turned around. Her new executive administrative assistant, Jackie Terrell, stood in the doorway.

She was a tall, regal African-American

woman in her early fifties, wearing an elegant lavender suit and matching pumps. When the two women had first met a few days ago, Jackie had seemed a bit stiff. Excessively formal, maybe. But she'd been Jim Rawlings's assistant for 18 years, which meant she'd be invaluable.

"Oh, good morning, Jackie. Yeah, I like to get in before the phone starts ringing. And please—I'm Cheryl."

Jackie smiled with prim cordiality. "Jim always arrived at nine on the dot, and I always get here by eight. But I'll make sure I'm in by seven from now on."

"Oh, don't be silly. Eight is fine."

Jackie nodded. "Please let me know what I can do for you."

For one thing, you can drop the Mrs. Danvers act, Cheryl thought. "I'd like to call a meeting of my executive team this afternoon."

"I'll send out the notifications." Jackie hesitated an instant, then said: "They'll be—well, traditionally, executive team meetings are held on Tuesday mornings, Ms. Tobin, but—"

"Tomorrow's fine," Cheryl said. There'd be plenty of opportunities to break some china before the week was out.

"May I get you a cappuccino? Jim always liked a cappuccino, first thing."

"No thanks." She indicated the paper cup defiling Jim Rawlings's desk. "I've had my hit of caffeine for the day. Too much makes me jittery."

"I see. Well, please let me know if there's anything I can get you."

Cheryl thought for a long moment and then said, "Actually, Jackie, there is something. Some information."

"Of course. What would you like to know?"

"Let's sit down for a moment." Cheryl walked over to the conference area and sat in a high-back black leather chair. Jackie perched at one end of a long black Chesterfield sofa and took out a pad.

Note to self: Get rid of the damned men's club furniture, Cheryl thought.

"Jackie," she began delicately, "when I was at Boeing, I heard certain rumors...about Hammond."

"Rumors?" Jackie cocked her head.

"Of course, you never know what's true and what's not when it involves a competitor. But what I often heard was that the reason Jim's sales team was so successful at landing foreign

Joseph Finder (joe@josephfinder. com) is an award-winning writer of best-selling corporate thrillers such as *Killer Instinct, Company Man,* and *Paranoia.* This fictional case is a prequel to his latest novel, *Power Play* (St. Martin's Press, 2007).

contracts was—well, to be blunt, that they weren't reluctant to give certain incentives."

"I'm not following you, Ms. Tobin."

"Off-the-book deal-sweeteners. Bribes, not to put too fine a point on it. There were whispers that Hammond kept a secret slush fund for payoffs to various foreign officials."

Jackie shook her head. "That sounds like watercooler gossip to me."

"Perhaps. But sometimes there's truth in gossip."

"People always love to trash the competition. Sour grapes, I'm sure."

"No doubt that's all it is. But now that I'm CEO, I need to be absolutely certain."

Jackie shifted, visibly uncomfortable. "Anyway, I was hardly in a position to know anything."

"You know what they say about you," Cheryl said lightly. "That you know where all the bodies are buried, right?"

Jackie seemed to be studying the rug. Cheryl had the distinct impression that her new assistant was holding out on her.

"Well," Cheryl said abruptly, getting to her feet. "Forgive me if I put you in a difficult position." She returned to the big black sarcophagus of a desk and, without turning around, added, "Given your loyalty to Jim."

"No—" Jackie said. "That's not it at all."

"You see, if the allegations are baseless, no one will be more relieved than I," Cheryl said softly. "But I want everyone to know that I won't stand for any coloring outside the lines. I want Hammond's reputation to be spotless."

A few seconds later, Jackie said in a small voice: "There might have been something."

• • •

Cheryl's new assistant spoke falteringly. "I've heard the rumors, too, of course. But I always ignored them. Until one day I found a folder on Jim's desk, and I picked it up to file it away." She added hastily: "I handled all his personal papers, even the most confidential. He knew he could trust me to be absolutely discreet. That's why I was so surprised when he told me to put the file down. He was quite...short with me. He said it was personal. Not like him at all."

"What was it?"

"Banking documents, it looked like. I mean, I had to look inside to know where to file it."

"Of course you did, Jackie," Cheryl said reassuringly.

"I saw some wire-transfer instruction forms. Sending millions of dollars from one of Hammond's accounts to a bank in Grand Cayman. I remember wondering about that because I didn't think we did any business there."

"What happened to that file?"

Jackie's eyes brimmed with tears. "I never saw it again."

After a few seconds of silence, Cheryl said, "Thank you, Jackie. I know it mustn't have been easy for you to tell me."

• • •

Hank Bodine was a big, bluff man of around 60, with a shock of silver hair, heavy black brows, and a large square jaw. He wore a perfectly tailored gray suit and a silver tie. He looked like a CEO. Cheryl had done her due diligence on him, though, and had heard he was a swaggering, foul-mouthed martinet given to explosive tirades. She wondered why the board had passed him over for the CEO job. Might it be his temperament? Or something else?

He looked around the office as he entered. "Haven't changed a thing, I see," he said in a booming voice.

"It's only my first day," Cheryl said. "In a month, you won't recognize the place."

She led him over to the men's club seating area, where they chatted aimlessly for a few minutes. Hank made little effort to conceal his hostility. "Well," he said, "I can't wait to hear what sort of changes you've got in mind."

"Who said anything about changes?" Cheryl said blandly.

Hank flashed his unnaturally white teeth, but the smile did not reach his eyes. "The board wouldn't have brought in an outsider to keep things the same."

"You know, I never like to mess with success. I mean, your order book for the SkyCruiser is over a hundred billion dollars, isn't that right?"

Hank nodded, waiting.

"I've got to tell you," she went on, "it's a lot better to be working with you than against you. Your division sure grabbed a lot of business away from Boeing in the past few years."

A hearty guffaw. "Hey, maybe we're selling a better plane."

Cheryl shrugged. "I hope that's it."

"Plus, I've got a crack sales force."

"So I hear."

"We're the underdog. We have to get up earlier. Work longer. Fight harder."

"I won't stand for any coloring outside the lines. I want Hammond's reputation to be spotless."

"As long as everything's on the up-and-up, you have my unqualified support. And gratitude, for that matter."

Hank's smile faded. "What's that supposed to mean?"

"We're both grown-ups, Hank. I think you know what I'm talking about."

"I'm not sure I do."

There was a beat of silence. "I just want to make sure," Cheryl said quietly, "that no laws have been violated. I'm talking about the Foreign Corrupt Practices Act."

Hank's eyes glittered coldly. "Is that an accusation?"

"Simply a statement," she said. "I won't tolerate any bribery, any payoffs to lock in deals. I want your personal assurance that nothing of the sort is going on at Hammond. To your knowledge."

He jutted his jaw, looked away. "I'm not going to even dignify that—"

"Hank, I want you to know that I'm considering launching an internal investigation."

"That some kind of threat?"

"Not at all. Call it a heads-up."

"You can't be serious."

"Deadly. Hank, let me remind you: I was at Boeing when someone tried a little too hard to land a big, juicy Pentagon contract—by offering a job to the woman in charge of air force acquisitions. Remember that? A couple of years ago?"

"Yeah," Hank said impatiently.

"Our CFO went to prison. Our CEO was forced to resign. Boeing had to pay millions of dollars in penalties. If it weren't for a great legal team, we'd have faced criminal charges, too. We lost probably billions in potential business. So I'm going to do my damnedest to make sure nothing's going on here."

Hank leaned forward, hunched his shoulders. "And what exactly do you think that's going to accomplish? You have any idea what's gonna happen to our share price when the word gets out that the new CEO's off on some witch hunt, looking into bribery or slush funds or whatever the hell?"

I never said anything about a slush fund, she thought. "But if it's not true—"

"Doesn't make a damned bit of difference if it's true or not. We'll lose contracts left and right. Soon as there's a drop of blood in the water, the sharks are gonna circle, believe you me."

She watched him in silence.

"You're barely here an hour, and already you're trying to tear the place apart," Hank said in a low, insinuating voice. "I've got news for you. You don't work for Boeing anymore."

Only later did Cheryl realize that Hank Bodine hadn't actually denied anything.

• • •

Hammond's general counsel was a trim, nervous man named Geoffrey Latimer. He was around 50, with graying light brown hair perfectly parted on one side and Brylcreemed into place. He shook Cheryl's hand, his grip firm and dry. His fingernails, she noticed, were bitten.

She'd dropped by his office unannounced, hoping to get to him before the rumor mill did. His office was a fraction of the size of hers. Neat stacks of papers and binders covered nearly every surface. He, too, had an ego wall of photographs of himself with various VIPs. This seemed to be standard issue on the 33rd floor.

Geoffrey listened gravely, his head bowed, like a priest hearing confession. When she finished, he looked up.

"I assume you're not talking about having *me* spearhead an internal investigation."

She shook her head. "It would have to be done by an outside law firm. It's the only way."

"I agree."

"Good."

"But I think it would be a mistake," Geoffrey said.

"How come?"

He leaned back in his chair and tented his hands. His brow was deeply furrowed. "To begin with, news of an investigation into possibly illegal conduct would inflict serious harm on the company."

Yes, she thought. Hank Bodine's argument. "But not if it's contained," she said.

"If you mean trying to keep the *fact* of such an inquiry a secret, I'm afraid that's just not realistic. Good Lord, there'd be forensic document examiners combing through years of files and archived e-mails, computer experts talking to our IT people...." He shuddered. "We're talking front page of the *Wall Street Journal.*"

Cheryl folded her arms, bit her lower lip. "But at the very least, don't you think I pretty much have to inform the board about my suspicions?"

Now he leaned forward in his chair and began toying with a paperweight. "Here's the thing, Cheryl. Once you do that, you escalate things to an entirely new level. The whole matter will spin completely out of control."

"How so?"

"The regulatory environment out there has gotten really brutal in the past couple of years. The courts have started to hold individual directors personally liable for any corporate malfeasance they know about and don't act on. That could mean potentially millions of dollars in legal fees alone—for each director. And all for what might turn out to be nothing more than a wild goose chase."

"You're kidding me." She tried to swallow, but her mouth had gone dry.

"Unfortunately, no. So look at it from their standpoint—you tell them about this suspicion of yours, and they'll have no choice but to take immediate and serious action."

"Which might not be such a bad thing, correct?"

He closed his eyes, gave a long, tremulous sigh. "Look, Cheryl. What they'll almost certainly do is take control of the company out of your hands. They'll feel as if they have no choice. You'll be the CEO of Hammond in name only—you'll have no power."

She watched him, didn't know what to say.

"Cheryl, if you have some sort of concrete evidence of corruption, then a probe would be not only responsible but imperative. Yet if you're going on nothing more than a hunch... oh, dear. The fact that there are stories out there about alligators in the sewers doesn't justify sending inspectors down the manholes. Trouble is, as soon as you repeat these tall tales, everyone's got to act as if they're true." He paused, gave the paperweight a final little shove. "And something else. Please forgive my bluntness."

"Go ahead," she said dully.

"A lot of people here are going to consider this just some clumsy attempt on the part of the new CEO to discredit her very popular predecessor. To blacken his name." He winced. "I'm not saying that's your intent, of course—far from it. But you'll start losing senior people. You'll become a pariah, Cheryl. And you have to ask yourself: Is it really what's best for the company?"

Her head had begun to throb. She thanked him and walked slowly out of his office, and

on the way a photograph caught her eye.

Geoffrey Latimer with Hank Bodine and Jim Rawlings. Aboard Rawlings's famous 400-foot, German-built yacht, their arms around each other. Like three frat brothers.

• • •

"Is everything all right?" Jackie asked.

Cheryl, surprised by the tenderness in Jackie's voice, attempted a smile as she passed her assistant's desk. She needed to be alone, to think. Late morning light flooded her office, making her headache worse.

Her first day as a CEO, and for the first time in years she felt almost paralyzed by indecision. She'd always been able to draw on an inner core of strength, to get through the hard times, to make the tough decisions. She'd once overheard a couple of guys at Boeing refer to her as Ice Queen, and no doubt people had said worse. She didn't particularly care. But her detractors, both men and women, wrongly assumed that beneath her sometimes-flinty exterior was even more flint. If only that were true.

She sat behind her desk and finally located the damned telephone. It was concealed in a desk drawer. Who knew what else Jim Rawlings was concealing? She picked up the handset, listened to the dial tone for a few seconds, then put it down.

Weren't quarterly filings due in a couple of weeks? The Sarbanes-Oxley Act required her to approve them, to certify them as "true, correct, and complete." But what if she signed a financial statement that she had reason to believe might be inaccurate—and then it turned out that there really was some kind of slush fund? Wouldn't she herself be in legal jeopardy?

Whom should she ask about this? Geoffrey Latimer wasn't her personal lawyer, after all. And after seeing that picture of him and Hank Bodine on Jim Rawlings's yacht, she had to wonder whether his real motivation was to protect his buddies.

But she couldn't just do nothing. Not anymore. She'd already started asking questions, and she couldn't exactly unring this bell.

Picking up the phone again, she dialed a Washington, DC, number: the direct line of a man named Hamilton Wender, a senior partner at the high-powered law firm Craigie Blythe. She'd gotten to know Tony, as he was called, when he did some brilliant defense

Her first day as a CEO, and for the first time in years she felt almost paralyzed by indecision.

work for Boeing. What a nightmare that was.
And this could be worse.

"Tony," she said, trying to control the anxi-ety in her voice. "It's Cheryl Tobin."

Should Cheryl initiate an investigation at her new firm?

Reprint R0710X
To order, call 800-988-0886
or 617-783-7500 or go to www.hbr.org

Index

Page numbers in italic indicate a figure.

For Product Safety Concerns and Information please contact our EU
representative GPSR@taylorandfrancis.com Taylor & Francis Verlag GmbH,
Kaufingerstraße 24, 80331 München, Germany

Printed and bound by CPI Group (UK) Ltd, Croydon, CR0 4YY

01/05/2025

01858426-0001